WITHDRAWN

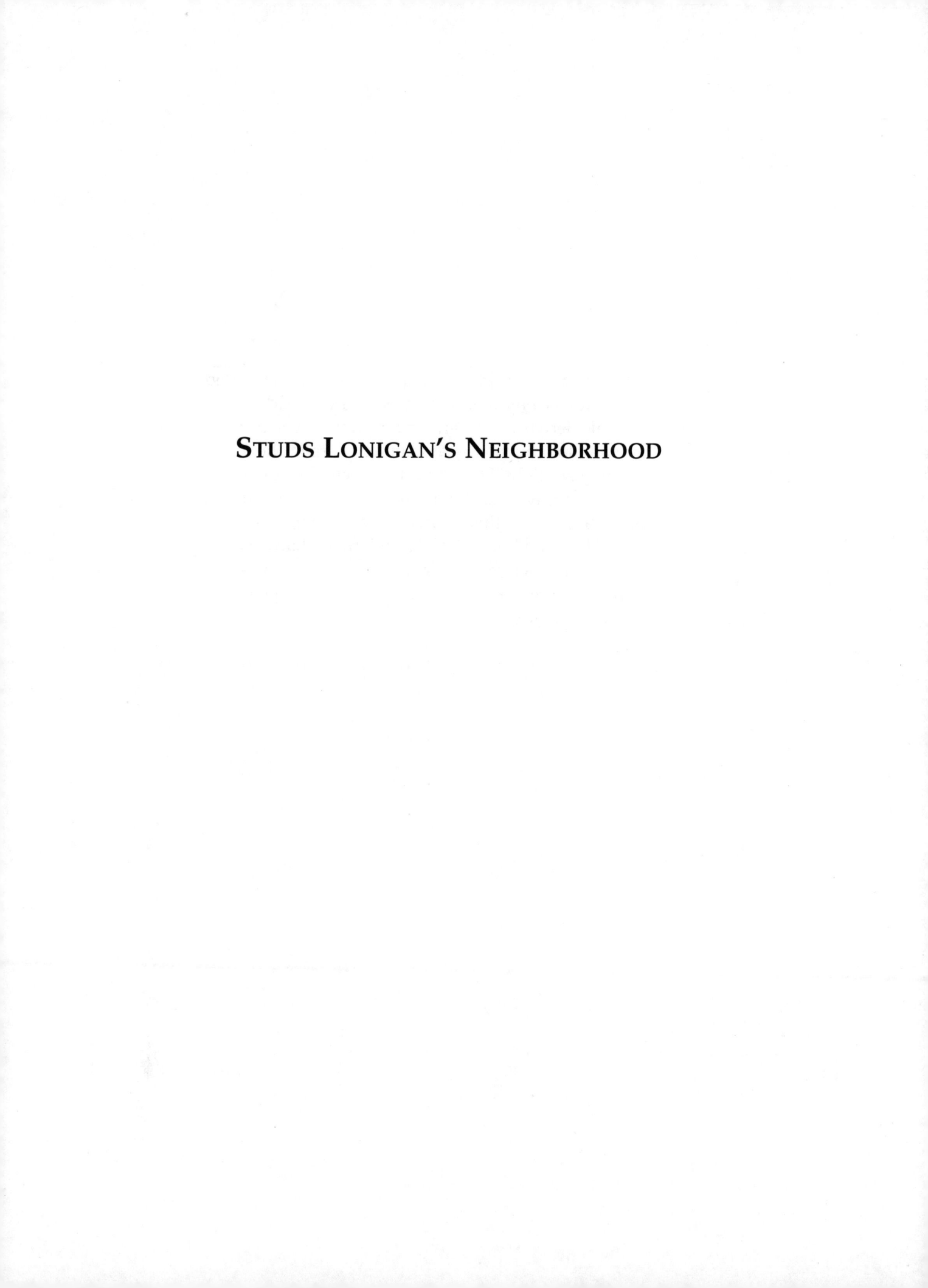

Studs Lonigan's Neighborhood

CHICAGO! He had once been a boy there, a frightened and ordinary boy, and somehow that boy had grown into this Bernard Carr, an American writer, standing here and looking across at Union Square in the morning sunlight. How had it happened? How had he found his road and won the confidence he now felt? The seeds of this change were not here in New York. They had been planted back there, halfway across this American continent. His heritage was there, not here, and not in the cultured Europe he was about to see.

—Bernard Carr in *The Road Between*

Studs Lonigan's

Neighborhood

and the making of
James T. Farrell

Edgar M. Branch

Arts End Books

TO MY GRANDCHILDREN

Matthew and Jeffrey Diez,
and
Robert, Olivia,
and Laura Williams

Front Cover Photo Credits:
"L" Train at 58th St. Station ca. 1948, photo by Edgar Branch
James T. Farrell ca. 1935, photo courtesy of Helen Farrell Dillon

Copyright © 1996 by Edgar M. Branch.

All previously unpublished writing by James T. Farrell copyright © 1996 by the James T. Farrell Estate.

All rights reserved, which includes the right to reproduce this book or portions thereof in any form whatsoever.

Library of Congress Cataloging-in-Publication Data

Branch, Edgar Marquess, 1913-
    Studs Lonigan's neighborhood and the making of James T. Farrell /
Edgar M. Branch.
      p.   cm.
    Includes bibliographical references and index.
    ISBN 0-933292-22-8 (pbk.)
    1. Farrell, James T. (James Thomas) , 1904-1979--Knowledge-
-Illinois--Chicago. 2. South Chicago (Chicago, Ill.)--In
literature. 3. Literary landmarks--Illinois--Chicago. 4. Lonigan,
Studs (Fictitious character) 5. Irish Americans in literature.
6. Working class in literature. 7. Neighborhood in literature.
I. Title.
PS3511.A738Z64   1996
813' .52--dc20   95-48322
                                                                   CIP

Publication of this book was made possible through a bequest from the Roving Fund.

Book Project Coordinator: Stephanie Greene
Book Design Consultant: Bob Oliver

Arts End Books Box 162 Newton, MA 02168 USA
Send a SASE for our free catalog.

Contents

Preface	i
Introduction	A Personal Statement: The Farrell Connection 1
Maps	"Studs Lonigan's Neighborhood" 8
	"Washington Park" 9
Chapter One	The Studs Lonigan Neighborhood: A Visual Record 11
Chapter Two	Studs and Danny 38
Chapter Three	The Grid and the Garden 50
Chapter Four	Jimmy Farrell in the Neighborhood, 1915-1919 63
Chapter Five	Coda: *Young Lonigan* on 58th Street 81
Chapter Six	Afterword 88
Abbreviations	93
Appendix "A"	94
Appendix "B"	95
Bibliographical Note	97
Index	98
Publisher's Note	104

Preface

WE SAY THAT STUDS LONIGAN's neighborhood was also Danny O'Neill's, and we know that Danny O'Neill, a consciously and carefully created character, in many respects is James T. Farrell's self-portrait. By most measurements, Studs is a failure; Danny becomes a writer, and Farrell was a great American author. Slow but steady degeneration marks Studs's life; explosive growth, Farrell's. Such contrasting, even antithetical, outcomes from what we think of as basically one source are far from uncommon. Yet when an author creates a character from his own enveloping neighborhood who seemingly is so diametrically opposite from himself and yet so alive that his name has become symbolic of an American way of life, we are led to ask: How, in this particular case, did it happen?

What we *know* from our personal experience, as opposed to what we often say, is that every individual, to a large extent, creates his own neighborhood. Farrell agreed. He believed that Studs and Danny and all individuals carry within themselves innate capacities and inclinations—different in kind and configuration in each person—which enable them to give their own particular form and meaning to the raw experience into which they are born. What Danny and Studs observe, think, decide, and do, constantly shapes and eventually transforms their personal worlds.

To explain so much about Farrell's belief is still necessary, because numerous critics for many years have tagged him as an environmental determinist, most often with reference to the character and death of Studs Lonigan. Farrell's vision made room for neighborhood, especially early neighborhood, as a major influence upon human growth as well as human degeneration. In his fiction, neighborhood is a vital ingredient of the ever ongoing process of his characters' development, but not an all-determining force strictly controlling that development. It is an energizing factor in the constant interaction between the outer and the inner in every person's experience.

In his writings about Studs and Danny, Farrell exposed the nature of each in voluminous detail. We know them thoroughly as individuals. We see what they bring to the world. We come to understand what their consciousness, their sensitivity, carves out for them as they progress through life. Even so, the neighborhood Studs and Danny and Farrell shared, the Chicago neighborhood found in much of Farrell's best fiction, has often been misunderstood and inadequately visualized. My hope is that this book will illuminate Farrell's early experience in that neighborhood and help the reader further appreciate what he made of it in his fiction.

* * *

Cleo Paturis, the executrix for the James T. Farrell estate, permitted me to quote from Farrell's unpublished manuscripts and letters, and for this I am especially thankful. For the many years we have known each other, she has been a steadfast friend and a supporter of my interest in James T. Farrell, as well as a hospitable hostess in her New York home. Cleo's knowledge and understanding of the man has been invaluable to me. She has always generously responded to my requests for information and for copies of Farrell's writings.

For several decades Neda Westlake, formerly the curator of the Rare Book Collection at the University of Pennsylvania Library, was a willing and efficient guide to the intricacies of the Farrell archives during my visits there. Her warm friendship and the hospitality she extended to me on the Pennsylvania campus and at her home are much appreciated. My gratitude goes out to Dorothy Farrell for her long-lasting friendship and her willingness to talk with me, as early as 1957 and as recently as 1995. Our talks provided useful details for this book.

Father Leander Troy, O. Carm., willingly gave me indispensable help. He provided valuable information about St. Cyril High School and the neighborhood it is in. He also provided the early picture of the high school building reproduced here, as well as the photograph of Farrell that appeared in the 1923 *Oriflamme*, the St. Cyril yearbook. I am grateful, too, to William F. Lederer for his thoughtful response to my inquiries.

Three persons now deceased deserve acknowledgment. Helen Farrell Dillon was exceptionally generous in devoting her time and concerned care in answering my questions about her brother, their family, and some of their Chicago friends. Mrs. Dillon also searched family records to supply certain birth and death dates of the Farrells and the Dalys as given in Appendix A. William Shannon encouraged my work and voluntarily sent me his correspondence with James Farrell. James Henle of the Vanguard Press also was encouraging and helpful. During the summer of 1957 in his Madison Avenue office he provided me with a comfortable chair, a table, a typewriter, and two packed file cases so that I might read—and copy some of—his voluminous correspondence with Jim Farrell.

Thanks also are extended to the following individuals: Michael T. Ryan, Director of Special Collections at the University of Pennsylvania Libraries, for his approval of my use of quotations from unpublished materials in the Farrell archives and of my reproduction of photographs from that collection; Nancy Shawcross, Curator of Manuscripts, and Dorothy Noyes, Manuscripts Processor, both of the Van Pelt Library at the University of Pennsylvania, for their helpful responses to my queries;

Richard L. Popp, Assistant University Archivist in Special Collections of the University of Chicago Library, for permission to reproduce two photographs; Maureen A. Harp, formerly Archives and Manuscript Assistant in the Special Collections Department of the University of Chicago Library, for helping me to locate those photographs; Margaret M. Sherry, Reference Librarian/Archivist, for permission to quote in their entirety two letters from James T. Farrell to be found in Samuel Putnam's *New Review* correspondence in the Manuscripts Division of the Princeton University Librairies' Department of Rare Books and Special Collections; and officials of the Chicago Park District for permission to print the photographs of Washington Park found in Chapter Three.

Patrick Morris, Map Cataloger of the Newberry Library, Chicago, and Emily Clark, Assistant Librarian of the Chicago Historical Society helped me locate a large 1904 map, and smaller maps of later dates, of Chicago's Washington Park. These were useful in the preparation of the park map in this book. Especially helpful were large 1914 and 1915 maps of the park provided by Bart Ryckbosch, Archivist, and Edward K. Uhlir, Director of Architecture, Engineering and Planning, both men of the Chicago Park District. Responding quickly to the request of my publisher Marshall Brooks, Ronald E. Grim, Head of the Reference and Bibliography Section, Geography and Map Division, the Library of Congress, forwarded copies of Sanborn Fire Insurance maps; and William A. Wortman, Humanities Librarian at King Library, Miami University, and the entire Interlibrary Loan Department there helped me locate and obtain microfilm reels of the indispensable Sanborn maps. To all these persons I am grateful for their crucial help.

Dean Judith Sessions, Director of the Miami University Libraries, and the entire Library staff of King Library, especially Miami's Special Collections Department, are owed a debt of thanks for their ever-willing help in forwarding the development of this book. During her last two years as a Miami student and as my assistant, Erica Lippincott provided essential technical services as well as efficiently exploring and organizing our common knowledge of some of the intricacies of Farrell's life and writings. For this I am most grateful.

Marshall Brooks, a knowledgeable man and a friend, a Farrell scholar, as well as the publisher of this book, has been involved in its development from the beginning. His advice and expertise were most helpful. He has gone the extra mile in making possible the artwork, the splendid maps, and the photographic reproductions in these pages. Stewart Brooks and Natalie Paynton-Brooks, read the entire manuscript and made important editorial suggestions. They also provided the index. Bob Oliver helped to produce the computer-generated maps and lent important book design assistance. I want to thank all these persons who were so essential in the production of this book.

My wife, Mary Jo, was with me most of the times my path crossed James Farrell's. Her interest in him was intense. Her understanding of him and her ability to formulate it in words often opened my eyes to profound levels of his nature that her insights laid bare. Her influence on the content of this book, as in everything I have written about him, is pervasive.

A Personal Statement: The Farrell Connection

JAMES T. FARRELL lived in Chicago for his first twenty-seven years, from 1904 to 1931. During the next quarter of a century he visited the city at least twenty-eight times. The pull was strong. After a 1954 visit he wrote: "The old Studs Lonigan neighborhood is a corner of America where many of my memories hide as though in blocks of stone and along dull and commonplace looking streets." It was, he continued, "one little corner of America . . . that . . . throbbed with significances of a personal past."[1]

Eight years later, Farrell wrote: "Thinking back over forty-seven years ago, it is startling to think of those quiet Chicago blocks around 57th and 58th Streets, and just west of Washington Park, as being 'the Studs Lonigan neighborhood'. . . . This boyhood milieu was tremendously and vividly real to me. It was as real as I was real to myself. It was important as life is important, because it was the encircling, surrounding fragment of the world in which I lived, with which I was familiar, and in which I played and grew, and dreamed. . . . If the reader will understand me here, in a feelingful sense, he will grasp why I cannot always fail to react when the boyhood environment in which I lived is carelessly falsified by others. It is as though I am being falsified."[2] What Farrell most frequently objected to was the belief that the neighborhood he had grown up in was a tenement-ridden slum overrun by gangs,[3] and the characterization of "that neighborhood and my life in it as something like, or akin to, a lower class Hell on the order of Dante's *Inferno*."[4]

During the mid-1940s at Miami University in Oxford, Ohio, I began teaching the upperclass semester course "Literature of the West." It was one of three regional American literature courses offered by the Department of English. We read American authors beginning with Mark Twain and leading up to the then-contemporary figures James T. Farrell, John Steinbeck, and A. B. Guthrie. Along the way we read writers like Edgar Howe, Joseph Kirkland, Hamlin Garland, Frank Norris, Upton Sinclair, Edgar Lee Masters, Vachel Lindsay, Carl Sandburg, Sinclair Lewis, Sherwood Anderson, and Ole Rolvaag, while giving special attention to William Dean Howells, Willa Cather, and Theodore Dreiser. In marking out "the West" we usually relied heavily on the ideas of Frederick Jackson Turner, but that did not stop us from defining *our* West so as to include, if we wished, almost any author not from the Eastern seaboard or the deep South.

The novel of Farrell's that we invariably read was *Studs Lonigan*. The students were impressed by its power. The trilogy had a strong shock value, and its cultural implications never failed to arouse genuine interest and intelligent, spirited discussion. I noticed, however, that a number of good students felt comfortable referring to Studs's Washington Park neighborhood as a slum, a word connoting blight and general human degradation. These students, and others, expressed sympathy for Studs because they tended to see the course of his life as having been largely determined by various "outside forces," among which was economic deprivation. Their sympathy may have been in order, but it seemed to me that they verged on picturing Studs's neighborhood as an Irish-Catholic ghetto, the womb of hordes of semi-tough semi-illiterates, and very little else. All of this, despite our awareness that for Farrell it was *spiritual* and not material poverty that saturated the neighborhood; and that he had vehemently denied—even in the introduction to the 1938 Modern Library edition of his trilogy which we were using—that Studs had lived in and been shaped by a slum.[5]

My feeling that the students' perceptions on this point left much to be desired grew out of my experience as a native Chicagoan and my personal knowledge of what has become known as "the Studs Lonigan neighborhood," a designation Farrell sometimes disapproved but repeatedly used. For my first twenty-five years I lived not very far from the streets Studs walked during his first twenty-seven years. My neighborhood was a small one, known as the Jackson Park Highlands. Four blocks by four blocks, it was restricted to large single family houses—no apartment buildings. It was tucked between Jackson Park to the north and the large South Shore district to the south and east. When, as a boy, I cut across a section of Jackson Park and followed the Midway past the University of Chicago, I found myself in Washington Park, which bordered Studs's neighborhood.

Moreover, in the 1920s as a kid, I was often driven in the family car through Washington Park, emerging along either the northern or southern boundary of Studs's neighborhood or, at times, going into the neighborhood itself. One of the routes my family and I took from Chicago's Loop or from my dad's office building at 1811 Prairie Avenue back to the Highlands was directly south down Michigan Avenue, which ran through the heart of that neighborhood. Later, in the mid-1930s when I was courting the Oak Park and River Forest High School girl who is still my wife, I often drove west down Garfield Boulevard (55th Street), the northern boundary of Studs's neighborhood, to eventually get to her home in River Forest. More often, however, I got there by taking the "L" train at 63rd Street and Stony Island Avenue and getting off at Lake and Harlem Avenues. This transportation gave me an overhead view of the Studs Lonigan neighborhood because the tracks crossed its entire breadth.

I knew all about the Washington Park tennis courts directly across the street from where Jim Farrell had lived on South Park Avenue (now Dr. Martin Luther

King Drive). Years later he told me that ever since his boyhood in the Corpus Christi parish he had known George Lott, Jr. [Ray Taite—see **A Note to the Reader,** below], the American Davis Cup star. In Washington Park he had played baseball with Lott, an accomplished all-around athlete; and, with other spectators, he had watched him—even when Lott was a boy in short pants—play tennis there with his partner Jim ("Shorty") Clark [Shorty Leach and Sad-Puss Brown]. I told him that in the late l920s I had spent two hours with Lott and his date because my best friend was that date's little brother. In those days I aspired to be a tennis star myself, played wherever I could—in the public parks, on University of Chicago courts, and at South Shore Country Club—and watched all the greats, especially Big Bill Tilden, when they came to Chicago.

And then there was my grade school friend, Smelly, a fast runner and a crack shot at marbles. He had moved from Studs's Michigan Avenue neighborhood to an apartment near my school, Parkside. His tennis shoes, worn in hot, cold, wet, or dry weather, earned him his nickname—and with no objection on his part. Smelly liked to talk about his exploits in the old neighborhood. One time when we were dropped off in Washington Park, he showed me where he had lived and where he had played baseball on the diamonds in the open meadow. Also in the mid-1920s I tried to teach him tennis on the park courts bordering South Park Avenue. On our way home we would sometimes walk down the lane leading across the Wooded Island, surrounded by the park lagoons.

Those are my earliest connections with the Studs Lonigan neighborhood. Today, looking back, I believe it is fair to say that in the mid-1920s I thought of it as an old, built-up district, plainer, more shopworn, less "modern" and less attractive than, for example, the expanding South Shore district, but nevertheless a respectable, mostly middle-middle class haven with a sprinkling of black residents. Generally speaking, the apartments and houses were well kept and pleasing. The streets were broad and clean. The stores of 58th Street, the central shopping strip for the neighborhood, were busy and served all the family needs of a striving, self-respecting community. In the late 1920s and the 1930s, to be sure, I observed the shift in the neighborhood's racial mix as white families moved a few miles south and east and black families moved in. But the neighborhood's outward appearance—its streets and buildings of all kinds—remained much the same. However, neither then nor earlier did I know of, or sense, the pervasive spiritual poverty Farrell found there: my knowledge of the neighborhood and its people was not that intimate.

So, girded with my memories and Farrell's protestations, how to explain what I believed to be my students' misunderstanding of the neighborhood?

I knew that part of the answer to that question was that very few of my students had read any of Farrell's four O'Neill-O'Flaherty novels published before 1948 and after the appearance of *Studs Lonigan* in 1935. These novels feature Danny O'Neill. Danny also lives in that neighborhood and knows Studs well, and no one would think of Danny as a slum product. He rises in life as Studs falls. As Farrell liked to say, Danny is Studs's "dialectical opposite." The students did not perceive the huge trilogy—powerfully projecting its dark malignity—as merely one panel in Farrell's more inclusive portrayal of human experience in a well-defined area of Chicago's South Side.[6]

A Note to the Reader

Many of Farrell's characters, like those of other authors, are imaginative projections of individuals he knew. Here and in following chapters names of real persons who served to some degree as inspirations for characters in Farrell's fiction are often followed by the relevant fictional names—within brackets—Farrell gave those characters. Similarly, names of fictional characters are often followed by the names—italicized, within brackets—of their real-life inspirations.

Had my students read the O'Neill-O'Flaherty novels, I conjectured, their understanding of Studs's neighborhood would have deepened. They would have appreciated the author's more balanced representation of all those ongoing human "destinies" (a word he liked to use) rooted in the neighborhood—the individual lives that with time spread out in many directions and that Farrell marked out in the total body of his fiction. After all, from the spring of 1929 when he wrote the short story "Studs," he saw the significance of Studs's tragic march toward an early death. But that story was only one among many in his imagination's repertoire. Farrell's literary intentions in his trilogy led him to focus upon Studs and his friends and what happened to *them*. It was a story, he came to realize, that he needed to get out of his system before he explored his personal past within his family and neighborhood. Danny O'Neill and his kind properly were given minor roles in *Studs Lonigan*. As John Chamberlain [Carl Jensen] put it, the Arnoldian view that art should see life steadily and see it whole—what some critics had asserted Farrell failed to achieve in his trilogy—"would deny the principle of literary division of labor. Why should a novelist, writing about Studs Lonigan, be required to drag in Velasquez and Joe Smith?"[7]

Even so, I wondered, shouldn't the trilogy, a self-contained work, have been self-sufficiently more detailed, more imagistic, at least in its portrayal of the youthful

Studs's physical surroundings: all those outward signs of what is or is not a slum—the streets, the apartment buildings, the stores, the churches and schools? Why was it, when some students (as well as some book reviewers and literary critics) read *Studs Lonigan*, they thought "slum" and imagined a deteriorated neighborhood, and I, for the most part, because I had been there, thought no such thing?

I came to believe that another key to unlocking the answer to this persistent riddle was an understanding of one consequence of the innovative objective method Farrell successfully employed in his trilogy. In a famous passage, the author observed that in writing *Studs Lonigan*, "I set as my aim that of unfolding the destiny of Studs Lonigan in his own words, his own actions, his own patterns of thought and feeling." He wanted to "recreate a sense of what life meant to Studs Lonigan . . . setting up as an ideal the strictest possible objectivity"[8]—an ideal to be realized by conveying the texture of Studs's consciousness and avoiding the direct authorial intrusion of commentary, analysis, and generalization. Several decades later, Farrell summed up his intention this way: "I was concerned with being concrete, specific, and accurate in detail, and in writing the entire story of Studs Lonigan in such a way, with only the use of such words and conceptions, that both language and conception were within the range of Studs' experience, mentality, knowledge and associations."[9] In most of *Studs Lonigan* Farrell adhered to this practice and, as scholars have recognized, forged his own distinctive manner of representing Studs's stream of consciousness or, when narrative progression required it, that of other characters. Farrell's total narrative method, in fact, permitted him, when called for, to transcend Studs's consciousness by various means, thereby placing Studs's mind and spirit in a social and psychological context that gives them added meaning and resonance.

Studs, the major character subjected to Farrell's method, has many feelings, but if they do not conform to the tough he-man ideal he came to live by, he customarily—although not always—shunts them aside. He has an average intelligence, but his ideas and beliefs are sluggishly conventional, and he rarely questions them. He is inarticulate. He knows that "he couldn't hit upon words that would say what he wanted to say" (*YL*, 199). Nor is he especially observant. His awareness is not multi-layered, nor is it attuned to the finer subtleties and nuances of human experience. His consciousness is not overly absorbent and wide-ranging. Its patterns and responses tend to be predictable. Farrell's objective method makes full use of those limitations in order to honestly explore the reality of Studs's psyche. The result is a stylistic and psychological triumph. As readers, we feel we are directly exposed to Studs's crippled being. We understand him from the inside out, and step by slow step we follow his decline to its deadly outcome.

An early and to me still puzzling criticism of Farrell's Studs Lonigan novels is that they sacrificed artistry to photographic realism, visual documentation. To the contrary, or so it seems to me, Farrell's very success in employing his method, his faithfulness to the ideal of projecting life "within the range" of Studs's limited consciousness, usually leaves most of the physical world Studs knows dim and shadowed. Studs lives his youth and young manhood in one small neighborhood. He is thoroughly familiar with it. It is not new to him. He knows his way around, and much of his life is routine. Usually he has little or no reason to register or mirror his surroundings (although Farrell's method ensures that we know where Studs *is* most of the time), so his conscious mind does not fully reflect those surroundings. This is true, for example, when he is riding around the neighborhood and its near environs with Mr. O'Brien and his son Johnny while Mr. O'Brien checks up on deliveries from his coal yard. And of course Studs does not go in for set descriptions of his immediate environment. When Farrell needs a detailed description—as when he wants us to see (and ironically appreciate) the material splendors of Father Gilhooley's new church building—his narrative method permits him to temporarily step outside Studs's consciousness, in that instance in an inter-chapter.

Only on rare occasions, as when Studs and Lucy go to the Wooded Island, or when Studs first gains admittance to the poolroom, or when he sits next to the mysterious girl during Christmas mass in St. Patrick's Church, does the emotional turmoil within intensify his sensitivity to the world around him. That world then becomes emblematic of the boy's inner experience as Farrell selectively clothes it in the language of visual documentation. In reading *Studs Lonigan*, we never doubt that the physical world is *there*. We never question that Studs, when sober, is normally aware of its enveloping particularity at any given time. As we read, we understand that it interacts with the flow of Studs's thoughts and feelings. But where, in *Studs Lonigan*, are copiously detailed realistic visual descriptions of the urban environment? Of street corners, poolrooms, bars, stores, brothels, city blocks, church exteriors, school or apartment interiors, park playgrounds, ball fields? Rather than *filtering into* Studs's consciousness to appear on the printed page in brilliantly sharp realistic detail, the bulk of the material world around Studs usually is *glazed over*, although never obliterated, by his consciousnesss as revealed by the author.[10] It is Studs's psychology and not what physically surrounds him, even though the latter unquestionably affects the direction Studs takes in life, that Farrell primarily wanted to capture by his method. The dominating end result of the author's method in the trilogy, as well as the intention behind it, was the exploration and exposure of Studs's inner reality—somewhat at the expense of visual documentation.

With such notions in mind, and desiring to provide a compensating visual record that might prove helpful to my students, I returned to Chicago in August 1948. While there, I took all the photographs included in this book that are not attributed to other sources. On four successive hot days, carrying a Kodak Brownie camera and a sheaf of notes, I walked through Washington Park itself and that portion of the Washington Park neighborhood that Farrell defined as his own in his writings. His usual practice of exactly locating the sites mentioned in his fiction provided me with a ready guide in my wandering. I discovered that the major scenes I wanted to photograph were still where he had indicated they were, although, to be sure, the businesses and the occupants of the 58th Street stores had changed. For the most part the buildings in the area appeared to be in good repair and recently painted. The building on the corner of 57th Street and Indiana Avenue that Danny O'Neill (and Farrell) lived in carried a sign reading "Royal 1, 2 and 3 Room Apts"—which suggested that the larger apartments formerly there had been divided up. In some places the street gutters and the parkways were littered with scraps of paper. Nevertheless, as best I could judge, it was evident that outwardly the neighborhood remained essentially the same as it had been during the time period spanned by the trilogy.

I recall seeing only blacks on the street. Those few that I talked with usually seemed friendly and interested, although wary. I asked a young man at the park boathouse landing why there were no boats out in the lagoon. He said something about the cost and the poor condition of some of the boats. At Danny O'Neill's (and Farrell's) apartment building on South Park Avenue I swallowed hard and asked an old man coming down the front porch steps if it would be possible to see inside his apartment because I used to know someone who lived there. He ignored my impropriety, looked at me blankly, did not even shake his head, and passed on by.

In the mid-1950s I drove through the neighborhood on a blazing hot Saturday in August. There were few cars moving. The sidewalks and streets on many blocks were crowded with children and adults escaping the withering heat indoors—far more people, it seemed to me, than possibly could have lived within the buildings that lined the streets. It was a sure sign that the neighborhood had been tenementized. In one block—I forget the street—the passage of my car was temporarily blocked by men and boys playing ball, riding bicycles, and talking in groups. I learned what I should have understood before coming: automobile traffic was not welcome there on a torrid weekend; the street, like the park, was a playing field.

I made my final drive through the Studs Lonigan neighborhood early in August 1992. Many, if not most, of the buildings—even those on once fashionable Michigan Avenue—looked deserted and crumbling, uncared for and with broken windows. Open spaces had replaced many other buildings. Danny O'Neill's apartment building on Dr. Martin Luther King Drive (formerly South Park Avenue) was gone. The stores on 58th Street looked bombed out or torched. Only a few cars were on the streets. A few men stood in small groups here and there, doing nothing. Now, at last, the Studs Lonigan neighborhood or what was left of it might with some reason be called a slum, or worse.

The present book also briefly puts the Studs Lonigan neighborhood into the context of the wider Chicago world that Danny O'Neill (and Farrell), but not Studs, entered into. It includes pictures of Danny's high school; the University of Chicago's Cobb Hall where, in the large lecture room, Danny took most of his courses; the campus Coffee Shop, where Danny tested his new ideas against those of fellow students; and the 57th Street Hyde Park Art Colony, the center of South Side Bohemia in the 1920s and for a brief period Danny's hangout.

This personal memoir of my connections with an important segment of Farrell's Chicago would be incomplete were I not to mention my four student years at the University of Chicago High School (known as U. High).[11] Those years roughly coincided with the years Farrell walked from his South Park Avenue home across Washington Park to his university classes. Later, in the mid-1930s, when Farrell's life was still virtually unknown to me, I, too, relaxed in the campus Coffee Shop and took university classes in the large lecture room of Cobb Hall. There one of my teachers was Robert Morss Lovett who, along with Professor Linn, Farrell credited with being "the spiritual godfathers of *Studs Lonigan.*"[12] I first read the trilogy at that time. Its appeal was instantaneous and emotional, coming as a revelation of identities and differences, of what I was and what I was not, of what I knew to be profoundly true and what I did not know at all, until then.

When I learned more about Farrell's life, I also learned that I shared his, as well as Danny O'Neill's, passion for baseball. I, too, was a faithful White Sox fan, often made the trek to Comiskey Park, took my grandmother there—she understood the game better than Julia Daly did, and listened on the radio to every game she did not see—and counted Eddie Collins, Ray Schalk, and Red Faber among my sports heroes. By tossing a tennis ball against a brick wall, I too invented imaginative baseball games between all-star lineups that I managed in my mind. Jackson Park, a block and one half from my home, with its wide open spaces, its two golf courses, its trails, its Lake Michigan beach, and the exhilarating ice-skating it provided on its sinuous lagoon, was my Washington Park and that of my gang of boys from Constance and Bennett Avenues.

My gang and I had our clubhouse, a shack we built in a vacant lot. We had our internal fights and cliques. We dug trenches and warred with a "foreign" gang. We had our poolroom too—benignly located, to be sure, in the basement of a member's house. Our juvenile neighborhood raids were at least as criminal as smashing windows with rotten tomatoes from my dad's garden. Sometimes we played with—and "rated"—the neighborhood girls. We gingerly experimented with sex. When puberty closed in on us, we made secret expeditions to those State Street burlesque houses bordering the Loop that attracted Studs.

Years after the end of World War I my gang and I, like Danny O'Neill and his friends, with spectacular bravado disposed of "Kaiser Bill" in play and song. In complete disconnection from our friendship with the sons and daughters of a large Jewish family in the neighborhood, most of us sang about Abie Kabibble, the King of the Jews, and what he did with the *Daily News*. With even more abandon, we sang the song beginning "Policeman, policeman, don't shoot me. Shoot that Nigger behind the tree." If prevailing conditions in Studs's and Danny's neighborhood help us to understand their prejudices, can that be said about boys growing up in the Jackson Park Highlands?

Upon reading Farrell's fiction, my recognition of the truth—and, in time, the artistry—of his depiction of Chicago and of the social and inner lives of his young people, especially the boys and young men, was bone deep. I was, I suppose, a happy and willing convert to the appeal of his fiction. Reading it, I felt I had been there before.

In 1938 at the University of Iowa I had the opportunity to read *Studs Lonigan* again while studying with Wilbur Schramm, a gifted teacher and then the Director of the Iowa Creative Writing Program. The trilogy still cast its spell, and I learned to appreciate it even more as an in-depth fusion of the psychological, social, and material worlds of Studs, a representative urban American.

Farrell informed me in 1957 that between 1928 and 1931, having moved out of the Washington Park neighborhood, he lived in at least three places—including one in the Jackson Park Highlands at 7046 Euclid Avenue—within three to six blocks from my home at 6829 Constance Avenue. There he labored mightily to write what became *Young Lonigan* and *The Young Manhood of Studs Lonigan*. He walked—and put into a portion of his fiction—the same streets and the expanse of Jackson Park I had frequented for years, and he went to the same movie houses and drugstores and beaches.

As these remarks may suggest, my personal Chicago past holds a warm and enduring place in my memory, not the least because of "the Farrell connection" it gave me. My experience of the city differed in major ways from Farrell's. But it helped cement my interest in him and my admiration for his writings. I hope this book adds to its readers' understanding of Farrell's work; and in particular, that its photographs enable readers to better visualize some of the streets, buildings, playgrounds, and institutions—all so meaningful to him—that help define and anchor the Studs Lonigan neighborhood as a vital presence in his Chicago fiction.

---

[1] "Farrell Revisits Studs Lonigan's Neighborhood," *New York Times Book Review*, 20 June 1954, p. 12.

[2] "Dut" (a fragment of Farrell's typescript of his abandoned book on *Studs Lonigan* intended for Dutton Publishers), p. 42.

[3] This notion persists even today. In his excellent book *Worker-Writer in America*, (Urbana and Chicago, 1994), p. 332, Douglas Wixson has written: "The decisive experience for Farrell had been urbanization with its tenements, street gangs, and thwarted ambitions." Unless extensively qualified, that characterization of Farrell's Chicago boyhood and young manhood inevitably is misleading. Moreover it carries with it strong overtones of our current awareness of contemporary massive urban decay with its dominance of entire neighborhoods by murderous street gangs.

[4] "Autobiography," completed 10 March 1973, p. 1019.

[5] Farrell's letter of January 13, 1961, to the editor of *Cue Magazine* typically disputes what he believed to be misconceptions about Studs's neighborhood: "Studs Lonigan did not live in an atmosphere without hope, nor was he a rebellious 'juvenile delinquent.' A large part of the trilogy deals with Studs after he had passed his twenty-first birthday. He did have a future and some of the characters envied him for it—he would take over his father's business. There was *no* gangsterism or vice in the neighborhood in which Studs lived. And Studs did not live in 'a slum-ridden South Side' of Chicago. The trilogy does not indicate any of this."

[6] For almost six years (June 1929 to February 1, 1935) Farrell worked on *Studs Lonigan*. During all that time he saw Studs's story in the context of the story of Danny O'Neill and his family, a tale that gradually took shape in his mind but one that he "was not then ready or able to tell." Nevertheless, while he was writing his trilogy, Farrell stated, "I conceived Studs and Danny O'Neill as opposites. . . . I saw in Studs an example of defeat and disintegration: in Danny, I saw the opposite. Studs loses; Danny wins" ("The Story of *Studs Lonigan*," pp. 3-4, the

Department of Special Collections, University of Pennsylvania Libraries).

[7] "Introduction" to *Studs Lonigan* (New York: Vanguard Press, 1935), p. x. During each period of his life, Farrell demonstrated a remarkable capacity to meet, know, stay in touch with, and remember an astonishing number of people. Referring to his boyhood in the neighborhood, he wrote, "[I] knew hundreds of kids. I couldn't put in all, whom I knew, in *Studs* and in my early stories" (Letter, Farrell to Branch, 4 Sept. 1976). Farrell repeatedly pointed out that the Irish and the Catholics were distinct minorities in the neighborhood. Many more kids went to Carter Public School than to St. Anselm. There is little doubt that Farrell knew most of them.

[8] "Introduction" to *Studs Lonigan* (Chicago: The Modern Library, 1938), p. xi. Farrell's aim, as stated above, should not be taken to mean that he wrote *Studs Lonigan* with a fully preconceived plan in mind or to illustrate "clear cut and firm general ideas and theses.... With me, the writing of a novel is an adventure and a discovery. I plunge into it with only a sense of the general direction which it will take." As he wrote, organized, and re-wrote, new meanings and new directions continued to emerge. ("The Story of Studs Lonigan," p. 7, the Department of Special Collections, University of Pennsylvania Libraries.) Whenever possible, quotations from *Studs Lonigan* and other of Farrell's published works will be cited in the text by title-symbols, identified in the section on "Abbreviations."

[9] "Introduction to Studs Lonigan," completed 16 Feb. 1972, pp. 38-39, renumbered from cancelled page numbers 132-133.

[10] The view expressed here is somewhat at odds with that of my friend Robert Butler who states in an excellent article that *Studs Lonigan* "provides a densely rendered, fully reified world" and "describes the urban setting in copious detail, providing a complete sense of external reality." See "Farrell's Ethnic Neighborhood and Wright's Urban Ghetto: Two Visions of Chicago's South Side," *Melus*, 18 (Spring 1993), p. 104.

[11] In 1919 Farrell's uncle, Tom Daly, tried to enroll his nephew in the University of Chicago High School, even though tuition was high. According to Farrell, no more admissions were being accepted when the application was made. Eugene Goodwillie [Albert Throckmorton] and George Lott, Jr. [Ray Taite], two boys Farrell knew from the time he lived in Corpus Christi parish, were admitted and became star athletes there. Goodwillie became a Rhodes Scholar and later a successful Wall Street lawyer.

[12] "Introduction" to *Studs Lonigan*, Modern Library edition (New York: Random House, 1938), p. xi.

Key to Map

Sixty buildings and landmarks are identified on this map illustrating the Chicago neighborhood Farrell depicted in many of his major novels and short stories—the very same neighborhood where Farrell lived for thirteen years. Fictional names have been set in **boldface** type; actual names in plain-face type.

1. Michigan Theater.
2. **Joseph's Ice Cream Parlor**. Here **Studs** and his gang jump their soda bill.
3. 55th St. Elevated Train Station.
4. Wolley Memorial Methodist Episcopal Church.
5. State St. **saloon**. **Paddy Lonigan** sometimes drinks beer here.
6. **Lonigans'** Wabash Avenue home.
7. William W. Carter Public School and Gymnasium.
8. Carter Public School playground.
9. **Lonigans'** Michigan Avenue home. **Mr. Lonigan** owns the bldg.
10. **"Can house"** (whorehouse) on 57th St..
11. First home of the **O'Flahertys** and **Danny O'Neill** in the "Studs Lonigan neighborhood." The **Le Gare**, **Borax**, and O'Dea families live here too.
12. **Johnny O'Brien's** home. The first of three two-story graystone apt. buildings.
13. **Helen Shires's** home. The second of three two-story graystone apt. buildings.
14. **Lucy Scanlan's** home. The third of three two-story graystone apt. buildings.
15. **Bill** and **Dan Donoghue's** home.
16. **Old Man O'Callaghan's** house.
17. **Red O'Connell's** home. **Mr. O'Connell** owns the building.
18. Vacant lot, neighborhood boys play here.
19. Three row-bldgs. whose back porch iceboxes are looted by **Studs** and his friends.
20. **Levin's Drug Store**. **Studs** and **Helen Shires** have sodas here.
21. Henry the Tailor's Shop. **Studs** and his gang sometimes hang out at Henry's. Egged on by **Studs**, Jimmy Farrell and Joe Baron had a fist fight here.
22. Prairie Motion Picture Theater.
23. **Iris's** home. Scene of the gang-shag.
24. Crerar Memorial Presbyterian Church.
25. Drugstore.
26. Palmer's Bakery.
27. **Gus the Greek's Restaurant**.
28. 58th St. Elevated Train Station.
29. **Bathcellar's Billiard Parlor and Barber Shop**.
30. Hirsch's Grocery Store.
31. Levy's Tailor Shop.
32. Savois's Drug Store.
33. Billy Maurer's home.
34. St. Edmund's Episcopal Church and playground.
35. **Cohen's Tailor Shop**. **Davey Cohen's** father is the owner.
36. Palm Movie Theater.
37. **Schreiber's Ice Cream Parlor**. **Studs** and his gang raid it in the owner's absence. (Spelled "Schroeder's" in YMSL.)
38. **Five and Dime Store**.
39. **Sternberg's Cigar Store**.
40. Home of Joe Cody and Tommy Barnes.
41. Home of the **O'Flahertys** and **Danny O'Neill** after May 1, 1917.
42. **Saloon** on State St. **Jim O'Neill** drinks here.
43. State St. Elevated Train Station.
44. Clarence Rowland's (Chicago White Sox manager) home.
45. **Kenny Killarney's** home.
46. Walter Rogan's home.
47. **Jim** and **Lizz O'Neill's** home after Spring of 1918.
48. Abraham Clarkson's house.
49. Natalie O'Reilly's home. Natalie was the prettiest girl in Jimmy Farrell's grammar school class.
50. John McDonough's home.
51. **St. Patrick's Parish House**. **Father Gilhooley** lives here.
52. **New St. Patrick's Catholic Church** built by **Father Gilhooley**.
53. Old St. Patrick's Church-School-Parish building. **Studs** and **Danny O'Neill** graduate from here.
54. **New St. Patrick's School**, built after **Danny O'Neill** graduates.
55. St. Patrick School playground.
56. **St. Patrick's Convent**. During the school year Sister Magdalen and Sister Bertha live here.
57. 61st St. Elevated Train Station.
58. Dorothy McPartlin's home.
59. SS. Constantine and Helen's Greek Orthodox Church.
60. Church playground.

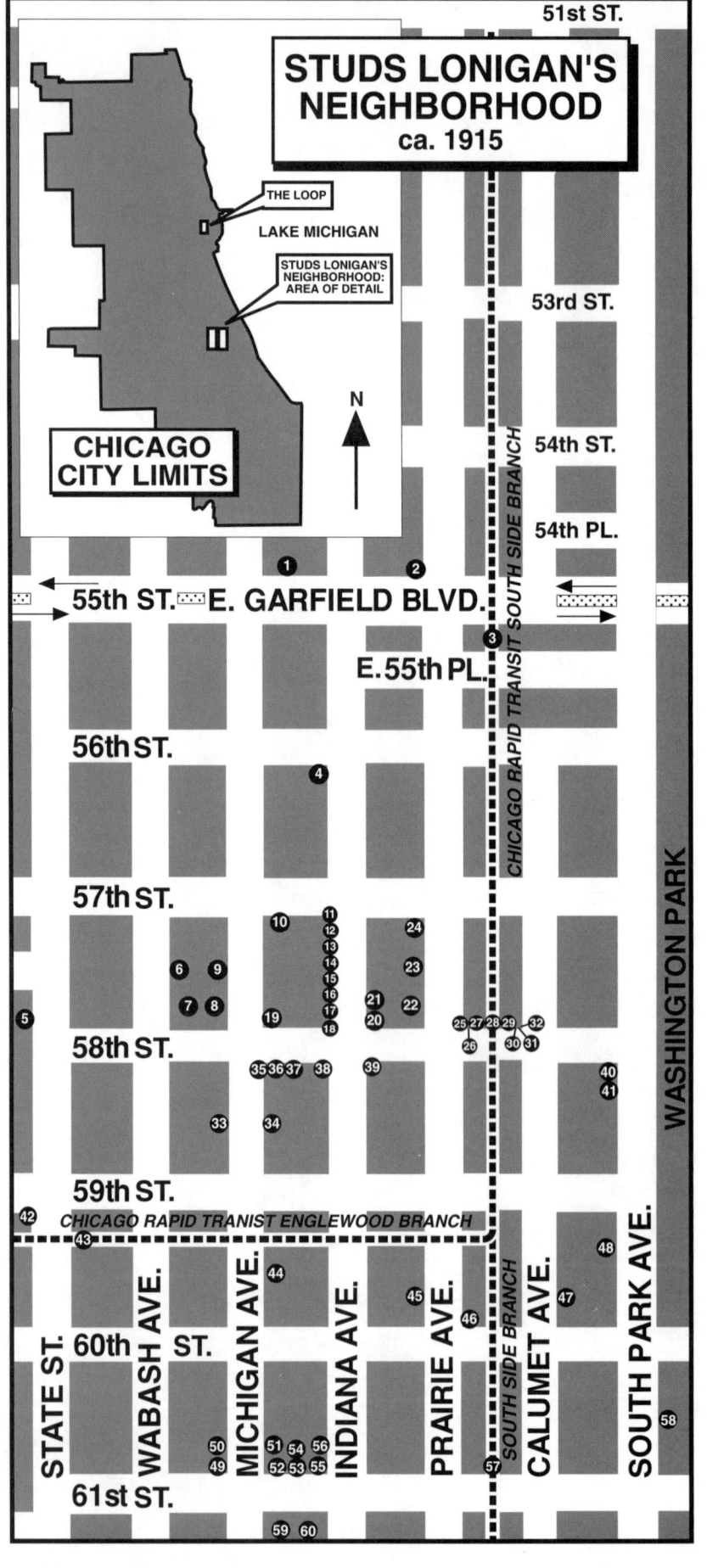

STUDS LONIGAN'S NEIGHBORHOOD
ca. 1915

WASHINGTON PARK
ca. 1915

Key to Map
1. Duck pond, wading pool, and sand court.
2. Tennis courts.
3. Refectory.
4. Playground.
5. Goldfish pond.
6. Ball field shelter.
7. Boathouse.
8. Log Bridge. Rustic Bridge.
9. Oak tree (**Studs** and **Lucy**).
10. Sheep pen.
11. Stone bridge. Farmstead Bridge.
12. Flag pole (78' high).
13. Armory.
14. Lawn bowling.
15. Rose Garden.
16. Conservatory and Greenhouse.
17. Bug Club.
18. Administration building.
19. Stable.
20. Power house.
21. Location of four roque courts.
22. Storage and machine shops.

While available archival materials fail to identify—conclusively—the "Lily Pool," it is more than likely the pool identified as such on this map is correct.

On a 1905 South Park Commissioners' map NORTH WEST and NORTH EAST DRIVES are labled **Bayard Ave.**; SOUTH WEST and SOUTH DRIVES, **Lafayette Ave.**; and SOUTH EAST DRIVE, **Palmer Ave.**, respectively. Later maps issued by the South Park Commissioners during —roughly—the Studs Lonigan era label the major Washington Park thoroughfares as they are shown on the present map.

South Park Commissioners' Maps dated 1905, 1914, and 1915, generously supplied by the Chicago Park District, provided many of the essential details found on the accompanying map of Washington Park.

Maps by Marshall Brooks and Bob Oliver.

Chapter One: The Studs Lonigan Neighborhood: A Visual Record

THE WABASH AVENUE HOME OF THE LONIGAN FAMILY

THIS TWO-STORY BUILDING is on the east side of the street in the 5700 block of Wabash Avenue. Its back yard is next to the fence marking the boundary of the Carter Public School playground. For almost twenty-two years it remains the home of the Lonigan family. They live on the first floor and rent the second floor. Paddy Lonigan [*Patrick F. Cunningham*; also the fictional Tom Jennings][1] the son of "a pauperized greenhorn" (*YL*, 13), is a first generation Irish American who, through his hard work, has made it in Chicago as a plastering and painting contractor. During the evening of June 16, 1916, an hour or two before Studs and Frances Lonigan are to graduate from nearby St. Patrick's [*St. Anselm's*] grammar school, he sits on his back porch digesting a juicy beefsteak and watching neighborhood kids in the Carter School playground on Michigan Avenue to the east.

In a mellow reminiscent mood, and proud of his success and all that he has been able to do for his children, Paddy recalls the old days of hardship when he had lived around 35th and Halsted and had fallen for Mary [*Bridget Feeney, the future Mrs.Cunningham*; also the fictional Julia Jennings]. He remembers one Sunday in 1900 when he had rented a buggy and had driven with Mary out to his present neighborhood. It was nearly all trees and woods then, he recalls, with hardly any people or buildings, and "Fifty-eighth Street was nothing but a wilderness" (*YL, 14*). He had bought their Wabash Avenue building before Studs was born;[2] and at that time, he remembers, "Wabash Avenue had been a nice, decent, respectable street for a self-respecting man to live with his family" (*YL, 19*).

While Studs Lonigan [*William ("Studs") Cunningham*] lives in this building, he wins and loses the affection of Lucy Scanlan [*Lucy Shannon*], feels elation at his first visit to Charley Bathcellar's [*Charley Batcheler's*] pool-

---

A NOTE TO THE READER
Most of the photographs (all taken in 1948 by the author except where otherwise noted) and commentary in this chapter reflect the neighborhood and its characters as presented in the trilogy *Studs Lonigan*. But other relevant works by Farrell, especially two of the O'Neill-O'Flaherty novels, also are drawn on. The order in which the photographs are presented roughly corresponds with the chronology of activities and interests in the lives of Studs Lonigan and Danny O'Neill. In keeping with this chronology, groups of street scenes alternate with groups of park scenes. Chapter Three contains additional photographs of Washington Park. Fictional names from *Studs* and other of Farrell's works appear within the photograph captions in **bold face** type. Names of actual people and places appear throughout the captions in *italics*.

The Wabash Avenue home of the **Lonigan** family.

room, plays hookey from high school, briefly runs away from home as "Lonewolf Lonigan," and, at 17, begins to work as a plasterer and painter for "the gaffer," his "old man."

Paddy sells his Wabash Avenue building in the late summer of 1922 and purchases a modern six-flat building on Michigan Avenue. Earlier, he had feared that "the niggers and kikes were getting in . . . And when they got into a neighborhood property values went blooey" (*YL, 19*). But he has faith that the expensive elegance of the apartment buildings on his new street and the coming construction of the nearby and imposing St. Patrick's Church will increase the value of his new investment.

THE O'FLAHERTYS' HOME ON THE SOUTHWEST CORNER OF
57TH STREET AND INDIANA AVENUE

On May 1, 1915, a little more than a year before Studs Lonigan graduates from St. Patrick's, Mrs. Mary O'Flaherty [*Julia Brown Daly*; also the fictional Grace Hogan Dunne] and two of her grown and unmarried children, Al and Margaret [*Thomas Richard Daly* and *Ellen (Ella) J. Daly*], move into the six-room, first-floor south apartment of this three-story, six-flat, red-brick building.

The **O'Flahertys'** home on the southwest corner of 57th Street and Indiana Avenue.

The family had come about six blocks south from their former apartment at 5137½ Prairie Avenue. Living with them here, at 5704 Indiana Avenue, are Mary O'Flaherty's favorite grandchild, eleven year old Danny O'Neill [*James T. Farrell*] and, after the fall of 1916, Danny's younger sister, Little Margaret [*Helen Farrell*] then ten years old. Because Uncle Al is often on the road and Aunt Margaret often works at night, Little Margaret is especially welcome in the household as a companion for Danny and her grandmother. Little Margaret and Danny are children of Mrs. O'Flaherty's daughter Lizz and Lizz's husband Jim O'Neill [*Mary Daly Farrell* and *James Francis Farrell*], who find it difficult to provide for all their children on Jim's wages. The move to Indiana Avenue brings this family of five from Crucifixion [*Corpus Christi*] parish into St. Patrick's [*St. Anselm's*] parish. Danny (like Jimmy Farrell) is permitted to finish the final month of his fourth grade schooling in Sister Carmel's class at St. Patrick's grammar school.

Danny welcomes the change. He had got in bad with the kids in the old neighborhood. They had teased him as a "goof," had called him "Four Eyes" (like Jimmy Farrell, Danny began wearing glasses in the spring of 1912) and had meanly laughed at him because his Aunt Margaret used to get loudly drunk. On the day of the move Danny comes from his old school to the new neighborhood to help with the moving. A half-block away from his new home, he meets two older neighborhood fellows, Johnny O'Brien [*Johnny Johnson*], a near neighbor on Indiana Avenue, and Studs Lonigan. After talking, they part on friendly terms—a good sign for the fresh start Danny hopes to make.

Also living in Danny's new apartment building are Andy Le Gare [*Andrew Dugar*], his older brother and sister, and his parents. Andy, a spunky kid and a good scrapper, is a year younger than Danny and goes to the Carter Public School. Ralph Borax [*Ralph von Borries*], his older sister Helen [*Helen von Borries*], and their mother, a public school teacher, also live in the same apartment building. Andy and Ralph are part of the Indiana Street bunch that Danny soon joins; and Ralph, in 1916, is the first kid—and, Danny claims, the last—to beat him in a fight. Helen Borax later has a crush on tough Weary Reilley [*Frank Egan*] and sympathizes with him after Studs licks him in a fist fight.

Two years to the day after moving to Indiana Avenue, Mary O'Flaherty and her brood, now augmented by another grown son, Ned [*William J. Daly*], move about four blocks away to South Park Avenue, on the western border of Washington Park.

VIEW OF THE O'FLAHERTYS' INDIANA AVENUE APARTMENT BUILDING

View of the **O'Flahertys'** Indiana Avenue apartment building as photographed in 1917. (The Department of Special Collections, University of Pennsylvania Libraries.)

On March 2, 1949, Farrell's boyhood friend Andy Dugar [Andy Le Gare] sent him this picture. In his letter Andy stated that it was taken by his brother Sid in 1917 when the Dugars lived on the first floor north of the building. The man standing by the mail box at the corner of 57th and Indiana Avenue is Andy's father. Mr. Dugar is a waiter in the Chicago Loop hotel where Farrell's aunt Ella is the cashier. Farrell gave him fictional life as the embittered but militant Mr. Le Gare, who in 1922 is unemployed and blacklisted because, as treasurer of his union and a strike committee member, he leads the strike against the hotel management (Inter-chapter VII, *YMSL*, 104-5).

VIEW FROM THE O'FLAHERTYS' FORMER INDIANA AVENUE APARTMENT BUILDING

Sid Dugar also photographed this view after his family had moved to the third floor. The picture was taken from the rear window of the Dugar apartment which was on the 57th Street side of the building. It looks to the southwest and shows the rear of the apartment buildings on the east side of Michigan Avenue. In his letter to Farrell, Andy Dugar points out that the picture shows Johnny Johnson's garage (lower right corner); the alley between Indiana and Michigan Avenues in which he and Jimmy Farrell used to chase up and down (above the garage); and Marion Shearer's [Marion Shires's] playhouse in the back yard of the Shearer's apartment building. After Studs licks Weary Reilley, he and some of the boys and girls who had cheered him on have a victory lunch in the playhouse. "It was a fine lunch, and afterward they played post office, and Lucy [*Lucy Shannon*, the girl Studs likes] gave her hero plenty of kisses. Life was fine and dandy for Studs, all right" (*YL*, 87).

View from the **O'Flahertys'** former Indiana Avenue apartment building, as photographed in 1918. (The Department of Special Collections, University of Pennsylvania Libraries.)

FATHER MICHAEL GILHOOLEY [*MICHAEL S. GILMARTIN*]

In Farrell's fiction the spiritual leader of young Irish-Catholic boys like Danny O'Neill, Studs Lonigan, and Johnny O'Brien, all of them residents of St. Patrick's Parish, is Father Michael Gilhooley [*Father Michael S. Gilmartin*]. Born in County Sligo, Ireland, in 1868, Father Gilmartin came to the United States as a young man of sixteen and received his classical and theological training in the East. After serving seventeen years in two other parishes (Holy Angels in Chicago and St. Mary's in Woodstock, Illinois), he was appointed pastor of the new St. Anselm's Parish on June 14, 1909. At that time the parish included some 400 Catholic families. Within little more than a month, Father Gilmartin had held his first services in makeshift quarters on Indiana Avenue and had purchased property for the construction of a combination church-school-parish hall building, and a rectory. Farrell characterized the pastor extensively in his fiction, especially in *Studs Lonigan* and the short story "Reverend Father Gilhooley."

Father Michael S. Gilmartin, model for **Father Michael Gilhooley**. (Courtesy of the Archives of the Archdiocese of Chicago.)

ST. PATRICK'S [*ST. ANSELM'S*] COMBINATION CHURCH-SCHOOL-PARISH HALL BUILDING

Acting for the Order of Providence, Father Gilmartin lost no time in constructing his combination church-school-parish hall building. Completed December 5, 1909, the building was a long, brown brick structure fronting on 61st Street between Indiana and Michigan Avenues. The street level basement provided an auditorium with a stage (where Studs and Frances Lonigan graduate in 1916, and Danny O'Neill in 1919) and other recreational rooms for dancing classes, social gatherings, and bazaars. The church, which seated 900 people, was on the first floor. Wide-step entrances led into it from the building's front and (near the altar) from both sides. The school, accommodating 500 children, was on the second floor. Classes began on September 9, 1910, with 200 stu-

St. Patrick's and **St. Michael's** [*St. Anselm's*] combination church-school-parish hall building. (Courtesy of the Archives of the Archdiocese of Chicago.)

dents enrolled.

Inside, as outside, the church was ordinary and plain in appearance. While waiting to take confession before the football game with the 47th Street Monitors, Studs is vaguely aware of the church interior as "a low-ceilinged structure of boxed-in gloom" (*YMSL*, 110). Jim O'Neill, a reluctant church-goer, stolidly observes the low, calcimined ceiling and sees the dim interior as "barnlike" (*F&S*, 290).

Some of Farrell's main characters seek their own brand of salvation in this building. Jim O'Neill's fanatically devout wife Lizz, while living nearby, is a daily visitor: praying, lighting candles, following the stations of the cross, and leaving generous cash gifts. Her son Danny O'Neill, whether in his period of unquestioned Catholicism or of guilty backsliding, is often a serious-minded church-goer. Studs, as a young boy, sings in the choir. We see him at twenty-one, bleary with a hangover, attending Christmas Day mass. Self-castigations, guilt feelings, conventional religious impulses, boyhood memories, and sexual yearnings stimulated by the presence of a "voluptuous blond" (*YMSL*, 192) seated next to him crowd together in his consciousness.

In the school upstairs the students, from the third grade through the eighth, are segregated in different classrooms by gender. Third and fourth graders of the same sex are combined in one classroom, as are students in the fifth and sixth grades, and those in the seventh and eighth grades. Narrow dressing rooms with wall hooks on either side separate the boys' rooms from the girls'.

For Studs, graduation means that he "was kissin' the old dump goodbye" (*YL*, 3), and for Weary Reilley school is "so much horse apple" (*YL*, 41). But Danny, after his graduation, leaves the building "almost crying" (*F&S*, 135) and alone, his emotions a chaotic mix of poignant loss and fearful anticipation.

St. Patrick's [*St. Anselm's*] Convent

The teachers at St. Patrick's School are Sisters of the Order of Providence, whose home convent is at Notre Dame, Indiana. The St. Anselm's [St. Patrick's] School Convent was built to house twenty Sisters. It opened in November 1911. The Sisters live there each year from early September through the school terms. The convent is a good-sized yellow brick building on Indiana Avenue, a little north of 61st Street and next to the school playground.[3] During the time Studs and Danny are in school, Sister Bernadette Marie, who teaches the seventh and eighth grade girls, is the principal. Sister Carmel teaches the fourth grade boys when Danny enters that class for about a month in May 1915. Sister Cyrilla is the boys' fifth and sixth grade teacher. Studs has the feared and disliked Sister ("Battling") Bertha ["Mauling" Martha] in the seventh and eighth grades, and Danny has her for the seventh grade. Sister Magdalen teaches Danny his final year and leaves an imprint for the better on his life that he never outgrows.

St. Patrick's Convent [*St. Anselm's Convent*].

VACANT LOT AT 61ST STREET AND
INDIANA AVENUE

This vacant lot lies across the street from St. Anselm's [St.Patrick's] Church and School and the adjacent playground. The sign on the fence reads: "Site of St. Anselm's High School and Community Center"—structures that were never built. The scene shows a littered street, bare parkway, broken fence, barren and dusty lot, and old flat buildings and frame houses. It illustrates a run-down portion of the Washington Park neighborhood some twenty years after Studs and Danny had moved to the South Shore district.

Vacant lot at 61st Street and Indiana Avenue.

THE NEW ST.PATRICK'S
[ST. ANSELM'S] CHURCH

For over a decade Father Gilhooley carefully nurtures the building fund for the temple he dreams of: "a church second to none, the envy of pastors throughout the diocese, . . . a magnificent church, with vaulted nave, marble pillars, a grand organ, a marble altar imported from Italy, stained glass windows, hand-carved woodwork, a marble pulpit from which he would deliver the first sermon" ("Reverend Father Gilhooley," *GP* in *SS*, 244, 253)—features closely tallying with Farrell's more detailed description in *Judgment Day* (p. 319).

The church cost $350,000. It was built in 1925 on the northeast corner of Michigan Avenue and 61st Street, and Father Gilmartin and Cardinal Mundelein of Chicago conducted the first mass the following February. There, in 1927, Father Shannon [*Father Stanton*], confident and aggressive, conducts his rousing mission as Studs and his friends listen and approve. In his talks he attacks the debaucheries of the Jazz Age, the sins of the flesh and of the intellect in the modern age, contemporary literature and universities. Four years later, Paddy Lonigan, confused and supplicating, and filled with a "sense of mystery" and "an awe of God, his God" (*JD*, 423), comes back to the church to pray for the life of his stricken son Studs. Within a year the church (and the new school) are entrusted to the Divine Word Fathers, the new spiritual guides in a parish now virtually all black.

The new **St. Patrick's Church** [the new *St. Anselm's*] facing Michigan Avenue at 61st Street.

The new **St. Patrick's Church** [*the new St. Anselm's*] facing Michigan Avenue. (The Department of Special Collections, University of Pennsylvania Libraries.)

THE NEW ST. PATRICK'S [ST. ANSELM'S] GRAMMAR SCHOOL

The new St. Patrick's [*St. Anselm's*] grammar school.

The new St. Patrick's [*St. Anselm's*] grammar school faces on 61st Street, just east of the new church. On a misty November night in 1928, five months after the Lonigans move to the South Shore district, Studs revisits the old neighborhood. He sees the new school—"a long, low building, now like a shadow, its shape distorted because of the night"—and the surrounding playground where he "used to play pompompullaway in the yard at lunch hour" (*YMSL*, 385). He and an old friend later lament that it is a school where "the pupils are all jigga-booes" (*JD*, 87).

THE WILLIAM W. CARTER PUBLIC SCHOOL

The *William W. Carter Public School* and playground.

Many friends of Studs Lonigan and Danny O'Neill go to the above school, located on 58th Street and Wabash Avenue. Its large playground is a center for neighborhood games. It provides slides and other equipment for younger students and, for the older ones, a baseball diamond and a basketball court. St. Patrick's students also play there because their own playground is cinder-covered—"tearin' hell out of your clothes and yourself" (*YL*, 42), as Weary Reilley observes. St. Patrick's playground also lacks baskets for basketball, and is off limits for baseball for fear school windows will be broken.

In the Carter School playground fifteen year old Studs Lonigan makes a momentous decision. Already a local hero for having beaten Weary Reilley in a fight, Studs licks Red Kelly [*Harold ("Red") O'Keefe*; also the fictional Torch Feeney] there. The victory gets him an invitation from Paulie Haggerty [*Paulie Harrington*] and Davey Cohen to hang out with the "lads from Fifty-eighth and Prairie" who have more fun "than the St. Patrick's guys from Indiana" (*YL*, 125). Studs accepts the invitation, having been stung by "the Indiana Avenue mopes" (*YL*, 117), including Danny O'Neill, who had scrawled signs on sidewalks and fences saying "Studs loves Lucy." He keeps to the new gang up to the end.[4]

JOHNNY O'BRIEN'S AND HELEN SHIRES'S INDIANA AVENUE APARTMENT BUILDINGS

Two doors south of where Danny O'Neill lives on the corner of Indiana Avenue and 57th Street, there begins a series of three almost identical double, two-story graystone apartment buildings separated by passageways leading to the back yards. Johnny O'Brien [*Johnny Johnson*] lives with his parents in the first of these buildings, partially shown, at the right, in the illustration. One afternoon while on business errands, Mr. O'Brien [*Mr. Johnson*], the wealthy owner of a coal yard at 63rd Street between Wabash Avenue and State Street, chauffeurs his son Johnny and Studs around the neighborhood in his

Johnny O'Brien's and **Helen Shires's** Indiana Avenue apartment buildings.

Lucy Scanlan's Indiana Avenue apartment building.

Chalmers. He impresses Studs as "a real old man" and "a regular pal to a kid" (*YL*, 95, 100). Johnny later graduates from high school and earns a degree at the University of Chicago. He goes into the coal business with his dad and marries Harriet Hayes, also from a wealthy neighborhood family and the younger sister of Roslyn Hayes [*Dorothy McPartlin*], whom Danny O'Neill idolizes.

Helen Shires [*Helen Shearer*], who is about Studs's age, lives in the second graystone house, just south of the O'Briens, with her parents and younger sister Marion. Studs, the eighth-grader, likes Helen because she is "just like a guy" and "a natural athlete . . . a lean, muscular girl, tall and rangy, with angular Swedish features, blue eyes and yellowish white hair" (*YL*, 9, 73, 74); and best of all, she is someone who "understood things" (*YL*, 76) and whom he can talk to—about girls and religion. She explains to Studs that her Protestant parents "say that it's all right what you believe, so long as you live up to that belief and don't do nothin' that's really wrong, or really hurt your neighbor, and if you do that, you ain't got nothin' to worry about from God" (*YL*, 79). When she outdribbles Weary Reilley [*Frank Egan*][5] with a soccer ball, he gets sore and hurts her, "bucking her breasts with his football shoulders" (*YL*, 81). Within moments, Studs and Weary begin the fight that makes Studs's reputation among the neighborhood kids.

Studs and Helen go their separate ways. In 1922, when they meet casually on 58th Street, Studs learns she is a stenographer in the Loop. To him she looks "mannish" and "whipped" (*YMSL*, 167, 168), but he still likes her. Four years later Studs hears the report that she is a lesbian. He is shocked, yet "All his old liking and respect for Helen from the old days returned. It couldn't be true" (*YMSL*, 330)—but he listens passively as Red Kelly condemns her as "'a disgrace to the human race. . . . That's worse than having a nigger'" (*YMSL*, 330, 331).

LUCY SCANLAN'S INDIANA AVENUE APARTMENT BUILDING

The Scanlans are a pioneer family in the Washington Park neighborhood, having come there before Father Gilhooley establishes St. Patrick's parish. Lucy Scanlan [*Lucy Shannon*], her sister Helen [*Helen Shannon*], and their widowed mother live in the third graystone apartment building, next door to the Shires family, at the time Studs and Lucy graduate from St. Patrick's grammar school in 1916. They move to the North Side in 1919. When Studs dates Lucy in 1924, seeing her for the final time, Mrs. Scanlan remarks to him in her parlor: "'You know, William, I never felt the same about any place I've lived in as I did about our home on Indiana. I wouldn't have sold it only for the girls. That neighborhood, there, it was just like home. I lived in it for over twenty years, and raised my family and buried my husband from it'" (*YMSL*, 275). Not long before his death, Studs learns that Lucy is married to an accountant and has three kids.

Lucy is Studs's girl for less than a month in the summer of 1916. They kiss playing post office at their graduation party, and they kiss during the summer afternoon they spend on Wooded Island in Washington Park, when Studs's newly discovered feelings of love run unrestrained within. But when Studs the "iron man" (*YL*, 117) takes over, Lucy in effect leaves his life, but never his consciousness, even up to the very end.

OLD MAN O'CALLAGHAN'S HOME

Old Man O'Callaghan's home, Indiana Avenue.

Two of Studs's best friends on Indiana Avenue, Bill and Dan Donoghue [*Bill and Dan Delaney*], live in an apartment building two doors south of Lucy. Two doors south of the Donoghues' home and set back from the sidewalk is the old-fashioned house of the O'Callaghans, an extremely rich couple who are among the very earliest settlers in the neighborhood. As a boy of fifteen, "Studs tried to think what the neighborhood had been like when old man O'Callaghan first settled there and built his house, cutting down trees and living alone just like a pioneer. It must have been like a forest. That must have been good except for the wind at night. . . . It must have sounded like a horde of ghosts rising from a rainy cemetery, or an army of devils and demons; and he didn't know how Old Man O'Callaghan and his wife stood it" (*YL*, 77).

RED O'CONNELL'S INDIANA AVENUE APARTMENT BUILDING

This three-story gray-brick apartment building, two doors south of the O'Callaghans' house, is owned by Red O'Connell's [*Red O'Connor's*] dad. Neither Studs nor Danny like Red, who graduated from St. Patrick's in 1915, a year before Studs. Danny calls him "a tall, lanky, cowardly kid" and thinks of him as a bully ("Studs," *GP* in *SS*, 350). Red likes to speed up and down South Park Avenue at fifty miles an hour in his dad's Chalmers. He specializes in shooting pigeons and boys with his beebee gun. He dislikes Studs because Studs had once licked him, and he yells for Weary Reilley during Weary's fight with Studs. Revisiting the old neighborhood in 1928, Studs passes the large building where Red had lived: "Red was a skunk, a no-do, no-work, crapping sonofabitch. He'd used to hang out down at the poolroom around Fifty-fifth the last Studs had heard of him, and he and a bunch of guys like him would be there, shooting their mouths off, selling the buildings around there and even real estate out in the lake with their line" (*YMSL*, 383).

Red O'Connell's Indiana Avenue apartment building.

THE VACANT LOT ON INDIANA NEAR 58TH STREET

Just south of Mr. O'Connell's apartment building, this vacant lot is near the corner of Indiana Avenue and 58th Street. On May 1, 1915, Danny O'Neill, on his way to help his family move into their new apartment, has just walked past the lot when he meets Studs Lonigan and John O'Brien. For Danny, that meeting begins a long and complex relationship with the older boy, Studs, who comes to typify much of "the world of Fifty-eighth Street" that Danny, twelve years later as a rebellious university student, "wants to purge himself completely of" (*YMSL*, 371). But as a boy, Danny plays happily in this lot with his friends—touch football, indoor ball,[6] and baby-in-the-hole. There they roast potatoes over fires.

As World War I is dying down in 1918, the Indiana punks—Danny, Andy Le Gare, Dick Buckford, Fat Malloy, Ralph Borax and Young Horn Buckford—dig opposing trenches and exuberantly wage war by lobbing sand-filled tin cans at each other. Studs, himself a would-be war-hero, watches and is "keen to join in the battle," but, as an older tough guy, "He couldn't play punk games any more" (*YMSL*, 24). As he watches, Lucy walks by. "Their eyes meet. She turns away, as if he were a total stranger" (*YMSL*, 26). Later that day, Studs returns to the empty lot, lonesome for Lucy and sore at the world and himself. As he kicks in the trenches and tears down the earthworks, Lucy again passes by and laughs at him, "holding her head high. His face a blazing red, he walked out of the vacant lot, past her . . . He was utterly miserable" (*YMSL*, 29).

The vacant lot on Indiana near 58th Street.

LEVIN'S DRUG STORE

Levin's Drug Store, 58th Street and Indiana Avenue.

Located at the south end of the 5700 block of Indiana Avenue, Levin's Drug Store (the actual name in 1916) was known for its good soda fountain. Here, shortly before Studs's fight with Weary Reilley, Studs and Helen Shires sip double chocolate sodas and talk about Lucy.

The Wooded Island

Wooded Island as seen from the southwest across the lagoon in Washington Park.

The lagoon shore on Wooded Island, showing an overhanging tree limb.

In the southern section of Washington Park, the Wooded Island that Studs and Danny know is landscaped on slightly hilly ground and planted with a variety of shade trees, especially along the shores of the surrounding lagoon. To the residents of nearby neighborhoods it is a major attraction. It offers a peaceful trail and a quiet place free from traffic and the life of the streets. A "cinder dirt-black bridle path that was flanked by wind-twisted trees and shrubbery" ("Autumn Afternoon," *TWIMC*, in *OSS*, 144) runs the length of the island through its middle and leads into the northern area of Washington Park, where it encircles the large open meadow there. A casting pond attracts fishermen. From May to November a flock of 100 or more Shropshire sheep are kept in a pen near the north end of the island. A shepherd tends them each day when they are let out to graze on the island or in the park grasslands to the north.

On a hot afternoon in early July, Studs and Lucy, hand in hand, walk from 57th Street through the park and over the log bridge at the northern end of Wooded Island. Coming to a mature, full-leaved oak on the lagoon bank, they climb it and sit on a large overhanging branch. They spend most of the afternoon there. The appeal of Lucy, her kisses, their sense of intimacy, and Studs's feeling of oneness with the natural beauty around him merge to make him feel that "this was a turning point in his life, and from now on everything was going to be jake. He had always felt that some time something would happen to him, and it was the thing that was going to make his whole life different; and this afternoon was just what was going to turn the trick; it was Lucy.... He wanted the afternoon never to end" (*YL*, 112, 113-14). But "Time passed through their afternoon like a gentle, tender wind, and like death that was silent and cruel" (*YL*, 114). The death of the first—and, while it lasted, the best—gentle, tender affection in Studs's entire life-to-be comes within forty-eight hours. Twelve years later Studs, blind drunk, stumbles over to Wooded Island looking for the same tree, but fails to find it.

Studs, Danny, and their friends often go to Wooded Island, crossing over the bridge at its northern end. The bridge pictured on page 21 is a replacement for the low wooden bridge they knew, which was named the Rustic Bridge and was condemned in the early 1920s. We can best visualize the older structure when Tim Kenny—a Danny O'Neill surrogate, in love with Mary Latham and in trouble with Sister Teresa and his classmates—walks over it to get to a nearby spring. "Its logs seemed old and even a little rotted.... What if it collapsed with him on it?... He walked on, crossed the stepping stones below the log bridge, and followed the little stream, which ran like an avenue through shrubbery from the small spring which was the source of the lagoon. The spring was clear, pure as the soul of Mary Latham. It gurgled up, causing small bubbles. A semi-circular mound of boulders surrounded it. Leaning over, he drank ... feeling that he was cleansing himself ... He felt as if he were drawing power and courage from a blessed and magic spring, ... a power that would make Mary Latham like him, love him" ("Autumn Afternoon," *TWIMC* in *OSS*, 146-47).

While Studs lives in the Washington Park neighborhood, park visitors approach Wooded Island from the south over "a squat stone bridge" (*YL*, 196) with an iron railing. This bridge, known as the Farmstead Bridge, was removed and replaced at an uncertain date before the accompanying photograph was taken in 1948. On a Friday afternoon in November 1916, while playing hookey from high school and about to drop out permanently, Studs, with Weary Reilley and Paulie Haggerty, wanders across the bridge onto Wooded Island. They stop "at the denuded Oak tree where Studs and Lucy had sat. It stirred memories in him that were sharp with poignancy and a sense of loss. Seeing the tree, all stripped like it was dying, made him doubly sad" (*YL*, 197). As darkness comes, the wail of the wind "sounded upon Studs's ears like that of many souls forever damned. . . . Studs wanted to get out of the park now" (*YL*, 199-200).

Twelve years later in the autumn of 1928 Studs, now living in the South Shore district, revisits the old neighborhood. "Niggers passed him on the sidewalk. They nearly all looked alike, as if they were the same person. The corner, their old corner, looked like Thirty-fifth and State. . . . He walked on. Niggers living in all these buildings, living their lives, jazzing, drinking, and having their kids, and flashing razors at each other" (*YMSL*, 381, 385). He wanders into the park as darkness closes down. Knowing that the guys in his old gang who are still around always meet at the stone bridge, he finds them there, seated on a bench and drinking. "'The jiggs drove us over here,'" Tommy Doyle [*Tommy Barnes*] informs Studs (*YMSL*, 388). Convening at the stone bridge, the alky squad of 58th and Prairie are making their last stand against the invading hordes from the north.

The bridge leading to the north end of *Wooded Island*.

The entrance to the bridge at the north end of *Wooded Island* taken from the island.

The bridge leading to the south end of *Wooded Island*.

THE LONIGAN'S MICHIGAN AVE. APARTMENT BUILDING

The **Lonigans'** Michigan Avenue apartment building.

In the spring of 1922, a few months before Studs's twenty-first birthday, Patrick Lonigan purchases the above three-story six-flat red-brick apartment building, located in the 5700 block of Michigan Avenue. It is on the other side of the block from the Lonigans' former Wabash Avenue home. Like the Lonigan's earlier residence on Wabash, its back porch overlooks part of the Carter School playground. The family lives on the third floor south. The rent from five tenants balloons Paddy's income, long since well over "a cool hundred thousand berries" (YL, 17).

The following December Paddy turns down an offer of $90,000 for his building. His oldest daughter Frances suggests he should accept it, because "this neighborhood is deteriorating" and the "best people in it are moving over to Hyde Park or out in South Shore."[7] Paddy disagrees: "The niggers will be run ragged if they ever try to get past Wabash Avenue." Moreover, he believes that Father Gilhooley's new church and the extension of Michigan Avenue as a boulevard will double the value of his building. "This is a good, decent neighborhood full of respectable people, and it will always be so. . . . Why this neighborhood hasn't even commenced to grow yet" (YMSL, 138).

But less than five years later, with Father Gilhooley's new church having been up for about two years, wealthy parishioners like the Lonigans are rapidly moving out as the blacks move in. Talking to Fat Malloy, whose family, Fat said, had already "moved out of this nigger neighborhood," Studs replies: "'My old man's thinking of selling the building, and buying one out somewhere south'" (YMSL, 366). Paddy sells it in the spring of 1928, no longer able to hold out against "'the damn niggers'" and "'the Jew real-estate dealers.'"[8] But he sells at a handsome profit. "'Yeah,' he told Studs, 'a shine offered the highest price for the building, so I let it go. But he paid, the black skunk'" (YMSL, 374, 375).

As the family waits for the moving van to come, "It seemed to Studs that his mother wiped away a tear." Paddy explains: "'You know, Bill, your mother and I are gettin' old now, and, well, we sort of got used to this neighborhood. We didn't see many of the old people, except once in a while at Church, but . . . they all sort of knew us, and we knew them, and you see, well, this neighborhood was kind of like home. We sort of felt about it the same way I feel about Ireland, where I was born'" (YMSL, 373). "'It's a shame,'" Mary Lonigan says. "'This was such a beautiful neighborhood. And such nice people. A shame'" (YMSL, 375).

In August 1931, with his son Bill dying at home and his money lost in a bank failure, Paddy Lonigan—preoccupied, bewildered and his emotions in turmoil—finds himself driving in his old neighborhood. "He halted the car in front of the building he had once owned, approached it. With his hand on the knob of the outer entrance door, he realized with the pain of loss that it was no longer his building and that all the life, hopes, expectations lived in this building, these were all gone" (JD, 427).

A Michigan Avenue apartment building in the 5800 block.

MICHIGAN AVE. APT. BLDG., 5800 BLOCK

Of all the streets in Studs's Washington Park neighborhood, Michigan Avenue is lined with the most impressive modern apartment buildings. The one pictured here in the 5800 block of Michigan is somewhat different in style from Paddy Lonigan's building, a block south. It may have been the home of Dick Buckford [*Dick Buckley*], one of Danny O'Neill's bunch; for Dick lives in that block with (like Danny) his maternal grandmother, apart from his parents and brother who live two blocks away. When Danny is new in the neighborhood and in love with ten year old Helen Scanlan, he and Dick taunt and buck each other in front of Helen's home on Indiana Avenue, with Danny thinking that "if he beat Dick up and Helen saw him, he would be her hero, and he would be one of the leaders of their gang, and then maybe she would like him . . ." ("Helen, I Love You," *CS* in *SS*, 6). But their encounter, unlike that between Tom Sawyer and the new boy on his street, comes to nothing; and Danny, feeling lonely and sad, walks over to Washington Park, where the wind "beating against the trees . . . seemed to him like an unhappy person, crying" ("Helen, I Love You," *CS* in *SS*, 8).

HOME OF THE O'FLAHERTY FAMILY AND DANNY O'NEILL

Early in 1917, Mildred [*Emma Wilkinson*], the wife of Danny's Uncle Ned O'Flaherty [*Uncle William J. Daly*] and the owner of a Milwaukee millinery shop, dies. Ned returns from his Wisconsin home to live with his Chicago family in the Indiana Avenue apartment. The apartment is now seriously overcrowded, and on May 1, 1917, after living two years there, the O'Flaherty family (Mary and her grown children Al, Ned, and Margaret), along with Danny and Little Margaret O'Neill, move four blocks away to a larger, more expensive second floor apartment at 5816 South Park Avenue. They live there until May 1928 when they move a few miles east and south into an apartment on the fringes of the then all-white South Shore district. Their new graystone building on South Park Avenue has a large covered front porch, as well as large back porches and a larger back yard than their home on Indiana had provided. The apartment has eight rooms, two more than before, and most of them are lighter and roomier. Danny's grandmother has her bedroom off the kitchen. Aunt Margaret and Little Margaret

Home of the **O'Flaherty** family and **Danny O'Neill** on South Park Avenue.

share a room off the dining room. And Danny now has his own small bedroom, halfway back along the hallway. But when his two uncles, both traveling shoe salesmen, are out of town, he occupies their spacious front bedroom overlooking the tennis courts across the street with the greenery of Washington Park immediately beyond. The O'Flaherty children earn good money. The family eat well and enjoy many comforts. The move gives Danny better access to Washington Park and the chance to know more and different kids in the neighborhood.

Living in the same building are the grocer Morris Hirsch and the large Sweeney family with whom Little Margaret and Danny become friendly. Living next door is Jim Gogarty [*Joseph Cody*], Danny's friend who, like Danny, will go to the University of Chicago and lose his religion.

A baseball game in *Washington Park*.

Washington Park

Most of the northern half of Washington Park that Studs, Danny, and their friends know is a large meadow. It extends between the park drives that exit at 51st and 55th Streets, an ideal open space for baseball, football, and soccer matches, with a field house located near the 51st Street side. It is here, on one of the two football fields, that Studs and his team, the 58th Street Cardinals, play Jewboy Schwartz and the 47th Street Monitors in the fall of 1922, a football game ending in a free-for-all. A soccer field is nearby. Numerous regulation size baseball diamonds flank the eastern and northern edges of the broad meadow. As a boy of seven, Danny O'Neill starts playing catch there with his Uncle Al in 1911. All the way through grammar and high school, Danny lives for the spring and summer days when he plays baseball in the park with a long succession of teams. Danny is a baseball fanatic. He sees himself in the future as a star who will hear the cheers of thousands and thus "show" all those who had put him down when he was a boy.

While walking across Washington Park in the summer of 1927, Eddie Ryan (Danny's reincarnation in Farrell's later fiction) "remembered himself in short pants, wearing the shirt of a gray baseball uniform with green letters across the front. He had caught fungo flies and imagined himself another Happy Felsch or Johnny Mostil, playing center field for the White Sox. He used to play in any game that he could get into, with kids or men. All his playing and practicing had been for a purpose; he had been preparing himself for the day when he would be a big league star on the Chicago White Sox" (*Lonely*, 205-6).

The boathouse as seen from *Wooded Island*.

Studs, Danny O'Neill, and their friends often enter Washington Park at 58th Street where a path, passing by the small goldfish pond, curves east and north to the boathouse, about two blocks into the park and located on the western shore of the lagoon opposite a point reaching out from Wooded Island. The boathouse "is a long, low, open structure, bounded on two sides by shrubbery" (*YMSL*, 48). Built of red granite concrete, it provides two boat shelters, one on each side of the landing. On the landing lined with cane chairs is a stall, where rowboat tickets are sold: fifteen cents an hour for two-oared boats and twenty cents for four-oared boats.[9] When Studs graduates from St. Patrick's in 1916, there are as many as sixty-five boats, greatly in demand for use in the lagoon from the end of April to the end of October. A barge, a police boat, and a lifeboat are also at hand. During the skating season, temporary wooden walls and wood flooring are installed in the boathouse, converting it into a steam-heated warming-house. One side of it is used by women skaters and the other by the men.

The boathouse is "one of the places where the young fellows from the neighborhood often gathered" to talk and lay plans. Eddie Ryan's [*Jim Farrell's*] friend George Raymond [*Paul Caron*] boasts there "of how he had laid Rosy" (*Lonely*, 14). The youthful Danny sometimes broods at the boathouse. Once, when it is almost deserted, he sees some blacks there. "He frowned. The shines shouldn't be allowed in the park. It was a white man's park" (*F&S*, 278).

As a boy of seventeen who is bored with the poolroom "gassing," Studs drifts over there and rocks in a cane chair. He sees some old men and women talking too much "in loud, cracking voices." He sees Coady the "flat-footed park cop," and "a couple of dinges. If the guys had come, they could have ganged the dinges. . . . He looked around: no chickens" (*YMSL*, 48). A "big guy, maybe thirty," tries to pick Studs up, "his hand ever-so-lightly running up Studs' thigh." Studs starts to haul off on him, but the guy "slipped into the bushes and disappeared" (*YMSL*, 50, 51). Again at the boathouse two months later, Studs invites "a lonesome-looking chicken . . . to go oaring" and is turned down flat with an icy stare and a cutting remark. He ends up with the neighborhood "bitch," Elizabeth Burns, in "a spot right near the tree where he and Lucy had been. She didn't offer him any resistance" (*YMSL*, 79, 80, 81).

Later, in the early 1920s, the guys from around 58th Street, now self-dubbed "The Merry Clouters," are singing and rough-housing at the boathouse when they learn that a single black has been seen nearby. They catch him, beat him up, and throw him head-first into the goldfish pond, where he slips and slides. They make "the Negro dance in the fountain until he slipped and splashed again. It was so funny they laughed until tears rolled from their eyes" ("The Merry Clouters," *GP* in *SS*, 231). That same night most of the Merry Clouters, with the exceptions of Andy Le Gare and Man Bleu, slink away from the invading Kenwoods, a tough gang from 55th and Ellis Avenue on the other side of the park.

The view from the boathouse landing.

The view above looks east, across the tip of Wooded Island and the park's "mainland" toward the University of Chicago and Hyde Park beyond. The 200 foot chimney in the distance belongs to the Washington Park coal-burning power house completed in 1907 and located on Cottage Grove Avenue at 58th Street. For years it supplied electric power to many parks in the South Park system, as well as to the Midway and to the major boulevards (Drexel, Oakwood, Grand, Garfield, Western Avenue) under the jurisdiction of the South Park Commissioners. It also supplied steam heat to park buildings.

THE MICHIGAN THEATER

Even before he lived in the neighborhood, Danny O'Neill is a movie fan. The day in 1915 when he moves in, one of the first things on 58th Street that he notices is the nickel show The Palm, which fails in 1918 and is replaced by a dry-goods store. But by then five-reel pictures have come in, and two larger movie houses have been built: the Prairie at 58th and Prairie, and the Michigan, on Garfield Boulevard (55th Street) between Michigan and Indiana Avenues. Also nearby, just east of South Park Avenue, is the Vernon on 61st Street.

The Michigan Theater is the kids' favorite. In 1918 a little scandal among the neighborhood Catholics breaks out when Sister Magdalen discovers that many of her eighth grade boys and Sister Bernadette's eighth

The *Michigan Theater*.

grade girls at St. Patrick's, so carefully segregated in their classrooms, go together in a group to the Michigan Theater on Sundays, a practice the Sisters try to stop when they learn about it. Studs, too, often goes to the Michigan Theater. He prefers those movies that permit him to identify with the adventurous hero and to fantasize about himself as a daring tough guy and an overpowering lover, with Lucy the willing recipient of his kisses and mastery.

THE ELEVATED

The *Elevated train at the 58th Street Station.*

The "L" train connecting Chicago's Loop with Jackson Park at 63rd Street runs through the Washington Park neighborhood above the alley between Calumet and Prairie Avenues, with stops at the 55th, 58th, and 61st

Street stations. Each weekday morning the many neighborhood businessmen, in suit and tie, take it to their work downtown. Danny's father, Jim O'Neill [*James Francis Farrell*], in workingman's clothes and carrying his lunch, also takes it to his job on the night shift at the express company. Danny's aunt Margaret uses it to get to her hotel job in the Loop. The "L" is Danny's route to Comiskey Park and the White Sox. He takes it south and east to get to his high school, and later as a university student he takes it north to the service stations where he works. For the Washington Park and other Chicago districts, the "L" "played a crucial role in the formation of the modern urban neighborhood with its characteristic brick apartment buildings, shopping strips, and a concentrated but highly mobile population."[10]

UNDER THE "L" TRACKS AT THE 58TH STREET STATION

The 58th Street "L" station is at the heart of neighborhood business and provides access to essential transportation for all the citizens. For the boys around 58th Street, however—and notably for those who like to hang out in the poolroom—the gloomy area under the "L" station and in the nearby alley is occasionally their dark street-playground, just as the park is their sunny playground. Sammy Schmaltz [*Moe Moritz*], toothless and with tobacco juice slobbering down his chin, sells newspapers at his stand under the "L" station. John Young, who grew up in the neighborhood, recalls that Studs and several others once kidnapped Sammy (named Toothless Nate in this story) "and hung him by the shoulders to a telephone post in an alley" ("Wedding Bells Will Ring So Merrily," *GP* in *SS*, p. 299). There, too, and also at 58th Street and Prairie, is where Mickey Flanagan [*Mickey McCarthy*], the neighborhood drunk, hangs out.

As Danny quickly learns in 1916, Three-Star Hennessey had been shagged by a cop under the "L" station when he and Paulie Haggerty were observed having a masturbation race there. Kenny Kilarney [*Kenney Kennedy*] is known for having taken Fat Jeff "back of the Fifty-eighth Street elevated station and crapped right in his ear" ("Curbstone Philosophy," *CGP* in *SS*, 481). In 1922 on Christmas Eve, Studs, drunk and staggering in the street, makes a public spectacle of himself in front of the station. More innocently, Danny and the other boys sometimes have their fist fights in the darkened alley. They hide there on a Halloween night when chased by an angry janitor they call "Bushwah."

BATHCELLAR'S POOLROOM ON 58TH STREET

Charley Bathcellar's [*Charley Batcheler's*; also the fictional Bert Calkins's] Billiard Parlor and Barber Shop, with barber poles outside, is two doors east of the "L" station (the location of the Met Music Shop in the photograph) on the north side of 58th Street. In the narrow front part of Charley's store are barber chairs, where Studs Lonigan has his hair cut by Frank. To the rear are two even rows of pool tables. Farther back are tables and chairs for poker players. Among Charley's patrons are confirmed and aging gamers, marginal community characters, and drifters. The poolroom is also a magnet for a sizable group of men and teen-agers who, like Studs in the summer of 1916, think of themselves as "young and strong . . . and the real stuff," the envy of the "old dopey-looking guys" (*YL*, 152) of the neighborhood.

At age fifteen and still in knee pants, Studs is ushered into the poolroom by the older habitués as a reward for having helped them fool moronic Nate, a grocery delivery man, into thinking that the dried horse manure given him for his pipe is a superior new kind of tobacco. "The pool room was long and narrow; it was like a furnace, and its air was weighted with smoke.

Under the *"L" tracks at the 58th Street Station*.

The site of **Bathcellar's poolroom** on 58th Street.

Three of the six tables were in use, and in the rear a group of lads sat around a card table, playing poker. The scene thrilled Studs, and he thought of the time he could come in and play pool and call Charley Bathcellar by his first name. He was elated as he washed his hands in the filthy lavatory" (*YL*, 150).

Charley sells out to George the Greek in 1919, the year Studs begins working for his father. George removes the barber chairs and replaces them with a shoe shine stand. He also hires the loutish and degenerate Mike to assist him. But otherwise the poolroom remains much the same—the same games, the same thrills, the same sex jokes, and the same plans for drinking and whoring. Occasionally there is novelty, as when an angry Red Kelly, after cursing his girl over the telephone, positions dim-witted and trusting Vinc Curley [*Vincent Curry*] against the wall and throws pool balls at his head.

In the spring of 1926 George closes his business. If Studs and his friends want to play pool, they must go to 55th Street. Early in 1931, most of them having moved away from the neighborhood, they learn that George had returned to Greece to live "like a big shot" on his earnings, but that, instead, he was shoved into the army. All the boys laugh, and Studs says: "'I never did like Greeks'" (*JD*, 19).

GUS THE GREEK'S RESTAURANT

Greeks were very much in evidence at Gus [*Mike*] the Greek's restaurant situated between Prairie Avenue and the "L" station on the north side of 58th Street, possibly at the location of Queen's in the photograph. Gus, the owner, runs a medium price, no-frills, fast-service eatery. Christy [*Takiss Georgis*,[11] known as *Pete*], the waiter, is "a tall, heavy-set, full-faced Greek in his forties. His hair had thinned out, and there was a bald spot on his head" (*YMSL*, 333). Christy is a well-read Greek language poet, a translator of Walt Whitman into Greek, and a political radical who believes "There are . . . two countries in the world. Greece and Russia. Greece is the world's past, Russia the future of the world" (*YMSL*, 335). Christy worked the night shift at the restaurant. He observes his customers closely and is critical of the 58th Street poolroom boys for scorning books and education.

Studs and his friends like Gus's as a place to "gas," or "barber." Danny, while at the University of Chicago, likes it because he and Christy can "talk of Plato or Socrates, Nietszche or Walt Whitman, modern Greece

The site of **Gus the Greek's** restaurant on 58th Street.

or classical Greece, Heine, Goethe, Shelley, Lord Byron, modern America, war" (*Lonely*, 46). Because the restaurant keeps late hours, it is a good place for Studs and his friends to sober up with "coffee an'" after a hard night's drinking, and for Danny to get a pick-me-up after working late at his service station.

When Studs overhears Christy criticize the United States as a country of greed, cheap journalism, and capitalist exploitation of the workers, he tells Red Kelly. Red convinces Gus to fire "that radical bastard" after threatening a boycott if Christy remains. Studs approves: "'Good stuff'" (*YMSL*, 365).

THE FIREPLUG AT 58TH AND PRAIRIE

The fireplug on the northwest corner of 58th Street and Prairie Avenue.

On May 1, 1915, his first day in the Washington Park neighborhood, eleven year old Danny O'Neill descends the "L" station steps, walks half a block, and sees "some kids around a fire plug" in front of the drugstore at "the corner of Fifty-eighth and Prairie" (*No Star*, 634). Very likely those kids are Red Kelly, Davey Cohen,

Paulie Haggerty, Tommy Doyle, Weary Reilley, Benny Taite, and Kenny Kilarney. This is the bunch in their early teens who like to meet there, talk, spit tobacco juice, and watch the girls go by. They call the place "their corner" or simply "the corner," within a few steps of the poolroom and Gus the Greek's restaurant.

Little more than a year later, Studs Lonigan joins this bunch, deserting his former friends around Indiana and Michigan Avenues. In Studs's life, "the corner" with its black fireplug comes to signify more than the gang's meeting-place. It becomes the fateful scene of important passages in the course of his existence. After he and Lucy fall out, she calls him "booby" at this corner. Studs responds by bottling up his real affection for her and sealing his shame at having his feeling for her made public. A few weeks later Studs, looking hard-boiled and spitting tobacco juice, sits on the fireplug, imagining that all the passersby admire him, the tough guy. A little later, gathered around the fireplug, he and his youthful band stand up to the boastful, intimidating fighter from the 47th and Cottage Grove Avenue gang ("Curbstone Philosophy," *CGP* in *SS*, 477-83).

In October 1928, after the Lonigans had moved to the South Shore district, Studs revisits the old neighborhood. At "their old corner... A gang of young niggers were gathered around the fireplug talking, kidding, laughing. He tried to frown," and he thinks "No other corner would ever be the same. Christ, and what wouldn't he give to have just one more night, with all the guys back again" (*YMSL*, 381-82). Studs, alone, staggers back again in the "gray dawn" of January 1, 1929, after leaving the violent debauch held by his gang on New Year's Eve "in a suite of three rooms at a disreputable hotel on Grand Boulevard in the black belt." The battered and besotted Studs is discovered in the heart of *his* old neighborhood "huddled by the curb near the fireplug at Fifty-eighth and Prairie, . . . bloody, dirty, odorous with vomit" (*YMSL*, 397, 411), and his once healthy body fatally weakened.

JIM AND LIZZ O'NEILL'S CALUMET AVENUE HOME

In the spring of 1918, Danny's parents, Jim and Lizz O'Neill [*James Francis Farrell* and *Mary Daly Farrell*[12]], with their children Bill [*William Earl Farrell*, known as *Earl*], Dennis [*Joseph E. Farrell*], Bob [*John A. Farrell*], and Catherine [*Mary Farrell*], move south from their wooden cottage at 45th Place and Wells Street. Their new home has five rooms and is on the first floor of a three-story, six-flat, yellow-brick apartment building at 5939 Calumet Avenue, on the east side of the street. The move places Jim and Lizz within two blocks of Lizz's mother, Mary O'Flaherty [*Julia Brown Daly*], and Danny and Little Margaret O'Neill, the two children living with their grandmother. In the O'Neill's former home kerosene lamps had provided the light. There was no plumbing or indoor bathroom. Water was heated and meals were prepared on a large kitchen stove which burned coal or wood and which warmed the cottage in winter. Heavy manila paper was spread over the floors in winter to keep the cold from coming up through the floor planks. But on Calumet Avenue the O'Neills have "a bathroom inside, running hot and cold water, steam heat, gas and electricity" (*F&S*, 3)—for $50 a month. Jim has his easy Morris chair, and the family enjoys an old horned Victrola. Jim is now in the supervision at the express company. He earns $175 a month, a sum soon raised to $225. Since August 1918 his oldest son Bill has also worked there, bringing in a monthly salary of $135. Dennis begins working at the express company in 1923, not long before Jim dies in this apartment in November of that year after a series of strokes.

Calumet Avenue is neither as "respectable" nor as impressive as Michigan Avenue. Nor does "old money" live there, as on Indiana Avenue. Its "lines of gray-, red-, and brownstone apartment buildings of two and three stories" show a certain lack of care. There are "many lawnless patches of dirt before the buildings," and on them "a few scabby trees" ("Jim O'Neill," *CS* in *SS*, 106). But the street

Jim and **Lizz O'Neill's** Calumet Avenue home.

is restful and domestic. Jim and Lizz take a stroll on "a mild summer evening at twilight. The street was very peaceful. People sat in front of a few buildings. Windows were opened, and from one of them came the sound of a victrola" (*F&S*, 261). Children play in the street. When Jim, returning home from his night shift, emerges from the "L" station, he sees the lamppost at Calumet Avenue still lighted, and, above the buildings, "he saw the fading moon disappear behind a cloud. He could make out the bushes at the edge of Washington Park ahead of him. . . . It was very quiet." Even 58th Street in the breaking light is "like some street in a dream." There is "something mysterious" about it. "A hidden meaning seemed to be lurking in it" (*F&S*, 12).

St. Stanislaus [St. Cyril] High School

Danny O'Neill attends St. Stanislaus [*St. Cyril* and also the fictional St. Basil] High School from September 1919 to June 1923.[13] The school was designed for boys and was under the direction of the Carmelite Fathers. It was founded in 1900 as St. Cyril College. It offered an eight year classical course, covering high school and college work, and a two-year commercial course. In 1918, the year before Danny matriculates, the college department was discontinued and the curriculum was limited to four years of high school instruction. During Danny's time there, the student body averages about 245. The priests at the school also serve the people of St. Stanislaus [*St. Cyril*] Parish in the surrounding neighborhood. A year after Danny graduates, the new Carmelite high school Mary Our Mother [*Mount Carmel*] is completed across the street from the old building, which was razed in 1969.

Danny's school building, a five-story graystone structure, is located at 6411-13 South Dante Avenue on the east side of the street. It is two blocks west of Stony Island Avenue and Jackson Park (which is used for football and baseball practice) and a half-block east of the Illinois Central tracks. The first floor (the half-basement) includes a parish chapel. St. Stanislaus [*St. Cyril*] Church occupies the second floor. Classrooms, a study hall, parlors, and offices are on the third and fourth floors. On the top floor are a refectory, the Carmelite community library and recreation room, a chapel, and cells for the priests and brothers. Behind the building is a brick-paved school yard surrounded by a high brick wall. A handball court and a basketball court are marked out on the bricks.

St. Stanislaus High School [*St. Cyril High School*]. (Courtesy of Father Leander Troy, O. Carm.)

Going to high school gives teenage Danny his first sustained experience outside the neighborhood he had lived in for four years. For him it meant new friends, particularly those in his high school fraternity Alpha Eta Beta, and new activities for his mind and body.

Loyola Academy

Unlike Danny, Studs does not want to go to high school. But his friend Helen Shires advises him to go, and his family pressures him to enter Loyola Academy in September 1916. [Farrell here used the name of a real boys' school.] Loyola—the building to the right in the photograph—is a premier Jesuit high school for boys, located on Sheridan Road far to the north of Studs's home. Within two months Studs is bumming from school. He is dropped from the freshman football squad for missing practice. To his friend Paulie Haggerty he confides: "they raise hell with you for not having homework and that stuff. You can't fake knowing Latin and algebra, and, Jesus, you have to write compositions for English. None of that for me. . . . It ain't worth it" (*YL*, 199).

Loyola Academy. (Courtesy of the Catholic Theological Union Library, Chicago.)

For some six months he plays hookey without his family knowing it. Then, for over a year, while still living at home, he looks for a job. After a bitter quarrel with his dad, Studs begins working for him as a plasterer and painter in the spring of 1919. He now has money in his wallet. Preparing for an evening out, he studies himself in the mirror: "He tipped his first straw hat at a rakish angle. . . . He arranged his blue tie. . . . Quite a guy, he thought. . . . Pretty well off too at seventeen" (*YMSL*, 63).

In 1922 Danny O'Neill is making a name for himself on St. Stanislaus's football team and Studs is quarterback for the 58th Street Cardinals in their violent game in Washington Park against the 47th Street Monitors. After that game Studs reflects: "Dumb, too, not to have gone to high school. If punks like O'Neill could make the grade, what couldn't he have done?" (*YMSL*, 131). Some nine years later in the Great Depression, Studs painfully learns the value of a high school diploma. Repeatedly given the "go-by" in his interviews for a job—any job—he finally lies about his high school background, claiming "Two years . . . [at] Loyola on the north side." It does not work. Studs wishes "he hadn't been such a muttonhead as to pass up the chance to get an education when he had had it" (*JD*, 360, 362). Despairing and filled with self-hatred, he twisted his lips "in a sneer at himself, and he thought that he was just a goddamn washed-up has-been" (*JD*, 383).

St. Paul's Academy [*St. Francis Xavier Academy*]. (Courtesy of the Catholic Theological Union Library, Chicago).

St. Paul's [St. Francis Xavier's] Academy

An article of faith for Studs and his friends is that, as Red Kelly insists, "the finest and most decent girls are Irish Catholic girls" who come from "a decent home, the right kind of parents," and have "the fear of God" in them (*YMSL*, 331). In this male judgment, consanguinity counts too. The boys honor their own and each other's sisters as "pure." Arnold Sheehan brags to the fellows while sitting in the Burnham brothel with a girl on his lap: "You know, I got four sisters, and they're all the most decent girls in the world. You know, my four sisters are as pure as a lily." Studs, occupied with his own girl, answers: "My two sisters are as pure as yours." The girl on Arnold's lap "curled her lips" in scorn (*YMSL*, 182).

The fellows are also convinced that the "best" Catholic girls on the South Side go to St. Paul's [*St. Francis Xavier*, also the fictional St. Matthew's and St. Hilda's] Academy. These are the girls who, as they say, "rate." By and large, as the boys seem to believe, they come from families with money and social standing. Among the girls known to Studs or Danny who go to St. Paul's Academy for their high school training are Studs's two sisters Frances and Loretta, Roslyn Hayes, Marion and Caroline Brown [*Dorothy* and *Virginia Butler*], Catherine Anne Freer [*Mary Louise Hunnell*], Eloise Russell, and Marion McGowan. Many of the Catholic girls who do not "rate" go to the Loretta Academy, located to the southeast at 65th Street and Blackstone Avenue. This school closed in the early 1970s.

St. Francis Xavier Academy for girls and women was founded in 1846 and operated by the Sisters of Mercy. During the time-periods of Studs's and Danny's boyhoods as represented in the fiction, it was situated just to the north of Washington Park, on Cottage Grove Avenue between 49th and 50th streets. Its four divisions included the preparatory school, the intermediate department, the academy, and the college.

Cobb Hall, University of Chicago

Eddie Ryan (Farrell's character in the Universe of Time series who is the equivalent of Danny O'Neill) matriculates at the University of Chicago in the summer quarter of 1925, two years after completing high school.[14] Eddie still feels that he is "living in a social world in which dispiritedness was like an invisible thing, powerful but unfelt." The University of Chicago will eventually transform his life. Immediately, it provides an "escape for a young mind and young feelings which had been swallowed up in the emptiness of too many passing moments, passing hours, passing days" (*Silence*, 89, 91).

That summer Eddie takes two history courses, "Early Medieval Europe" and "Later Medieval and Early Modern Europe," taught respectively by Professor Kraft [*Professor Einar Joranson* and the fictional Professor Cotton] and Mr. Thornton [*Mr. John Wesley Hoffmann*], a visiting instructor.[15] His classes are held in venerable Cobb Hall, the university's first—and in 1892 its only—building. Cobb Hall is a favorite place for students to congregate before and between classes. To Eddie, now twenty-one, hoping on his first day to make friends and to find a girl of his own, everyone in the crowd around him outside Cobb Hall looks young and happy. As they all walk inside to their classrooms, their talk is "like a gush of gaiety" that breaks over his loneliness (*Silence*, 97). During the next four years the Cobb Hall classrooms and Harper Memorial Library[16] will become the centers for Eddie's university education.

After classes, while lounging on the fresh-cut grass of the quiet campus and surrounded by the "gray Gothic buildings and towers," Eddie feels "far removed from the depressing and rackety-rack-rack noises of his neighborhood, in which dullness had become like seediness" (*Silence*, 61-62).

When he matriculates in 1925 Eddie is a young man "full of simple faith and simple beliefs.... His mind was open to accept truth ... He had no desire to be unconventional, or to isolate himself from others because he would study and learn. He was not a young rebel ... He wanted to like people and to be liked by them. He wanted to learn and to succeed" (*Silence*, 57). But his studies at the university turn Eddie into a rebel—against his church and the dominant social order. It also leads him to the threshold of his future profession: writing.

It is outside Cobb Hall on January 9, 1927, that Danny O'Neill reads a note from "the famous Professor Paul Morris Saxon" [*James Weber Linn* ; also the fictional Joseph Paxton Lyman] that admits him, on the basis of submitted writing, to the professor's creative writing course, English 210 (*Anger*, 297). Now, he feels, "he was setting out in earnest to be a writer.... For good or for ill, this was the aim in his life.... This was a vow ... which Danny O'Neill, knowing no gods, made to Danny O'Neill" (*Anger*, 299-300). Elsewhere Farrell stated he decided to be a writer[17] on March 16, 1927, the day Professor Linn, his first publisher, included his sketch "Pie Juggling in the Loop" in Linn's column "Round About Chicago" in the *Chicago Herald-Examiner*.[18]

Cobb Hall, University of Chicago. (The University of Chicago Archives.)

Hutchinson Hall Coffee Shop, University of Chicago. (The University of Chicago Archives.)

HUTCHINSON HALL COFFEE SHOP

The Coffee Shop,[19] specializing in shorts orders, is a favorite student hangout, where the discussion is often lively. Danny goes there with his first campus friend—Walter Broda [*Felix Kolodziej*; also the fictional Walter Brovid], a Pole and a sophomore philosophy student. Their talk turns to Joseph Conrad's writings. Broda, Danny, the single tax advocate Gardiner [*John Monroe* and also the fictional Harry Oldering] and the brilliant philosophy student Carter [*Albert Dunham*, Katherine Dunham's brother and also the fictional Norman Allen], later discuss Alfred North Whitehead's writings over a Coffee Shop table.[20] When Danny becomes an atheist in 1926, his new ideas are put to the test there by Francis Xavier Murphy, the Secretary of the Campus Catholic Club. Murphy, a skilfull debater, out-argues Danny to logically prove God's existence. But Danny comes away "convinced that all the arguments of the Church, all the reasonings of the medieval schoolmen, all the books of Saint Augustine and the other saints could not shake him in his denial" (*Anger*, 232).

During the last week of the 1927 winter quarter, Danny tells his writing teacher, Professor Saxon, that he has quit his job at the gas station and has decided "'that I'm going to become a writer or nothing'" (*Anger*, 301).[21] The professor thinks Danny is foolhardy: "'Writing is a cruel profession. If you stake your life on the hope of being a writer and fail, you can ruin your whole life'" (*Anger*, 304). Danny then goes to the Coffee Shop with Marion Willingham [*Martha Dodd*], a professor's daughter and "a beautiful girl of talent" in his writing class whom he quickly finds himself "thinking of marrying" (*Anger*, 306).[22] Marion tells him his stories are "always cold and terribly unpleasant," always "about uncivilized people" with nothing spiritual in them. She wants him to write "'so that a story has aspiration, so that it lifts you up.'" Danny realizes that his "hopes of knowing her had been idle" (*Anger*, 308) and that he must continue writing about the reality he has known in his Chicago. Neither the reasonable professor nor the beautiful girl will deter him. He leaves the Coffee Shop.

The 57th Street Hyde Park Art Colony.

THE 57TH STREET HYDE PARK ART COLONY

In 1893 twenty-six small, flimsily constructed, one-room, single-story shops, each with its embossed triangular roof-facade, were built to accommodate the crowds coming to the World's Columbian Exposition in Chicago. Serving as refreshment booths, souvenir stands, galleries, curio shops and restaurants, they were located a few blocks east of the University of Chicago campus on both sides of 57th Street between the Illinois Central tracks and Stony Island Avenue at Jackson Park. When the Exposition ended, the shops were boarded up for almost two decades. But in 1913 this relic of the World's Fair was reborn as the Hyde Park Art Colony, sometimes known as the Jackson Park Art Colony (Farrell usually called it the 57th Street Art Colony). It became the home of Chicago's flourishing South Side Bohemia.

With monthly rent pegged at $12.50, writers, painters, sculptors, booksellers, choreographers, and artisans of all sorts could afford to live there or set up shop. Others came as guests, to read from their works, or offer musicals, or dance, or exhibit their paintings, etchings, and sculptures. Among the Colony's literary luminaries during its first decade were Floyd Dell, Ben Hecht, Thorstein Veblen, Edgar Lee Masters, Vachel Lindsay, Theodore Dreiser, Carl Sandburg, Sherwood Anderson and Margaret Anderson. Later on, among many others, came Harriet Monroe, Clarence Darrow, Maxwell Bodenheim, and James T. Farrell. The structures were razed in the mid-1960s, a sacrifice to urban renewal.[23]

As early as March 1927 the rebellious Eddie Ryan begins going to Uasia, a bohemian forum, with his friends George Raymond [*Paul Caron*] and Alec McGonigle [*James ("Jack") Sullivan*]. Ironically christened the Slow Down Club by George and Alec, Uasia is nearby on Cottage Grove Avenue a few doors off 57th Street. There, one evening, Eddie extemporaneously debates a well-known socialist on the topic "Is Life Worth Living?" The next year Eddie, with his girl Marion Healy [*Dorothy Patricia Butler*] also develops a liking for Jack Jones's [Dick Dickson's] resort for bohemians, the Dill Pickle [Sour Apple] Club in an alley off Bughouse Square on Chicago's Near North Side. There the patrons discuss and debate avant garde subjects.[24]

Danny O'Neill (like Farrell) is also drawn to the unconventional life followed by the residents of the Hyde Park Art Colony. At times Danny hangs out there even after the 1929 spring quarter when he dropped out of the university in order to concentrate on his writing. The stand-in for Danny in the story "The Open Road" comments on his bohemian friends there: "When they had parties they talked. When they didn't have parties they talked. They always talked, and generally the conversation was about somebody else's sexual life" (*GP* in *SS*, 195-96).[25] As hard times grow during the Depression era, political radicals and Communists infiltrate the Colony, a development reflected in Farrell's tales "Comrade Stanley" and "Getting Out the Vote for the Working Class." In the story "Comedy Cop" the Colony's Communists are targets for Red Kelly and some of the 58th Street boys. In a night raid they smash windows and harass the radicals.[26]

A large apartment building at 5642-8 Harper Avenue lodged many members of the Hyde Park Art Colony. In his autobiographical memoirs and elsewhere, Farrell variously named it the Coudich or Kuditch Culture Center [Schmolsky Culture Center], after its owner. It was an old building recently purchased by a French Jew who cut it into small apartments intending to make it a haven for artists. He inveigled local bohemians—painters, writers, sculptors, critics, dancers, and other "free spirits"—to live there.[27] Farrell's novel *New Year's Eve/1929* catches much of the flavor of ongoing life in the Coudich Culture Center and in the Colony at large in the late 1920s.

On February 10, 1928, Nicholas ("Nick") Matsoukas [Pete the Greek; Cyril Thearchos], a student friend of Farrell's at the university, opened the Cube [Square Circle; Diagonal] a little theater in one of the Colony buildings situated between the Illinois Central tracks and Stony Island Avenue.[28] The Cube became a fully integrated campus center for bohemian gaiety, and for the cultural events that attracted the young crowd. Its patrons freely hung monickers on each other. Among them were Clarence the Poet who went about with an Indian blanket draped over one shoulder, a bit of Taos on the Midway; Ouida, of the brilliantly colored coiffures, an occasional leading lady in the Cube's plays and a dreamy purveyor of French songs; Chan, the quiet-lipped Chinese; and the Michigan Virgin, the serious farm girl who adored listening to intellectual conversations.[29]

The Cube had a makeshift stage and uncomfortable red-smeared wooden benches. It featured authors' readings, musical evenings, modern dance, and productions of plays by modern masters, some of them directed by Farrell's close friend Mary Hunter [Joan Jackson; Lenora Jackson].[30] Katherine Dunham [Doris Carr or Carney; Sarah], then a university student, acted and danced there. Jim Farrell[31] acted in an adaptation of Hemingway's "Today is Friday." Jim's girl, Dorothy Butler [Marion Healy; Marion Brown; Elizabeth Whelan] took the part of Mrs. Solness in Ibsen's "The Master Builder."[32] Jim and the eighteen year old Dorothy met at the Cube in July 1928. The meeting came at a reading by Maxwell Bodenheim [Benjamin Mandlebaum], the subject of an English paper Dorothy was working on. Farrell vividly recalled the attractive strawberry blonde with a round, fresh face, who was wearing a wide straw hat, with a band of flowers around the brim, and an ankle-length chiffon dress splashed with red flowers.[33] The Cube closed shop in January 1929. Its stage was dismantled, and its benches sold for kindling. By then, Farrell was well on his way to rejecting bohemianism as a way of life for the serious writer.

Following their secret marriage at the Chicago City Hall on April 13, 1931 (witnessed only by their friend Theodore Marvel [Mordecai Janeway; Bob Whipple]), Jim Farrell and Dorothy Butler sailed for Paris April 17 on the H.M.S. *Pennland* and docked at Cherbourg on April 25. The voyage was made possible by money supplied by Dorothy. While they were in Paris, Jim completed his revisions in the manuscript of *Young Lonigan* [Jud Jennings] and wrote the first draft of *Gas-House McGinty* [Loudmouth Cannon]. He received contracts for both books from James Henle [Leo Berger] of the Vanguard Press [Advance Press]. The Farrells sailed from Boulogne-sur-mer April 9, 1932, on the S.S. *Statendam* and disembarked at Hoboken April 17.[34] *Young Lonigan* was published four days later.

---

[1] The Cunningham [Lonigan] family included the father, Patrick F., the mother, Bridget Feeney, and five children: Mary, William [William ("Studs") Lonigan; Jud Jennings], Frances [Frances Lonigan; Elizabeth Jennings], Loretta [Loretta Lonigan; Teresa Jennings], and Martin [Martin Lonigan]. Patrick was a native of Castle Bar, Ireland. His wife Bridget was born in Chicago. Patrick became a successful plastering and painting contractor and the owner of apartment buildings. He drove a Packard, a mark of distinction. In the Studs Lonigan neighborhood the family lived first at 5733 South Wabash Avenue and later at 5730 South Michigan Avenue. Patrick's place of business was nearby, at 6232 South Michigan Avenue.

Mary, the oldest child, is not a character in Farrell's fiction, and his memory of her was vague. After *Studs Lonigan* was published, he learned from William Murphy, a Congressman in the 1960s from the Second Illinois Congressional District, that Murphy had dated her. Mary remained single. Characters based on the four other children all appear in *Studs Lonigan* under their real first names.

Loretta Cunningham married Louis Lederer [Phil Rolfe; Lester Rothberg]. Frances Cunningham married the well-to-do Bernard O'Connell [Carroll Dowson]. Martin, like his brother William, remained single.

[2] The death certificate for William ("Studs") Cunningham reveals that he was born September 13, 1902, in Chicago. He was a painter and plasterer who worked for his father. He remained single, was not in the U.S. military, and at the time of death still lived with his parents at 7822 Luella Avenue in the South Shore district. He died during the afternoon of March 10, 1929, when approximately twenty-six and-a-half years of age. Dr. W. F. Hewett [Dr. O'Donnell; Dr. Dolan] certified his last illness as four days of bronchial pneumonia preceded by seven days of influenza. The undertaker was Frank O'Reilley [Old Man O'Reedy] on

79th Street. Willliam Cunningham was buried from Our Lady of Peace Church in the Holy Sepulchre Cemetery. In *Studs Lonigan*, although not in the tale "Studs," confusion in the author's dating of various events may lead to the reader's erroneous conclusion that Studs Lonigan is portrayed as having been born in September 1901.

3 The significance of the convent to Farrell is suggested by a passage in *The Silence of History* in which Eddie Ryan, Danny O'Neill's equivalent in Farrell's later fiction, reflects on his feeling for various periods of history he had studied in courses taken at the University of Chicago. When reading about the Middle Ages, he had "felt an emotional richness as contrasted with later periods, and in that richness, there was more of the familiar. I had been feeling the ages of the past through the Church since I had been a little boy . . . I had been taught by nuns dressed in their black habits, and living in convent homes where they spent hours in prayer. I had heard the echo of the nuns at prayer in their chapel at the yellow brick convent home . . . The echo of women's voices in unison of sound, that of prayer and song, had stirred me with emotions I did not understand, but knew in their immediate truthfulness, with their true but almost quelling sadness." This sadness "was related to the heart of life, to the trueness of hearts, and to the timed and yet forever important life of Christ on Earth, . . . a poetry of the centuries which I could not recognize as such, but which was the first poetry of my life" (pp. 263-64).

4 Among Studs's main friends in the 58th Street gang were Slug Mason [*Slug Specker* and the fictional Big Cracker], Arnold Sheehan [*Roland Powers*], Hink Weber [*Hink Weberg*], Tommy Doyle [*Tommy Barnes* and the fictional Gerry Nolan], Harold ("Red") Kelly [*Harold ("Red") O'Keefe*; the fictional Torch Feeney], Stan Simonski [*Al Bernudi*], Paulie Haggerty [*Paulie Harrington*], George Gogarty [*Ed Kenny*], Tubby Connell [*Tubby Collins*], Art Behan [*Paul O'Brien*], Joe Thomas [*Joe Lyons*], Ike Dugan [*Mush Cullinan*], Big Rocky [*Herb Mosher*], and Young Rocky [*Al Mosher*].

5 Frank Egan lived near 63rd Street and was a member of the 63rd Street gang. Farrell met him at Teresa Dolan's [Louisa Nolan's and Marguerita Mooney's] dance hall over the drugstore on the southwest corner of 63rd Street and Stony Island Avenue. Frank committed the brutal rape recorded in the final chapter of *The Young Manhood of Studs Lonigan* and was sentenced to prison for it. In Farrell's trilogy he is directly involved in the rise and fall of Studs Lonigan. Farrell noted that he was the one major character whom he "imported" into the 58th Street neighborhood. It was Frank's brother, an engineer for the City of Chicago, who was nicknamed "Weary." (Interview, 27 December 1955; letters, Farrell to Branch, 23 November 1964 and 27 October 1976).

6 Indoor ball was played outdoors with a larger ball than the regulation softball.

7 Hyde Park is the neighborhood bordered by 47th and 60th Streets to the north and south, and the lakefront and Washington Park on the east and west. The South Shore district extends south of 67th Street from Stony Island Avenue to the lake, and south to 79th Street. (Dominic A. Pacyga and Ellen Skerrett, *Chicago City of Neighborhoods* [Chicago: Loyola University Press, 1986], pp. 370, 375, 384.)

8 Patrick Cunningham also sold his Michigan Avenue apartment in 1928, the year before his son William died. He moved his family to 7822 Luella Avenue in the South Shore district. Although *Judgment Day* shows Paddy Lonigan on the verge of financial ruin in 1931, Farrell stated to James Henle, in his Chicago letter of April 3, 1936, that Patrick Cunningham was still listed in the Chicago telephone directory as a plastering contractor.

9 Farrell described the boathouse in his unpublished novel "When Time Was Young": "The boathouse was not enclosed. It was spacious. It had a stone floor, and was covered by a heavy roof, which was supported by round bulky looking pillars. In front, and a few steps down, there were two small piers . . . A sidewalk was between the front end of the boathouse . . . and the piers and the landing. . . . At the landing, and on either side of the piers, there were many row boats . . . and they were held by a rope to stakes on the landing. Two attendants, wearing light tan khaki uniform suits and uniform caps, with badges, sent the boats out, pushing them with a hook, and brought them in closer, using the same hooks" (typescript, p. 215).

10 Pacyga and Skerrett, p. 336.

11 Takiss Georgis, Farrell believed, was an outstanding "carrier of culture," the kind of person whose own interests and accomplishments infected others with a love of books, learning, and ideas. "Pete's friendship was valuable to me," Farrell wrote. "In time, I came to treasure it. . . . Perhaps no one, when I lived around 58th Street, other than Paul Caron and Joe Cody, gave me more moral support in my effort and drive to gain an education" ("Since I Began," completed 17 July 1975, pp. 2297-98, 2303). The two men became good friends and kept in touch over the years. Takiss moved to Roseville, California, and in his old age managed his own restaurant in San Francisco.

12 Mary Daly Farrell was one of nine children born to Julia Brown Daly, and the oldest of Julia's three daughters to survive beyond infancy and early childhood. Two boys and two girls died before the age of three.

13 When Farrell entered St. Cyril's, his main ambition was centered on athletic success. He became known for his athletic ability and was commonly called "Jumps." His high school grades were average. During his senior year he averaged in the high seventies, with his best grades (in the mid-eighties) earned in English and Rhetoric. In his memoirs he wrote: "At the time, St. Cyril did not have a reputation for athletics. It did not have a gymnasium. It fitted within the category of Catholic high schools that were socially acceptable" (Undated, untitled MS, pp. 2-3). St. Cyril's basketball team practiced elsewhere. Farrell's final participation in organized sports came in 1925. After a brief time on the University of Chicago freshman basketball squad, a severely wrenched knee forced him to withdraw from practice.

14 Farrell registered for the Summer 1925 quarter on Saturday, June 20, 1925, in the university's Bartlett Gymnasium. He supported himself by working for the Sinclair Oil and Refining Company [Rawlinson Oil and Refining Company] as a service station attendant at 42nd Street and Michigan Avenue. Danny O'Neill's and Eddie Ryan's experience at the university, as seen in Farrell's fiction, closely parallels that of the novelist.

Before enrolling at the university, Farrell had completed the first semester (1924-25) at De Paul University while working at the Express Company. He hoped to become a lawyer. His five courses at De Paul included Economics I-II, Economic History, Sociology I, English History, and English Composition I-II. His highest grade was 95 in English Composition, taught by Jeremiah J. Buckley. His lowest grade of 75 came in Sociology. His overall average was 87. During the second semester, Farrell attended a handful of class meetings in each of his five courses (Sociology II, English Literature, Political Science, Economics II, and Economic History) before dropping out because of the danger of a nervous breakdown through overwork.

15 Edward Arthur ("Eddie") Ryan [*Farrell*] in *The Silence of History* (p. 131) claims that he received an "A" in both of his summer 1925 courses.

Farrell's University of Chicago transcript records that he earned an "A" from Professor Joranson and a "B" from Mr. Hoffmann. From the summer of 1925 through the spring of 1929, his final quarter, he enrolled in nine quarters at the university, dropping out and then resuming work three times after his original matriculation. He made nine "A's," nine "B's," and two "C's," for an average of 3.37 (the Registrar's calculation) on the current formula of grading based on the 4-point system. Based on the system of marking then in effect at the University, he made 21 1/2 major credits and 96 points. When he had made 18 major credits he passed from the Junior College (first and second years) into the Senior College (third and fourth years) and was awarded Honorable Mention for Excellence in Junior College Work. The university granted him a tuition remission three times: for the Spring and Summer 1928 quarters and the Summer 1929 quarter.

16 During this time, Farrell read hundreds of books in the library. After June 1928, when he began writing his trilogy, he also used empty classrooms and landings in at least two university buildings, Harper and Classics, to work on his mega-manuscript—what became the then undivided narrative of *Young Lonigan* and *The Young Manhood of Studs Lonigan*. "I used to read, with holes in my pants, in Harper's, and write *Young Lonigan* in a room on the second floor of Classics, it being usually full of cigarette smoke and Jewish law students arguing cases, while I pounded away at the typewriter. Arguments about cases, briefs etc. would go on, and I would slug the keys, not hearing a word of it" (Letter, Farrell to Ralph Marcus, 25 Aug. 1943).

Farrell's campus friend George Brodsky wrote of him: "I can still see him, a burly lone figure sitting at the long oak table on one of the landings in the west towers of Harper, a cigarette hanging from the corner of his mouth (perhaps in unconscious imitation of Teddy Linn), banging away at the keys, with the metallic ring of the machine echoing up and down the stone stairwell. . . . What attracted me to Farrell was his singleness of purpose to be a writer. I admired his innate honesty, his lack of guile, his childlike belief in the causes he singled out to champion, but above all I held his prodigious industry in awe" (Letter, George Brodsky to Branch, 3 Feb. 1976). At times Farrell also wrote in the branch public library at 63rd Street and Kimbark Avenue, where Katherine Dunham worked. For two and-a-half years before he and Dorothy left for Paris in April 1931, Farrell plugged away at his long manuscript, as well as many short stories, in the three apartments on the fringe of the South Shore district which he and the Dalys occupied during that time. He also read and wrote so much in the Chicago Public Library at Randolph and Michigan that his sister Helen called it his office.

17 During the Spring quarter 1926 at the university, Elsa Chapin, Farrell's first composition teacher, gave him exceptionally high grades on his themes. She especially liked his "Brisbane University," a satire on the platitudinous writings of Arthur Brisbane, columnist for the Hearst newspapers. She persuaded him to send it to the *New Republic*. It was the first time he submitted his writing to a commercial magazine for publication. It was rejected.

18 Farrell took five composition courses at the University of Chicago. The quarter offered, course number, title, catalog description, instructor, and grade are given for each: Spring Quarter 1926, English Composition 103. Required of all candidates for degrees who have completed nine majors in the Junior College, including English 101. (Farrell received transfer credit from De Paul to meet this requirement.) Elsa Chapin, "A"; Winter Quarter 1927, Advanced English Composition 210. Open to students in the Senior Colleges and the Graduate Schools who have attained a high grade in composition or who otherwise satisfy the instructor as to their ability. James Weber Linn, "B"; Summer Quarter 1928, English Composition 202. Advanced composition: exposition. Prerequisite: 18 majors including English 103 (or its equivalent by advanced standing). Martin Joseph Freeman, "B"; Summer Quarter 1928, English Composition 210. Prerequisite: the equivalent of 202 or 205 and the permission of the instructor (Robert Morss Lovett was course director). Llewellyn Jones [Jason Hastings], literary editor of the *Chicago Evening Post* [*Chicago Carrier*], "B"; Spring Quarter 1929, English Composition 211, Advanced Course. Prerequisite: English 210. The student must satisfy the instructor as to his abilities upon entering the course. James Weber Linn, "A." During the Winter 1926 quarter Farrell took his only course in literary history, English 140, Survey of English Literature. In his autobiographical writings he identified the instructor as Mrs. Munsey, who led the class from the Romantic writers through the late Victorians. (The time schedule for the Winter quarter gives Mrs. Katherine Graham as the instructor. The university Registrar finds no record of a Mrs. Munsey in or associated with the English Department at this time.) He received an "A" grade.

19 The Coffee Shop, now known as the C-Shop, is technically in Hutchinson Hall, which also houses the large Hutchinson Commons. Hutchinson Hall is one of a group of buildings (known as the "Tower Group") designed and constructed together, including the Reynolds Club and Mandel Hall. Because the Coffee Shop opens on a central hallway connecting directly to the Commons, the Reynolds Club, and Mandel Hall, it commonly is thought of—and Farrell often referred to it—as being in Mandel Hall.

20 As Jim Farrell continued his studies, the circle of his campus friends grew. His closest student and faculty friends at the university included Joseph Cody [Joe Coady; Jim Gogarty; Peter Moore], Felix Kolodziej [Walter Broda; Walter Brovid], George Brodsky [Bertrand Glass; Bertrand Gold], Virginius Frank Coe [Lucretius Harry Roberts], Charles ("Bob") Coe [Tom Roberts], Katherine Dunham's brother Albert Dunham [Norman Allen; David or Daniel or Dennis Carter, Carr or Carney], Professors Frederick L. ("Fritz") Schuman [Stanley Frederick] and Rodney Loomer Mott [Donald W. Torman], Stanley Newman, Alvin David [David or Daniel Arenberg], Martin J. ("Tom") Freeman [Fred Trendell; Frank M. Morton], Alden Stevens, Paul Rosenfels [Nathan Lewisburg], Arthur Karstens, and Milton Peterson.

Cody was a pre-law student and a long-time friend from the 58th Street neighborhood who became a Chicago attorney. He was a high jumper on the university track team. Farrell, Kolodziej, and David met during the Spring Quarter 1926 while enrolled in Political Science 103, Comparative Government, offered by Professor Harold Lasswell [Professor Pearson], who had replaced Jerome Kerwin as the instructor. Farrell earned an "A" in the course. The Coe brothers, Kolodziej, Brodsky, and David were active members of the campus Liberal Club. Kolodziej was on the university wrestling team. He and Brodsky teamed up to convince Farrell to join them in Professor Linn's English 211, Advanced Composition, during the Spring Quarter 1929. They defended Farrell's stories read by Linn in class. Brodsky became the owner of the Chicago firm George Brodsky Advertising, Inc. The Coe brothers were brilliant college students in Political Science and Political Economy. Charles Coe, Frank's younger brother, joined the Economics Department at Brown University. In 1945 Frank was appointed Director of the Division of Monetary Research in the U. S. Treasury Department and the next year Secretary of the International Monetary Fund. Both Coe brothers were named in the 1948 Congressional espionage investigation of Harry Dexter White.

Schuman, like Rodney Mott, was an instructor in the Political Science Department. He later became an outstanding authority in his field and the Woodrow Wilson Professor of Government at Williams College. In 1941 Freeman became Chairman of the Hunter College

Department of Journalism. He published several books. While Farrell was on campus, both Freeman and Schuman and their wives invited Farrell and his girl, Dorothy Butler, into their homes. In turn, they attended a party given by Dorothy in her mother's Blackstone Avenue apartment. Stanley Newman became a distinguished anthropologist who taught at the University of New Mexico. Albert Dunham, a protégé of his teacher the philosopher George Herbert Mead, earned his Phi Beta Kappa key at Chicago, studied at Harvard under Alfred North Whitehead for his doctorate in philosophy, and was appointed a professor at Howard University. In 1935, he suffered a mental breakdown and was institutionalized as a paranoid schizophrenic in St. Elizabeth's Hospital in Washington, D. C., where Farrell visited him in 1944. He died in 1949.

21 At this time Farrell gave up his job at the Standard Oil Company [National Oil Company] service station on the southeast corner of 25th Street and Morgan Avenue. He had been earning a salary of $145 a month plus commissions on the sale of oil.

22 Farrell identified Marion (named Thelma Carson in *The Silence of History*, pp. 282-90, 316-61) as his fictional equivalent of Martha Dodd, the daughter of Professor of history and later Ambassador William Edward Dodd. In 1933 Farrell read her story "Brother and Sister" in *Story*. Writing to Martin J. Freeman on November 1, 1933, he stated "The gal has talent," but he found her story "as thin as would be expected."

23 During the post-war years many of the artists went to Greenwich Village and similar places. In the mid-1920s the colony enjoyed a revival. As Farrell wrote in 1929, "Artists again gathered to these famous haunts. Life took on a fast swing. Pictures were painted, gin was drunk and there was dancing until the small hours of the morning.
"Yearly Madhatters parties were held, in which all the studios were thrown open and large crowds followed the orchestra from place to place" ("Stony Island Colony of Art Sheds Glories," *Chicago Herald-Examiner*, 4 Mar. 1929).

24 George Brodsky wrote that during this period "Farrell was known to our U. of C. group as Jimmie. He signed his letters that way.... My recollection of him in his youth, based on virtually daily intimacy for some two years, reveal him as an unkempt character, combative, defensive, scornful of the 'clean boys and girls' around him, given to maudlin moments of curious sentimentality, but awesome in the way he was driven to write day or night, sober or otherwise, the hectic words, misspelled or whatever, tumbling from the typewriter keys" (Brodsky to Branch, 6 Nov. 1979). Farrell's self-description in his autobiographical writings and his account of Danny O'Neill and Eddie Ryan in his fiction is largely in line with Brodsky's description.

25 In 1929 Farrell wrote the unpublished satirical sketch "The Do-LESS Ones." In it, characters based on Jim's friend Paul Caron and Paul's wife Sarajo, and on others, are shown in a Colony studio talking about art and "The Fountain of Time," Lorado Taft's sculpture on the Midway.

26 Reminiscing about his and Farrell's group of close campus friends in the late 1920s, Frederick Schuman wrote: "All of us were young 'rebels' against a status quo which promised only poverty and war. None of us, I believe you will agree, regarded Communism as the 'way out' or embraced the Communist cult in either theory or practice" (Schuman to Farrell, 12 Sept. 1960). Farrell's early criticism of Communism and its practitioners may be found in notebooks written before he left for Paris in April 1931.

27 This information was provided to the author on April 4, 1956, by Mr. Clark of the Clark and Clark Book Store on 55th Street. Clark's store served the university community. In 1926-28, he employed Farrell to deliver handbills in the neighborhood. Among Jimmy Farrell's better friends in the Coudich Culture Center were Mary Hunter, Vladimir Janowicz, the painter Emil Armin, and the art critic J. Z. Jacobson.

28 Matsoukas would soon date Virginia Butler, sister of Dorothy Patricia Butler, Farrell's wife-to-be. He was known as The Campus Aesthete. Art critic, campus playwright and journalist, scene designer, impressario, idea man, and reputedly a dweller in a studio where doves flew about the eaves, Matsoukas was caricatured in the *Daily Maroon* as affecting lavender ties, a black mustache, and a long-necked, languid, intellectual air. He satirically dubbed Jim Farrell "Jimmy the Genius" and "The Founder of the Four-letter School of Literature." Farrell, in turn, good-naturedly ribbed him in the student publication *Phoenix*. Matsoukas became Publicity Director for Skouras. Sterling North portrayed Matsoukas as Demetrius Dardanus in his novel *Seven Against the Years*.

29 Stanley Newman and his wife belonged to the Cube group. Newman reminisced: "The Cube crowd was an assorted bunch of writers, painters, sculptors, and advanced thinkers or hangers-on, all of us strongly influenced by the Nathan and Mencken atmosphere of maintaining gaiety in the process of tearing down idols.... Nobody in the Cube group, to which he [Farrell] did belong as a kind of peripheral member, took his literary efforts seriously" (Newman to Branch, 24 April 1956).
Newman also recalled that most members of the Cube group prided themselves on their "sophisticated" moderation in drinking in contrast to the behavior of "philistine" fraternity boys, but that Jimmy Farrell sometimes drank too much at their parties and, while "pie-eyed" and "stinking drunk," was given to loud and belligerent assertions of his rebellion against the church. In Farrell's unpublished novel "The Call of Time," the university student Eddie Ryan feels a tide of bitterness rising in him because of the "time he felt to have been wasted on him when he had been in parochial schools." But by 1930 he is beginning to realize that he could "reclaim the waste by making something out of it in his writing" and thereby understand more about his past. He was learning that bitterness "was an obstacle... thrown in the path of understanding" (pp. 994-995).

30 Mary Hunter was the niece of Mary Austin. She married Farrell's friend Jack Sullivan, later a New York lawyer. In a pioneering effort at the Cube in the early spring of 1929, she directed three one act Negro plays with all black casts, including the talented Katherine Dunham, who also acted in a dramatization of F. Scott Fitzgerald's "The Man Who Died at Twelve O'Clock." Farrell described Mary Hunter at this time as "a plump, handsome, black-haired girl with shining dark eyes" ("Norman Allen" in *ADW*, p. 96). She lived in a second floor apartment of the Coudich Culture Center. Among other plays she directed at the Cube were Pirandello's "Six Characters in Search of an Author" and Ibsen's "The Master Builder." She later became a Broadway director. Lit by candles and paper lanterns, the Cube also staged such plays as Strindberg's "The Stronger," Ibsen's "Ghosts," Paul Green's "The No 'Count Boy," O'Neill's "The Dreamy Kid," and "East Lynne." It presented musical programs featuring Debussy's "Afternoon of a Faun" and Stravinsky's "Firebird Suite," and a dance interpretation of part of Robinson Jeffers's "The Roan Stallion."

31 In his fiction published before he died, Farrell did not write about either Danny O'Neill or Eddie Ryan at the Cube. Had he done so, it is likely that the portrayal would have paralleled his experiences there.

32 Dorothy matriculated at the university in the autumn 1927 quarter at age seventeen. She was enrolled through the winter 1929 quarter as a pre-law student. Living at 5600 Blackstone Avenue, she had a short walk both to the campus and to the Cube. During this period she and Katherine Dunham were members of a ballet class in an Art Colony studio across the street from the Cube. The class was taught by Mark Turbyfill, Katherine's first ballet teacher. Dorothy later enrolled in the university for the winter 1947 quarter but did not earn a degree. At the time she acted in "The Master Builder," her boy friend, Jimmy Farrell, counted Ibsen as one of his literary heroes. He had read Ibsen's greatest plays during the summer of 1926 and later felt that the playwright had exerted a profound influence on his own writing.

33 In his unpublished novel "The Call of Time," Eddie Ryan [*Farrell*] says of Marion [*Dorothy*]: "She was a very good looking girl, if not a beautiful one. Her red hair, almost a Titian red, was splendid, if not gorgeous. And she had a neat, appealing figure" (p. 245). Similarly, Eddie says of Marion in the unpublished "Innocents in Paris": "Marion's hair fell down about to the level of the small of her back. It was golden red, a light red, and somewhat like the color of the hair of one of Titian's nudes" (Text 1, Vol. VII, Chapter 1, p. 15).

Shortly after meeting Dorothy, Farrell wrote an eight-page letter to her from Gary, Indiana, while on his abortive trip to New York with Paul Caron and Elkin [*Selby*, a former instructor at the University of Michigan] in July 1928. Farrell was writing his letter, he said, "at eleven o'clock on Wednesday, the very hour I had a date with you in the coffee shop. The fact that I'm unable to see you at this moment disappoints me." His letter analyzed Bodenheim's personality and leading features of his poetry. He included a bibliography of some twenty items on Bodenheim and his writings, and offered, while in New York, to "look up the files of a magazine in which Bodenheim wrote most of his early poetry" (Farrell to Dorothy Butler, 28 July 1928).

34 Douglas Wixson reports Jack Conroy's claim that Dorothy Farrell's wealthy uncle, the chain foodstore tycoon John Roney [Tom Gregory and Mike McWeeney], funded the Farrell's "European sojourn" in 1931-32. Wixson also reports Conroy's claim that in the early 1940s Roney told him "that Farrell still owed the money lent him, and that Farrell had told people he earned his upkeep in Paris writing for the *New York Herald Tribune*" (*Worker-Writer in America* [Urbana: University of Illinois Press, 1994], p. 546). Dorothy Farrell emphatically denies that John Roney loaned the Farrells any money or was asked to do so (Interview, Dorothy Farrell, 22 July 1994).

From the late 1920s on, no love was lost between the wealthy entrepreneur and Farrell, who portrayed Roney satirically in his tale "Can All This Grandeur Perish?" The Farrells' 1931-32 correspondence and records in Farrell's Paris address book reveal their sources of income during their year in Paris: substantial advances from James Henle for *Young Lonigan* and *Gas-House McGinty*; generous gifts from Dorothy's mother Margaret Butler [Tessie Healy] and Dorothy's good-hearted uncle Art Althouse [Uncle Jack]; modest earnings by Farrell; small sums given by Martin J. Freeman [Fred Trendell; Frank M. Morton], Felix Kolodziej [Walter Broda; Walter Brovid, Gus Inwood], Edward Bastian [Alvin Dubrow; Bob Estrelle], Lloyd George Alfred ("Bus") Stern [Frank or Fred Morris], and Vladimir Janowicz [Comrade Stanley; Stanley Gradek; Jan Varsky]; and small loans or gifts from several of the Farrell's Parisian friends. Farrell repaid loans from Rev. Harold Belshaw [Rev. Whitehall], the Episcopalian Director of the U.S. Students and Artists Club in Paris, and from Dr. Horatio S. Krans, the Director of the American University Union in Europe, which helped cover the expense of the return trip to America. He also repaid a rent remission from his Sceaux landlords Madame Prévost and her son Albert [Madame Leblanc and Albert Leblanc].

Farrell wrote book reviews in 1929-30 for the *New York Herald Tribune*. No credible evidence known shows that Farrell ever reported, or claimed to have reported, for that newspaper while he was in Paris in 1931-32. Even had he wished to make that claim, he would have known that it easily could be disproved.

Chapter Two: Studs and Danny

DANNY O'NEILL, Farrell wrote, is "an autobiographical image." To Farrell the phrase meant that his portrait of the character bore a close resemblance to his own person, but was not "a strictly accurate autobiographical representation"—an impossible goal to achieve, he believed. "I had to invent."[1] By extension we may say that Studs Lonigan is a biographical image, but no doubt one with a more plentiful admixture of invention than that which went into Danny's creation. Studs's character and actions were drawn in part from Farrell's knowledge of William ("Studs") Cunningham. But as he freely and correctly admitted, Studs Lonigan was "a combination of myself and Studs Cunningham."[2]

On May 1, 1915, at age eleven, Danny O'Neill first meets Studs Lonigan. It happened on Danny's first day in his new home at Indiana Avenue and 57th Street. Thirteen years later, about 9 P.M. on an evening in early November 1928, Danny talks with Studs for the final time in front of the old Central Chicago Public Library at Randolph Street and Michigan Avenue. Their meeting is described in the tale "Studs," where we also learn that Studs dies not long afterwards and that Danny goes to his wake the next night. Change the names above to Jimmy Farrell and Studs Cunningham, and you emerge with the same "facts." Studs Cunningham died on Sunday, March 10, 1929. The next day, while on the University of Chicago campus—Farrell was then taking Professor Linn's Advanced Composition course—he learned of Studs's death from his friend Joe Cody. That night the two went to Studs's wake in the South Shore district.[3] But in the trilogy Studs dies in August 1931. Farrell "invented" the Depression-era Studs Lonigan of *Judgment Day*.[4]

The differences between Danny O'Neill and Studs Lonigan, and their dynamic relationship—no matter what their specific admixture of "reality" and "invention" in any fictional episode—are at the heart of Farrell's picture of the neighborhood's significance for human development. "The principal fact to keep in mind," he wrote, "and the most general, or inclusive one, concerning Studs Lonigan and Danny O'Neill is that they both come from the same general kind of boyhood background. In the broadest sense, theirs is the same kind of an environment," but, he added, by no means exactly "the same"; for here "We are dealing with values."[5]

Initially in the 1920s Farrell wanted to explore his own boyhood through the character Danny, and Studs was conceived merely as one of the minor characters in the later years of that story. He soon realized "that he should get outside of himself" and not begin "by licking his own wounds and lacerating his own adolescence on paper."[6] In part fortuitously—responding to Studs Cunningham's death and to the warm reception given his tale "Studs" by Professors Linn and Lovett—Farrell focused his imagination on Studs Cunningham's life. He began to adapt his newly conceived "objective" manner to his character's special traits and limited consciousness, and inevitably he came to see Studs and Danny as potential "dialectical opposites of one another. Studs fails and dies; Danny lives and fights. Studs usually makes the wrong decisions where his fate and destiny are concerned; usually Danny makes the right ones. Studs is defeated in life; Danny is undefeated."[7] These two fully realized characters eventually became the major symbols embodying the potential for spiritual enrichment and spiritual poverty at work in Farrell's own neighborhood; for self-discovery and meritorious accomplishment on the one hand, and tragic weakness and self-evisceration on the other. Their lives dramatize the contradictory "tendencies" Farrell discerned in his boyhood past.

One way that Farrell anchors these larger themes in his Chicago fiction set in the Washington Park neighborhood is to bring Danny O'Neill and Studs Lonigan together, face to face and from time to time, over the sixteen years bridging their first meeting in 1915 and Studs's death in 1931. An eighth-grader in 1915, Studs was "the kind of kid the other kids liked."[8] Blue-eyed and with blond curly hair, he was a school leader, the quarterback on the school football team, and "liked by the girls." Fairly short in stature, he was sturdily built. He could "fight like sixty and . . . never took any sass from Tommy Doyle, Red Kelly, or any of those fellows from the Fifty-eighth Street gang" ("Studs," *SS*, 349).[9] Three grades behind Studs in 1915, Danny is called "goofey." "He wore glasses, was a dreamy-eyed kid, whose attention was always evaporating in a misty and even stupid, look of self-absorption."[10]

The narrator of the tale "Studs," a Danny surrogate, recalls that his "first concrete memory" of Studs is when Danny and his friend Dick Buckford are bumping each other with folded arms in the street (a scrap also reflected in "Helen, I Love You") and Studs, coming by with Red O'Connor, Bill Delaney, and Tubby Collins, "urged us into fighting." Danny wins, and Studs later praises him as the best fighter among the younger guys. "'You're too good,'" Studs says. "'You can crap the whole bunch of them.' Danny beamed."[11] Danny is taken on "as a sort of mascot" by Studs and his bunch ("Studs," *SS*, 349). Eager to strengthen Studs's friendship, Danny invites him to his twelfth birthday party in February 1916, only to have his grandmother, who had heard bad things about Studs, disinvite him. Danny gets her to relent and he visits Studs's home to tell Mrs. Lonigan that Studs was welcome to come. But Studs, who seems to have understood and is not angered, declines.

From then on, into the summer of 1916, as we learn in *Young Lonigan*, Danny continues to bask in

Studs's approval. He cozies up to Studs by talking to him about Three-Star Hennessey's public masturbation, and about Rube Waddell, the baseball great. He engages Studs in an imaginative baseball game. Studs, in turn, in a sparring match, "trains" Danny to fight, and he promotes a boxing match between Danny and Three-Star Hennessey, and a wrestling match between his mascot and TB McCarthy. When Studs fights Weary Reilley, Danny is present, rooting loudly for Studs.

The turning-point comes when Danny laughs in Studs's presence while reading the graffiti saying "Studs kissed Lucy a million times." Studs socks him, Danny bawls, and Studs, blaming Danny and others in the Indiana Avenue bunch for his public "shaming," vows "to pay that little droopy-drawers back yet. . . . He was through hanging around with the Indiana Avenue mopes" (*YL*, 116-17).

After their breakup, Danny and Studs meet only rarely. When Danny starts going to the 58th Street poolroom in 1922, during his junior year in high school, Studs rags him, cuts him down. Later, Danny is praised there by Wils Gillen [*Wilson Gilligin*] for his basketball prowess. Chalking his cue, Studs says: "That's all spelled C R A P, punk" (*F&S*, 277, 432). Ironically, three years later in June 1925, Studs, who was patrolling Michigan Avenue with his friend Jim Nolan [*Jim Barnes*] the cop, keeps Nolan from shooting Danny at Danny's service station at Michigan Avenue and 42nd Street: Nolan had mistaken Danny for a robber. But in March 1927, on the night Danny resolves "to drive this neighborhood . . . out of his consciousness with a book," Studs, Red Kelly, and Barney Keefe pass Danny on the street and "called him goof and told him to leave it alone" (*YMSL*, 372). Danny, who has discovered his life-mission at the University of Chicago, and Studs, mired in old habits, are now hurtling through life in opposite directions. Not once in *Judgment Day* do they meet face to face.

But even though Studs and Danny rarely meet after 1916—also true of Jim Farrell and Studs Cunningham—Farrell indirectly makes sure that his readers never forget for long the tension-laden love-hate relationship of the two. Studs, who has no dog, loves Danny's Airedale, Lib ("a damn sight smarter than Danny," he thinks), plays with Lib in Washington Park, and "couldn't think of hurting it" even to get even with Danny (*YL*, 121). Studs relishes the punishment Danny receives from the nuns at St. Patrick's School for having kissing games at his 1917 birthday party. In 1918 as a tough guy too old to play with punks, he envies Danny and his friends waging trench warfare in a vacant lot. He admires Danny's skill at catching fungoes in the park ("He was a perfect judge of fly balls, and he never overran the pill" [*YL*, 171]), and he sees Danny outbox the older Red Kelly and Tommy Doyle.

On Armistice Day 1918, Danny wishes he were with Studs in Chicago's Loop "raising hell" at war's end. In 1922 Studs overhears Danny praise his play as quarterback in the football game with the Monitors. Pleased, he tries to open up with the punk O'Neill who "wasn't so bad" after all, but the effort is sidetracked (*YMSL*, 131). On various other occasions Studs mentions Danny disparagingly: for being goofy or being an atheist, or for not making Father Shannon's mission. The two see each other casually on the street or at the meeting of the St. Patrick's Young People's Society. In another device Farrell uses, Danny's thoughts are turned to Studs by the actions of other characters. In Andy Le Gare's letters to Danny from Los Angeles, Andy remembers Studs as "the best whitest guy of the older guy who hung around that pool roome den of iniquieties and the only one of them guy who treat me decent when I was a kid" (*YMSL*, 184). Danny and his boyhood friend Jim Gogarty plan in 1925 to become law partners and then go into politics. Jim suggests they hang around the poolroom and "laugh and kid with the boys," because "After all, Studs Lonigan and the boys are future voters"—a suggestion Danny rejects (*Anger*, 52).

In August 1931, as Studs is dying at home, Chicago cop Jim Doyle tells Paddy Lonigan that Danny, who "went to the A[merican] P[rotective] A[ssociation] University" was "probably responsible" for Danny's younger brother and sister marching in the Communist anti-war parade Paddy is watching (*JD*, 441). This is Danny's only presence in *Judgment Day*. As Paddy watches the marchers, Studs, who has received Extreme Unction, enters heaven, where he will be miserable because "there are no whores or poolrooms" ("Studs," *SS*, 354) and because of the guilt he carries for having destroyed his better self. At this very moment, Danny, as we learn later, is married, living in Paris, and revising the manuscript of what will become his first novel.

In such terms Farrell dramatizes the "dialectical opposition" of Studs Lonigan's and Danny O'Neill's "destinies" and simultaneously plumbs his own buried feelings about his past relationship with Studs Cunningham. The pattern is clear. The "goofy," often lonely and introspective younger boy admires and emulates the popular older boy, who at first accepts and "adopts" him, only later to reject him, displaying hostility and contempt. In turn, the younger boy, having grown beyond early limits, rejects the older boy and his way of life. Eventually, we are tempted to assume, he (like Farrell) will use the entire experience creatively (and as self-justification) in portraying the course of Studs Lonigan's "destiny" and that of Danny O'Neill.

Farrell's retrospective analysis of his family-related motivations lying behind his portrayal of Studs Lonigan occurred immediately after the death of his mother, Mary Daly Farrell, on January 9, 1946. Living in Chicago with her daughter Helen and Helen's husband Matt Dillon, Mary suffered a massive stroke late in December and remained in a comatose condition for almost two weeks. For ten days her children (Earl and Joe, with their wives, and Mary from California, and Jim and Jack from the East Coast), as well as her brother and sister, Tom and Ella Daly, gathered in Helen's home waiting for her death, during what Farrell called the longest wake in history. To his friend George Gross he wrote: "I have lived my life to date three times. In reality. In my books. And in the ten days of my mother's last illness and death." The experience, he continued, was a scalding one in which loves and hates of the past boiled over and exploded, a train of memories thundered through his mind, and concealed motives which had driven him came to light.[12]

Farrell went into detail with his publisher James Henle about the memories that "unrolled in my mind . . . with no strain, no striving for remembrance" during "those traumatic days in Chicago when Mama[13] died." Many of his memories, he confided to Henle, referred to "the inner motivation . . . behind" Studs Lonigan, and many of them centered on male figures important in his youth, one of whom was his older brother Earl. Simmering up in his mind were old resentments: "Earl as a big brother generally did not protect me. He usually took the side of others, sometimes of bigger boys, against me. He played cruel jokes on me, dominated play, even cheated to beat me . . . Sometimes he socked me and kicked me . . . in brief rejected me." Earl was a pal of Red O'Connor, and the two older boys once shot Jimmy with a beebee gun. It was Earl who persuaded his grandmother not to allow Studs Cunningham to come to Jimmy's birthday party. Farrell believed that his "father considered Earl a better boy, and a Farrell."[14]

"I was always proud that my father could fight," Farrell told Henle, "always afraid of him, afraid that he would hit me, beat me, and was never at ease with him when I was a boy."[15] "My father and I were never really close. We did not communicate much, for years. He never could forgive me, I feel, because he could not forgive himself for letting me go to my mother's relatives."[16] "When I was nineteen, after I had gotten drunk (described in *Father and Son*) he called me 'The jerkings of a Chinese jackoff against a lamppost.'"[17] "My love of and respect for a father was transferred to Uncle Tom Daly."[18]

Feeling partially alienated from Earl and his father, as Farrell explained to Henle, he turned at age eleven to Studs Cunningham as a protector and a model. Like Farrell's father, Studs could fight—"he was one of the best fighters of the boys who hung around Indiana. . . . I wanted Studs to be a good fighter. . . . Studs used, sometimes, to tell me I could fight. For a period, he treated me better than Earl. I was always interested in him, and wanted his good will. . . . As I recall now, there were times I felt as if Studs were like an older brother. . . . Studs was a melted [melded?] real and ideal brother-father image here, and [an] alternative to the Farrell images in my mind.[19] . . . Later, in the pool room days, he used to treat me as did Earl when I was a boy. The only time he changed would be when we talked of Vincent Curry [Vinc Curley], the moron. That—talking of Vincent's imbecility—gave me a bond whereby I could get approval."[20]

After exposing these intimate resurgent memories to Henle, Farrell cautioned him that he could not say they were "absolutely true, but rather . . . a remembrance and recreation of things past, emotions, feelings, inner drives as these returned to me" in the days following his mother's death. In addition, as Farrell wisely recognized, the meaning of *Studs Lonigan* was far from exhausted by an understanding of these selective and very personal motivations. The trilogy's meaning, he insisted, primarily inhered in "the plane of objective social behaviour. *Studs* is to be seen as on the objective plane of the outer world. This analysis doesn't then . . . damage any interpretation of . . . its other meanings. . . . [It is] a story of a boy and a young man."[21] The trilogy, he explained to Henle on January 21, was based on observation as well as on his personal impulses. It gave an objective picture of boys' behavior and moods typical of many American boys of that time. Past Farrell criticism has born out Farrell's caveat. It has repeatedly explored the spectrum of social themes (those "other meanings" related to "objective social behaviour") that it has found to be structural in the body of his fiction.[22]

A. Some Background Considerations

Farrell believed that "The artist seeks to defeat time and death, and to create moments of experience that will live as long as there is living. He grasps after reality, even though it be the reality of dream or fantasy, because he wants to preserve what has been living."[23] As we have just seen, Farrell was fully aware that such an exalted formulation of the artist's goal might and indeed did have, for him, a dark underside: the intimate psychological ground of intensely personal motives—a valid and deeply rooted part of "the reality of . . . what has been living."

Consider, as another example, the experience recounted in the painfully honest autobiographical tale

"The Stuff That Dreams Are Made Of," written in 1955.[24] There we learn that twenty years after *Studs Lonigan* was published, Farrell recalled a dream he had had twenty-eight years earlier, in July 1927. That year he (the narrator is an unnamed Danny O'Neill persona) had hitchhiked to New York City with his friend Paul Caron [Ed Lanson in the story]. Having only one dollar between them, they spent their first night there in Union Square sleeping on a bench. When he awoke, stiff and dirty, he remembered with "painful clarity" the dream still echoing in his head. In it he had "wanted to be back in Chicago and living in circumstances that were familiar to me." He had dreamed of Frances, "one of many girls who represented the world I had consciously rejected and left"—his boyhood neighborhood—and he wanted to be with her. In his dream Frances had been merged with Roslyn and Texas, two other neighborhood girls he had secretly loved but who, like Frances, had either ignored or scorned him. In the twenty-eight years since 1927, the memory of this dream had surfaced in his mind several times. When he began his story in 1955, he asked himself why.

That question, he wrote, spawned "a few random associations; and suddenly these lead me into a deep morass of associations, connections, names, fragmentary recollections of incidents. I am lost in an inner chaos of the past." He realized anew "that the lives of others, innumerable others, become inextricably entangled in the very structure of our personality. . . . They are lodged in our lives like ghosts who can return at any moment to haunt us with the memory of what we never had, with shame and moral agony or with joy."

With the female "others" of this dream in mind, Farrell reasoned that his own "Intellectual emancipation had not erased the aching and never forgotten pains of frustration and loneliness of my boyhood. And out of that boyhood had emerged the dream of a girl" who had rejected him. "But," Farrell recalled, "by becoming a writer I would not only express my own feelings and prove myself: I would also show them. Whom would I show? Everyone who had ever hurt me, insulted me, ignored me. . . . Most especially, I would show girls. . . . Out of the vanity I felt concerning these girls, I found my purpose in life."[25]

This acute self-scrutiny by Farrell in 1955 lays bare an important psychological source of his Chicago fiction about his experience in the Studs Lonigan neighborhood.[26] Also it recognizes the associational processes, those fermenting memories of the "inner chaos of the past" bubbling up from the subconscious, which drove the artist's creation forward, and out of which he shaped the final product. It exposes what was simultaneously a burden and a great gift: his vulnerability to memories of his boyhood spent in that neighborhood."[27] Striving to portray the reality of that past through the representation of his characters' immediate experience, he poured those memories into his fiction.[28]

Farrell knew that it was impossible for the artist to "remain true to reality in the sense of literal fact . . . To create," he wrote, "requires an alteration of reality in order to fashion a new structure of events and characters. . . . The invented reality of fiction can mirror the raw, direct reality of life, but it is a reflection, as though at an angle."[29]

The invented reality Farrell sought to create in *Studs Lonigan* and the O'Neill-O'Flaherty novels was three-dimensional. He wanted to bring together, through the development of his characters, their physical, social, and psychological worlds. His highly selective, symbolic use of images from Studs's physical environment is widely recognized as a feature of his realism. But, he wrote, "Reality is not merely the outer physical world; it also encompasses the social and the psychological world. The reality of a person includes his or her inner life, the silent, private life of hope and fear, of all the content of the currents of consciousness. Belief and faith support, confirm, uphold realities. Faith in God made God a reality in my boyhood."[30] As we have seen, Farrell's use of his objective method to expose Studs's inner life was a major accomplishment of his trilogy.

Farrell used the terms "temperament" and "character" interchangeably to designate the unique combination of psychic elements that gives to each person his individuality. Each person's temperament, he believed, was a product of native predispositions interacting with, and therefore partly shaped by, surrounding conditions, physical and social. An individual's temperament or character, then, was in part a social product; and in turn, temperament reacted to, and gave direction to, surrounding social conditions. Human development occurred through this dynamic, continuously interactive relationship.[31]

Farrell learned from experience what he later found formulated in the writings of John Dewey and George H. Mead [Emerson Dwight]: the scope and depth of a person's development depends upon the extent to which he can first absorb the attitudes and values of others with whom he interacts, and then shape his beliefs and habits—and indeed his very character—accordingly. He became aware that by incorporating what Mead termed the "generalized other," one's self gains flexibility, range, and an expanding identity. As a young teenager, Danny shares Studs's conviction that only whites belong in Washington Park; but unlike Studs, he outgrows the rigid personality patterns of bigotry that beget racial aggression.[32] His "generalized other" becomes far less restrictive than is Studs's.

When trying, then, to create realistic characters (of whatever degree of psychic limitation) Farrell believed that his task was to let his characters "reveal themselves in thought, speech, conduct, and dreams . . . set inside of the social situation in which they are involved." In doing so much, the writer will consider these questions: "What course do the conditions of life permit these differing temperaments to take? What are the limits within which these differing temperaments can manifest themselves?"[33]

Farrell's portrayal of Jim O'Neill, Danny's biological father, and Al O'Flaherty, his surrogate father (both of whom live in the Studs Lonigan neighborhood), is merely one example of his skill in translating the answers to these questions into fictional terms. Jim O'Neill, a "working man" in overalls committed to the Teamsters' Union, belongs to the "working class." Al O'Flaherty, a dapperly dressed salesman, belongs to the "lower middle-class." By use of his objective method Farrell mobilizes those concrete details of their clothing, their possessions, and their domestic arrangements to illuminate the contrast in their socio-economic status. We see that the status of each man—based on the money he earns and the work he does—is a powerful determinant of his values and convictions; and these, in turn, are vividly implicit in what each man says to Danny and does with him or to him.

Likewise, as Farrell's method reveals through many details—for example, the contrast in the kind of clothes worn by Studs and by Danny, and the higher status of Studs's high school compared to that of Danny's—the "differing conditions of life" surrounding Studs (from a well-off middle middle-class family) and Danny (from two related but divergent families, both less affluent than the Lonigans) have a role in shaping the temperament and affecting the self-esteem and the actions of each boy. In turn, the developing psychology of each boy helps reshape the surrounding conditions of his life.

B. A Question of Values

In eight novels and numerous short stories Farrell detailed the contemporaneous lives of Danny O'Neill and Studs Lonigan which spanned more than a decade in the same neighborhood. Because these two characters are closely tied to the same general environment, readers have searched the fiction for clues to a satisfactory answer as to why Danny is able to rise above a world he never made and Studs suffers an early and inglorious judgment day. In the fiction Danny's life is presented in even more minute detail, from the inside out, than is Studs's; and his involvement with the institutions of family, school, and church is the more sustained, and his psychology the more fully explored. Consequently, perhaps most readers have felt that the direction his life takes is relatively understandable and convincing. On the other hand, matters are not so clear with Studs. He is favored by personal, social, and financial advantages Danny lacks. Nevertheless, by almost any measure, his life leads to early failure. Readers have observed that gang values, the culture of the poolroom and of manual labor, cheap liquor, sex, and the stereotypes of his class and religion count heavily with and against Studs.[34] For that reason, and for reasons given earlier, some readers have fastened on the easy and mistaken explanation that Studs is the product of a slum environment and of economic deprivation. Pinpointing more credible causes of Studs's fatal decline that are woven into the fiction has proved troublesome for some.

It is safe to say that Studs Lonigan is not presented as a ghetto dweller, "an animal of the Chicago jungle; a back-alley bum" or "a shanty Irish punk."[35] He and his gang—Weary Reilley sometimes excepted—do not pack guns; nor—Hink Weber seemingly excepted—do they take drugs, or push them. Nor are gang warfare or crime their chronic pursuits. Farrell once referred to Studs's companions as "more or less small-time amateur hoodlums" ("Studs," *SS*, 350). That may be a characterization too harsh to fit the totality of what Studs is. He has his obvious and serious failings, but he works for his money, is relatively well-to-do, and on most occasions and in many places is socially acceptable.

Although Farrell rejected the "slum theory" as an explanation of Studs's failure, his general theory of human development always allowed for the vital role played by social classes, "surrounding conditions," and institutions in the shaping of human character. As early as 1930 he argued that in a commercial civilization which stressed acquisitiveness and money, "there must be social organization that directs what is most generous and social in man, and which sublimates what is not."[36] He believed that the components—both those that were humanly cohesive and compassionate and those that were humanly hostile and disruptive—of a person's "milieu" affected the direction taken by that person's life. His fiction and commentary repeatedly make the point that in Studs's case what is learned from the media (newspapers, movies, radio) and in the home, school, church, and playground too often reinforces rather than counteracts the malignancy of unexamined ideas as well as the influence of the street and the poolroom. They fail to give adequate answers to Studs's constant question: "What'll we do now?", and he is caught rudderless, floating in the sluggish stream of time. For Farrell, then, the failure of social institutions and of the national or parochial ethos to adequately advance what is humane and "generous and social in man" is one root of the spiritual poverty that brought Studs down.

Studs, Farrell wrote, is "a young man who is concerned only with himself ... he was spiritually poor, which means that at the core of [*Studs Lonigan*] there is the question of values, the values by which people live, or are supposed to live."[37] Elsewhere Farrell said: "Spiritual poverty has to do with values ... It has to do with a sense of past, present, and future. Spiritual poverty is the failure to understand that the most important thing we can do ... is to develop the mind."[38] In Farrell's autobiographical tale "Kilroy Was Here," Danny's friend Bryan, the black poet who lives on South Park Avenue near Danny's former home there, remarks about the neighborhood boys: "They don't care about much of anything, anything that you and I would care about." Danny replies: "There's something more important than their not caring. They don't know. That's the point about the boys I grew up with—they didn't know" (*Vicious,* 83). Farrell thought of the spiritual poverty that affected Studs as a cultural malnourishment and an intellectual dehydration that conditioned Studs to willingly subsist on the ideological hardtack—the clichés and stereotypes—of his circumscribed time and place.

As Farrell worked his way through the final two volumes of *Studs Lonigan* in the early 1930s, he began to develop in greater detail his concepts of destiny and of neighborhood as concerns of central importance in his literary labors. He spelled out his ideas in a series of letters to his St. Cyril's high school classmate Richard Parker [Bart Daly].[39] In his writings, he explained, he wanted to trace the destinies of scores of characters. His concept of "destiny" ruled out "all extra-experiential and supernatural" causes; rather, his common-sense and generalized meaning of the word was "the pressure ... of many things that have happened in the past ... exerting itself in a present." A person's "internal compulsion and weakness, and external force are both parts or factors of this pressure.... Individuals are born with a temperament, ... a set of capacities, which delimit what they can, and what they cannot do." Society's institutions tend to organize and direct those capacities. They shape "the goals of action of any human being ... So I think that destiny can ... be considered as the pressure of events, and events are a complex of what we'll call the social, and the natural. Geography, heredity, and a whole past of historic developments then are the causes of an individual destiny, whether it be Studs, or the destiny of any one else."

Farrell emphasized to Parker that destinies play themselves out in specific neighborhoods.[40] "My concern," he wrote, "is the milieu and environment in America that I know and can assimilate, and characters only in the ways they fit into it.... I've got the ambition of doing a whole series of works that will run perhaps between thirty to fifty volumes of plays, stories, novelettes, and novels, and series of novels, all of which is a loosely integrated picture of the life of a society, all of which tends to extend outward from the neighborhoods of my boyhood, and particularly from that Fifty Eighth street neighborhood, which I am treating as a miniature of the world at large." At this early time, Farrell believed that his assimilated knowledge of the Studs Lonigan neighborhood was the vital center of his current and future fictional portrayal of human life.

Some twenty years later, a quarter of a century after Farrell had written of Studs's life and death in "Studs," he stated what he had come to believe: why a person develops as he does is at bottom an insoluble mystery impervious to reasoning. "The unfolding of human destinies is awesome to me," he wrote. "Why we become what we are, and how we ride out of our childhood, is still a mystery to me. I think it is a mystery to everyone." And, he added, even when he was writing *Studs Lonigan* years before, that mystery "hung in my mind."[41] Farrell still acknowledged the importance of neighborhood. He knew that general theories advance our understanding of human development, but he believed that they cannot adequately account for the complexity of the particular engine that powers a particular person at a particular time and place along the road of his "destiny." However, he remained convinced that "Studs was a victim of a kind of spiritual poverty," and "that if *Studs* is a tragedy, it's a tragedy of weakness and indecision ... because of some defect in his temperament, or because he just didn't have the capacity."[42]

In 1961 Farrell returned to the problem of why Studs Lonigan was the way he was. He concluded that "a man lives and dies according to what he is as a person, and circumstances surrounding him will not alter his basic personality." He argued that "the conditions of a specific time in which a man exists" will change the externals of his life, but do "not change what he is as a person." Studs today, for example, "beneath the surface ... could not be any different from the Studs of 1926.... Studs would be a tragic figure today as yesterday."[43] The ultimate mystery still remains, but Farrell came to believe that what counts the most in the never ending interchange between the "outer" and the "inner" of human experience, what is most decisive in shaping the "destiny" of a Studs Lonigan or a Danny O'Neill, at any time-period, is the individual's "basic personality," the unique mix of ingredients in his native temperament. By expressing itself through experience in the social realm, that temperament spawns an individual's character traits and becomes the profoundest source of the values by which he lives.

Farrell's fiction about Studs and Danny, the two

boys from the same neighborhood, supports his theorizing. Their interwoven stories convey a sense of two distinctly opposite characters, each with an irreducible temperament that underlies and helps to direct the surface changes in each boy's life. For example, Danny nearly always "wants to know," while Studs usually is not interested in knowing or assumes he already knows. This difference is evident in Danny's growth, and Studs's lack of growth, in intellect and in religious conviction. Danny learns to understand and to break inadequate childhood patterns of thought as, for example, what constitutes "manliness." Respecting religion, Danny's odyssey from fervent belief in Catholic doctrine to atheism reflects his intense desire to uncover the truth about God's existence. But Studs, despite being relentlessly battered by experience and suffering insurmountable losses in his physical, personal, and financial well-being, does not question his habituated faith.

The difference is seen clearly even in Studs's self-proclaimed area of superiority—toughness and physical prowess. Danny, the survivor, is the really tough one. Studs, in a fist fight, relies on lumbering roundhouse swings; but Danny, who has studied and practiced the techniques of boxing, can manage his footwork, land more punches, and avoid the wild swings of his opponent. Although he makes false starts, Danny eventually makes and sticks to the right decisions in order to achieve what he wants. Sister Magdalen, Danny's eighth grade teacher, may have had this capacity in mind when she told Danny he was loyal and had "stick-to-it-iveness" ("Sister," *Judith*, 343-44). Studs occasionally makes the right decisions, but then relapses into the old bad habits.

Studs, in fact, exemplifies the psychological type John Dewey labeled as the savage who still exists within civilization—an idea Farrell had come across in reading Dewey's *Human Nature and Conduct* soon after he began working on *Studs Lonigan*. The savage, Dewey wrote, is the man enslaved by hardened customs, by "inflexible tribal habitudes in conduct and ideas." But habit and custom cannot possibly cover "all the changing detail of life"; they do not provide ready responses to the novelty that constantly erupts, whether in primitive or civilized human experience. In civilized society when the regulation of that novelty is left to "appetite and momentary circumstance," the civilized savage is born. In him "enslavement to custom and license of impulse exist side by side. Strict conformity and unrestrained wildness intensify each other." He becomes "known in his degree by oscillation between loose indulgence and stiff habit."[44]

On the other hand, Danny is a partially alienated individual who increasingly feels that he lives in a standardized, stereotyped culture. He and others like him "seethe with a kind of inner restlessness, an inner chaos.

Often, they grope towards finding in culture, especially in books, something which will aid them in discovering themselves, in objectifying their problems . . . and the nature of the world in which they live."[45] Danny is then able to utilize his feelings and impulses to modify and reorganize old habits and thereby form new ones. No longer a law unto themselves, as Dewey observes, impulses and feelings become, for Danny, "an indispensable source of liberation . . . in giving habits pertinence and freshness."[46]

Like Studs, Danny experiences adversity and shame. Often called "Four eyes" or a "goof," Danny is moody, introspective, painfully "different" in some ways from the other guys, unpopular with the girls, and ashamed of his father's "working class" job, his mother's aggressiveness and coarseness, his aunt's loud cursing and public drunkenness, and the fighting that goes on among the O'Flahertys.[47] He wants acceptance by his peers. But sometimes the other boys ditch him, and he often feels like an outsider, and lonely.[48] Yet he has the intellect and the inner resources of imagination and resolve to figure out his own strengths and to act on them, even to the point of becoming a leader—as in certain sports. Moreover, he is able to turn adversity and shame to positive account. He forges new and elevating habits precisely because he has known insecurity and anxiety. He constantly extends the range of his experience and interacts with an ever-expanding range of persons he comes to know. In all these respects Danny achieves self-transcendence and is, indeed, the "dialectical opposite" of Studs.

In 1954 Farrell touched directly on this point in his intimately personal story "Kilroy Was Here." While walking the old neighborhood with his friend Bryan the poet, Danny looks up at the back porch of his former apartment at 5816½ South Park Avenue. "He thought of his Airedale dog, Lib. She was dead so many years. Behind that porch, inside the door of that flat, so much of his life had been lived, and all that life with its agonies and fears and worries had gone into making him what he now was. Once he used to think of the agonies of those days. Now he realized that inside that flat on the second floor he had dreamed, and his ambition had flourished" (*Vicious*, 87-88).

Farrell believed that "Spiritual poverty has to do with . . . a sense of past, present, and future."[49] Danny's vision of his future self evolves through many avatars—as star athlete, businessman, lawyer, politician, and writer, among others; but at any given time he tries (not always with complete success) to base his shifting goals on his best realistic appraisal of his capacities and his deepest desires. Studs, too often and at almost any time, seriously misreads both his past and his future. His vision of his future self is mostly stagnant and unreal, one that is mired in stale stereotypes rather than founded in real capacities he has developed in the past. Danny is able to discard what proves useless to his dominant ambition. Studs cannot do that. By 1927 when Danny determines to become a writer, he has largely freed himself from the domination of his family and especially Uncle Al, from business ideals, from the Church and the supernatural, from dependence on his friend Jim Gogarty and the Nietzscheanism of Ed Lanson,[50] from many old prejudices, and from fear of what others may think, though his imagination remains tied to many ghosts of his past and a romantic idea of himself as an unyielding Atlas. Perhaps Sister Magdalen, Danny's sympathetic and insightful eighth grade teacher, sensed this very ability of his to cast off the fetters of outgrown pasts when she repeatedly informed him: "'Daniel, you have the germs of destruction in you'" ("Sister," *Vicious*, 349).

[1] From an untitled section of Farrell's projected book on *Studs Lonigan* meant for Dutton Publishers, p. 13. Farrell often asserted there was more invention in his trilogy than customarily recognized. For example, he wrote: "In *Studs Lonigan* there was the intensity of re-lived experience, with the added fiction of imagination. Some have made the mistake of treating *Studs Lonigan* [four illegible words] as literal recording" (Autobiographical fragment, p. 16). In an undated letter to Victor Weybright Farrell emphatically stated: "The truth is that *Studs* is full of imagination and invention—not a record of a boy's life as that life happened actually." While recognizing the artistic inevitability of altering the "reality" presented in memory, Farrell nonetheless maintained that the Danny O'Neill books in general were extremely accurate in their portrayal of his personal life and that of his family (but with notable exceptions, as in the final chapters of *My Days of Anger*.)

On the other hand, accuracy was not a primary consideration in the writing of the Bernard Carr books. The origin of that trilogy, he said, was more casual than compulsive. It lay in a conversation with Weldon Kees about writing and what happened to writers like Robert Cantwell. In *Bernard Clare*, Farrell stated, Bernard was an imaginative construct combining his own experience and characteristics of his friends Paul Caron and Jack Sullivan, mixed with elements of Studs Cunningham's character. Bernard's family was not Farrell's. In an early version of *Bernard Clare* Farrell introduced Danny O'Neill as a character who "showed Bernard up"; then he removed Danny from the story. Moreover, when writing the Bernard books, Farrell was often besieged by domestic and financial troubles and problems of self-identity. So severe were his troubles, he believed, that it was a miracle he wrote the Bernard books; and to have followed his original intent of having Bernard slowly degenerate would have crushed the author (Interview, 13 March 1957).

[2] Farrell's statement made to the writer in New York on 10 June 1957. Studs's story, Farrell wrote, "uses and re-fashions much that I saw and felt at a time when I was growing, when I was finding my own way in the maze of life" ("The Story of *Studs Lonigan*," p. 3, the Department of Special Collections, University of Pennsylvania Libraries). Despite the radical contrast in the abilities of Studs Lonigan and Danny O'Neill to shape their personal futures as they want them to be, the two have much in common.

[3] Joe Cody stated that Studs's wake was just as Farrell described it in the tale "Studs" (Interview, Joseph Cody, 3 Apr. 1956). The wake was held in the Cunningham's apartment on the third floor of the building at 7822 Luella Avenue owned by Mr. Cunningham. While at the wake, Jim Farrell felt the hostility of several of Studs's friends toward him—a University of Chicago student and an oddball who wanted to be a writer. In Farrell's account of the wake in his unpublished novels "The Call of Time" and "The Distance of Sadness" Jud Jennings [*William Cunningham*] was still working for his father when he became ill and his father was still in business, in contrast to their desperate situations in *Judgment Day*. Nor is there any indication that Jud, like Studs Lonigan, had a girl who was carrying his child.

Later that spring, before his composition class with "Teddy" Linn was over, Farrell wrote "Studs" in the Hyde Park apartment of his friend Mary Hunter, an aspiring actress, a director of plays produced at the Cube in the 57th Street Art Colony, and later widely known as Marge in the television series "Easy Aces." "I was ready to write—I had completed 'Mary O'Reilley,' 'The Open Road,' another hitch-hiking piece in Dorothy's hands, 'Slob.'" Present when Farrell wrote "Studs" were several friends: James Jerome ("Jack") Sullivan, who married Mary Hunter in October, 1933, and the painter and poet Chuck Colahan and his wife Jean [Frank and Teresa O'Dair; Donald and Rose Hennessey] from Chicago's North Side. Farrell submitted the story to his teacher, Professor Linn, who, like Farrell at that time, wrote for the *Chicago Herald-Examiner*. Before the story was returned, Farrell called Professor Linn about an item in the newspaper, but could not get him. Linn "apologized in class (English 211), and said he presumed that I was calling him on story [i.e., about "Studs"]. It was an impressive story—Sherwood Anderson could make it great. Almost great. It should be kept confidential, he said. It was 'great.' (Sense of his remarks)." (Letter, Farrell to Branch, 23 July 1960.)

[4] Many, perhaps most, of Farrell's characterizations of his fictional people are based on living persons or a combination of living persons. For example, Lucy Scanlan of *Studs Lonigan* whom Studs loved, he said, was a combination of Helen Shannon, whom the young boy Farrell liked, and her sister Lucy Shannon. As a consequence of Farrell's effort to achieve desired effects, his characters inevitably diverge from the living models. An example is the character Andy Le Gare in *Studs Lonigan*, modeled on Andy Dugar. In a letter to Farrell of November 23, 1947, Dugar, who had just read *Studs Lonigan*, humorously points up the difference between himself and the fictional Andy Le Gare by admitting to Farrell that he knew he was dumb and goofy as a kid but did not know that he was a half-wit. In a letter of 29 May 1976 to the author, Farrell stated: "I usually start from the character [the reference here is to the real person] and work away from him, and create him or her. Most of my characters are ones I didn't know well. As a matter of fact, I did not know Studs Cunningham well." Farrell went on to say that all the characters of *What Time Collects* except Anne Duncan Daniels were invented, and he scarcely knew her during the period of her life that he wrote about. The minor character Jewboy Schwartz of *The Young Manhood of Studs Lonigan* was invented. Some of the other characters who, Farrell maintained, were either totally invented or grew from models he scarcely knew were Ellen Rogers, Tommy Gallagher, Clackey Metz ("The Fastest Runner on Sixty-First Street"), and the central character in "The Scarecrow." "On the whole, except in the case of my family, and a few others, I have done best with characters, the models of whom I scarcely knew" (Letter, Farrell to Branch, 15 June 1976).

[5] "Dutton Final," pp. 23-24. In "The Story of *Studs Lonigan* " Farrell wrote: "Danny wins in the sense that he escapes from an environment

of spiritual poverty [and] finds a confidence within himself to try and chart his course and to take a hand in making the kind of destiny for himself that he wishes." But Studs lacks the resources to "take sufficient nourishment [from] . . . the values of his milieu . . . to wage a more successful fight with his destiny than the one which he did wage . . . . He does not break through the crust of stereotypes which are the content of the conformism according to which he lives. . . . Conformity, religious rigidity and sentimental clichés nourish the spirit of Studs no more than they nourish other spirits" (pp. 4-11, Department of Special Collections, University of Pennsylvania Libraries).

[6] From a deleted portion of the manuscript of the Introduction to *Studs Lonigan: A Trilogy*, intended for the Modern Library edition (New York: 1938). For years before Farrell composed *A World I Never Made*, plans for novels reflecting his own life simmered in his mind. In 1933, for example, he wrote: "I've been thinking of [a] novel dealing with my life down around Corpus Christi from First to Fourth grade. It has the material, only my memory of it is kind of vague now. . . . This would cover 1911 to 1914." Anticipating his "Universe of Time" series, Farrell added: "I think I ought to do a Remembrance of Things Past of America, with 20 or so books, including several autobiographical, and family, Lonigan, McGinty, etc." ("Notebook—Novel—Am. Ex. Company," p. 86, dated Nov. 21, 1933).

[7] "Dutton Final," p. 2.

[8] Unpublished and untitled early story (1929?) about Studs and Danny (Department of Special Collections, University of Pennsylvania Libraries.)

[9] In "When Time Was Young," Farrell put Jud Jennings's [*Studs Cunningham's*] height at between 5'6" and 5'7" (p. 218, second page of that number), and in "The Distance of Sadness" he wrote that Jud was "a short fellow, with broad shoulders and a broad face" (p. 248). Farrell's sister Helen recalled seeing Studs Cunningham "lots of times in the neighborhood. He and a group of fellows hung out at the pool hall on 58th Street and were in front of it often. He looked just like Jimmy Cagney—swaggered sort of when he walked. He was tough and most likely the leader of his group—Red O'Keefe, Shrimp Harrington and maybe 8 to 12 others. He was a fighter and I recall seeing him fist fighting on the streets" (Letter, Helen Farrell Dillon to Branch, 7 July 1994).

[10] Unpublished and untitled story about Studs and Danny (1929?), op. cit.

[11] Ibid. In his letter of 17 January 1973 to William L. Lederer, Farrell confirmed that Studs and his friends, including Tubby Collins, used to get him into fights in order to see fights and to see him fight. Fortunately, when that happened, Farrell added, he won the fights.

[12] Letter, Farrell to George Gross, 14 Jan. 1946.

[13] After being taken to live with his grandmother Julia Daly when he was three, Farrell learned to call her "Mother" and her husband, John Daly, "Father." He called his mother, Mary Daly Farrell, "Mama" or "Ma," and his father "Papa" or "Pa."

[14] Farrell's characterization of Earl in his letter to James Henle should be qualified by our knowledge that Earl and Jim were not only close in their boyhood days but also in later life. Earl was genuinely liked by his brothers and sisters as a kind and considerate man of rare understanding and ability.

[15] Letter, Farrell to Henle, 15 Jan. 1946. (Vanguard Press Archives, Rare Book and Manuscript Library, Columbia University, owner of the letter.)

[16] "Autobiography II," an undated notebook, pp. 105-06.

[17] Letter, Farrell to Henle, 15 Jan. 1946.

[18] "Since I Began," completed 30 Dec. 1970, p. 1341. Farrell's alienation from his father (and mother) is in sharp contrast to his sister Helen's feelings for their parents. Helen lived with them until 1916 when, at ten years of age, she moved in with the Dalys, returning to the Farrells in 1926. (In *The Death of Nora Ryan* [1978], p. 346, Clara [*Helen*] states "I never liked living at the Dunnes" [*Dalys*].) It was from her parents, Helen wrote, that she received oceans of love and affection, as well as her values. Her father was enormously proud of all his children "and wanted so much for all of us to have a fulfilled life and did much to keep us all together . . . Our father and mother took Joe, Jack, Mary, Frankie when we had him, [and me] to Lincoln Park many a Sunday when we lived on La Salle Street. Some Sundays he would take Joe, Jack and me to Michigan Avenue to see automobiles going up and down. Back then there were horses and wagons and it was always a treat to us to see autos. Our Mother had a great sense of humor and often had us laughing. She also joined us in our play and allowed us to make up games and play store or house or soldiers or anything [that] stirred our imagination" (Letter, Helen Farrell Dillon to Branch, 24 Aug. 1994).

[19] In *The Death of Nora Ryan* Eddie Ryan has "a fit of anxiety" immediately after his mother's death. He talks about it with his brother Steve [*Jack*], a psychiatrist "committed to Freudian psychoanalytic interpretations." He is led to admit that his anxiety is associated with memories of Jud Jennings, his older brother Jack, and Torch Feeney [*Harold ("Red") O'Keefe*], who in 1928 had told him, in a bullying way, that "I should take care of my mother," and in 1933 had threatened to shoot him. Steve suggests that for a time in Eddie's feelings Jud became "a substitute older brother," and Eddie admits that he "associated Jack [his older brother *Earl*] with the old man." Steve draws the conclusion that "It could be that the underlying theme of Jud Jennings [*Studs Lonigan*] is the slaying of the father." Eddie replies: "No, Steve, not the theme, but the motive, if that." Eddie reflects that this interpretation of his trilogy "was at best a partial truth. . . . He thought of Jud Jennings. Torch Feeney. Maybe there was some underlying connection between them and his brother Jack and his father. He didn't know. It might all be in his unconscious. But even if it were, it would not change Jud Jennings. Jud Jennings was behind him." Even so, Eddie asks "Was there something involved here that he didn't want to know?" He realizes "There was much in him that he didn't know, the unconscious" (pp. 369-75).

[20] Letter, Farrell to Henle, 15 Jan. 1946.

[21] Ibid. "When I began working on this material, I envisaged one long novel, ending in a scene similar to that described in the story *Studs*. . . . I began to see Studs, not only as a character for imaginative fiction, but also as a social manifestation. . . . There were numberless changes and expansions of the original conception, alterations in emphasis, reconstructions of the structure of events from the time that the work was first conceived until the last line was written" ("Introduction," Modern Library edition of *Studs Lonigan*, p. xi).

[22] Farrell wrote "a psychoanalytic account . . . of the writing of *Studs Lonigan* " which presumably may have paralleled the memories he detailed in his letter to Henle and reconstructed in his novel *The Death of Nora Ryan* (1978). The account was destroyed in his apartment fire.

Referring to it later, he commented: "This kind of approach will not tell a reader much about the content and meaning of a novel. Specifically, by probing my memory, and presumably by recalling and re-feeling infantile rivalries, angers, fears, and yowlings, I will not help readers to understand more, that is, unless they happen to find it more interesting to play amateur psychiatrist, than to read a book as a created, constructed, imagined reality about human destinies" ("Dutton. How I Wrote Studs," a cancelled title of a fragment of his typescript on *Studs Lonigan* intended for Dutton Publishers, p. 1). Farrell's observation is cogent, but our knowledge of what he outlined in his letter to Henle helps us to better understand the origin of his trilogy and his development of major characters.

23 "Dut," pp. 42-43.

24 Published in *Side*, 106-115. The names of the girls mentioned in the discussion that follows are their fictional names used in the story. In a January 12, 1976, note to the author, Farrell volunteered the belief that in this tale the "analysis (Freudian) of a dream [was] relevant to the biography [i.e., his biography]." He confirmed that the dream in the story was "a real dream I had, when I spent my first night in New York, sleeping in Union Square" (Letter, Farrell to Branch, 29 May 1976).

25 Having published his first novel and broken with his publisher, Bernard Carr in New York City feels dispirited and uncertain of the future. He feels that he is looking for that "one pair of eyes to look into, one pair of ears into which he could pour words expressing all that was unexpressed in his being." Only his unresponsive boyhood love Elsie Cavanagh "had had those special eyes, those special lips, those special ears, that special face. The loneliness of his boyhood came back to him." He thinks that "Every man must have an Elsie Cavanagh in his life, a little girl made . . . of innocent dreams. And he hadn't gotten over this astounding fact. He guessed that was why he wanted to be a writer. Yes, his wounded dreams of love had hurt him more than all the lies he had been told. And so here he was, with the emotions of a boy of ten or twelve driving him, driving him with ambition to want to be a great and immortal American writer." Later, Bernard reflects that "Not only girls, not only Elsie Cavanagh, but the Church and his family, almost everything in his boyhood had made him feel unimportant. . . . And didn't this all help to explain why he wanted to write?" (*The Road Between*, pp. 92-93, 151).

26 Joe Cody, Jim Farrell's next door neighbor and companion on the University of Chicago campus, suggested that Jim's "awakening interest in girls" was one source of his determination to become a writer (Interview, Joseph Cody, 3 Apr. 1956). In his unpublished tale "Term Papers" Farrell depicts Eddie Ryan, shabby, broke and struggling to write, on the University of Chicago campus. For ten dollars he writes excellent term papers on Walt Whitman for two wealthy students, Mildred Mayer and Bernice Denehan. He is sexually attracted to both of them, but after rudely paying Eddie they dismiss him like a servant, a nobody, to his humiliation. He thinks: "His writing had to stand for itself, speak for him, become his justification. This meant 'showing them' and it meant more than this, in fact, much more. His writing meant fulfilling his destiny. And when he really achieved that, then everyone who had slighted him . . ."

27 In the 1978 novel *The Death of Nora Ryan*, Eddie Ryan is in New York thinking of his boyhood in Chicago. "He could remember it all. Whenever he thought of Chicago he remembered scenes from the past" (p. 20). Farrell affirmed in an autobiographical sketch written for the Nobel Prize Committee that he could remember in time sequence, and that his memory went back to 1907-08, and -09. He stated that the depth and detail of his memory was extraordinary. He could remember the dresses worn by all the girls at a 1917 birthday party (pp. 4, 10, 11).

28 Although Farrell's unaided memory was formidable and often self-sufficient in the recall of details, he sometimes solicited family members and friends for supplementary information for use in his fiction. For example, he went to his brother Earl, an employee of the express company, for helpful details on major characters in *Gas-House McGinty*. For the text of *Judgment Day*, his friends Dr. Noah D. Fabricant of the University of Illinois College of Medicine in Chicago (the author of *Modern Medication of the Ear, Nose, and Throat* and *Why We Became Doctors*) and Dr. Jacob M. Klapman, a Near North Side physician (the author of *Group Psychotherapy; Theory and Practice*), checked the medical details and supplied Farrell with a list of symptoms of pneumonia, with fever charts. Nathaniel West and Nathan Asch corrected details in the movie scene. Sam Ross researched contemporary bookie outlets—Farrell was unfamiliar with them—and checked the details, as did Nadine ("Deene") Young, of Studs's visit to Phil Rolfe's place. Felix Kolodziej researched Chicago newspapers for details of current events, song titles, radio programs, etc. Tom Sulkie was the religious "expert" Farrell turned to, and Herb Klein helped out with the demonstration scene witnessed by Paddy Lonigan as Studs is dying.

29 "Dut," p. 43.

30 Farrell's typescript labeled "S.D." [Studs Dutton], p. 18. "Reality," Farrell wrote, "is both external and internal. Our thoughts are part of reality. The reality of the outside world is only part of reality. From the standpoint of the writer, reality is external and internal. Also, in my case, reality is not out there, as something coherent, cohesive, and all of a piece, as set against what is in the mind of the character. The character interacts with the world. The reality is a relation between aspects of the outer world, including others, and the characters, and some of the things that go on in the mind of the character" (Letter, Farrell to Branch, 3 Feb. 1976).

31 In 1940, responding to Edmund Wilson's criticism of his O'Neill-O'Flaherty novels, Farrell wrote: "I hold a functional conception of character, viewing it as a social product embodying the reciprocal play of local influences on the individual, and of the individual on society. I am concerned with the concrete processes whereby society, through the instrumentality of social institutions, forms and molds characters, giving to the individual the very content of his consciousness." From "James Farrell on James Farrell," *New Republic*, 103 (1940), 596.

32 "I had grown up in a social universe of bigotry and prejudice, concerning religions, races, and nationalities. I more or less thought that the Irish were superior to the members of all other nationalities; that Catholics were better than Protestants; that Christians were better than Jews; that white men were better than black men. . . . But [by the spring of 1926] I had begun to lose, to abandon, some of these notions, and I was steadily moving away from others of them. For one thing, I was beginning to drop my racial prejudices. This meant, most specifically, prejudices against Negroes; but it also encompassed what remained of anti-Semitic prejudices of my boyhood and adolescence" ("Since I Began," completed 14 Oct. 1975, pp. 2607-14).

Farrell recorded that he began to lose his anti-black prejudices while working at the Sinclair service station at 25th and Wabash in Chicago's black district. There he observed the poverty and poor living conditions of blacks, and his sympathy was aroused. His conversations on racial prejudice with Joe Cody, his reading of such books as William Graham Sumner's *Folkways*, and his University of Chicago course work reinforced his changing view.

Hoping to prepare himself for a career in law and politics, Farrell took Professor Bertram G. Nelson's English 116, Public Speaking, in the spring 1926 quarter. According to the university catalog, the course was designed "to train to gather, select, arrange, and present material in order to affect a given audience in a given way within a given time." The students took turns speaking for about five minutes before the class from the stage in Mandel Hall. Their talks were then evaluated by their classmates and Professor Nelson. Jim Farrell's poise and presentation in his talks on Robert Browning's poetry and on Karl Marx were harshly criticized He was awkward, nervous, shaky, and talked too fast. But Professor Nelson praised his content. Jim Farrell's next speech was on the evils of racial prejudice, which he had come to believe was "one of the worst, the most pernicious and malignant of the evils of the times." He argued that one race was not natively better than another, and he emphasized the lack of economic and environmental opportunity for blacks. He centered many of his observations around the discrimination which kept blacks out of University of Chicago fraternities. His speech, he wrote, was "brief and passionate," and it evoked "a turmoil of indignation" in the class. It was the outward sign of a profound and ongoing change in his thinking about American society. During his final years, Farrell judged the University of Chicago to be "a great liberal university, one of the greatest in the history of American education," a place where the professors strove to make their "students think, and to think freshly" ("Since I Began," completed 1 July 1976, pp. 82, 129-130, 134, 136-37).

[33] "An Introduction to Two Novels," *University of Kansas City Review*, 13 (Spring 1947), p. 223.

[34] To underline this point in *Studs Lonigan*, Farrell portrays Studs's younger brother Martin Lonigan, beginning to follow in Studs's footsteps—working for his father as a painter and emulating Studs's toughness. Yet Martin Cunningham's personality and his "destiny" contrast to Studs Lonigan's. Farrell's sister Helen remembered Martin as a friendly classmate at St. Anselm's grammar school, a jolly companionable boy nicknamed Butz. She remembers that he became active in the Democratic party and had a good job in City Hall (Letter, Helen Farrell Dillon to Branch, 7 July 1994). William L. Lederer, Martin's nephew, writing to Farrell on January 13, 1972, noted that his Uncle Martin overcame his alcoholism and became a gentle, simple, and religious man. Martin took care of his aging father Patrick, who died in his nineties. Thereafter he lived with his sister Mary. In his letter to James Henle of April 3, 1936, Farrell wrote that he believed Martin at that time was working "somewhere out south" for the Union Carbon and Carbide Company. In 1994 William L. Lederer stated that Martin had worked in the Cook County Clerk's office, presumably his more permanent place of employment (Letter to Branch, 10 June 1994).

[35] James T. Farrell, "Studs Lonigan Today," *Climax*, 8 (April 1961), p. 32.

[36] "Thirty and Under," *New Freeman*, 1 (2 July 1930), p. 374.

[37] "Studs Lonigan Today," p. 33.

[38] "Streets Still Studded with Studses: Farrell," *New York Daily News*, 8 March 1979, p 9. An interview by Michael Daly.

[39] The quotations in this and the following paragraph from Farrell's correspondence with Parker are found in his letters to Parker dated 7 February 1934 and 19 August and 13 November 1935. At St. Cyril's, Parker took First Honors in all his subjects, was president of the Literary and Debating Club, the Class Orator, and a basketball star. He took his doctorate at the University of Chicago and became a noted Egyptologist at the Oriental Institute and Brown University.

[40] Referring to his books published by 1939, Farrell wrote to Yves Picart on March 11, 1939: "I wrote these books with the aim and hope of recreating a sense of the life I had known, the neighborhoods in which I had lived and grown up, in order to reveal how human destinies unfold in such social conditions and environments, to reveal the meaning of institutions, the church, the school, the family etc., as these have meaning concretely and specifically on the lives and the personalities of human beings."

[41] "Farrell Revisits Studs Lonigan's Neighborhood," *New York Times Book Review*, 20 (June 1954), p. 5.

[42] From the discussion period after Farrell's lecture "The Writer and His Audience," State Teachers' College, Indiana, Pennsylvania, 12 June 1958.

[43] "Studs Lonigan Today," p. 32.

[44] John Dewey, *Human Nature and Conduct*, Modern Library ed. (New York: Random House, 1957), p. 99. In an early notebook of uncertain date (1929-30?) Farrell commented on this book and other writings by Dewey. He drafted an article titled "Toward an Interpretatiion of Popular American Art." In it he wrote that American savages "are forced to perform tasks which canalize their impulses in rigid undynamic habits, thereby establishing a tightly-clamped neural set-up. Impulses break loose from this narrow, drudgery-driven confinement, and are unattached. America, being socially chaotic, with cheap aesthetic standards, fails to provide social meanings sufficient for free impulses." Suffering strain and fatigue from mechanical work, Farrell argued, the American savage on Saturday nights turns to brothels, speakeasies, taxi dances, and cheap cabarets. He finds "excess gratification" in waves of brutality, rape, and murder. Farrell later submitted a version of the essay to the *International Journal of Ethics*, edited by the philosopher T. V. Smith, whom Farrell had known while Smith was on the faculty at the University of Chicago. It was rejected.

[45] Farrell, "Literature and a Greek Waiter," *Thought*, 14 (17 Nov. 1962), p. 13.

[46] *Human Nature and Conduct*, p. 100.

[47] Farrell's initial choice for the title of *A World I Never Made* was "The Fighting O'Flahertys." "I heard of a sign the Norman conquerors left in the Aran Islands after they met the clan of O'Flaherty, which reads— From the Fighting O'Flahertys, good Lord deliver us" (Letter, Farrell to James Henle, 14 Mar. 1935).

[48] Helen Farrell Dillon, thinking of the loving relationship she had with her parents and younger brothers and sisters, astutely observed of Farrell that "He must have been very lonely at times and I hurt a little to think of it because Joe, Jack, Mary and Frankie for the short time we had him and myself had so much" (Letter to Branch, 24 Aug. 1994). In *The Death of Nora Ryan* (1978) as his mother lay dying surrounded by her family, Eddie Ryan "suddenly felt isolated. The rest of them had lived with Mama and Papa while he had lived with the Dunnes. They had not shared a childhood." Eddie also re-lives the "sadness"—an emotion deeper than embarrassment—he had felt for all of them "ever since he was a little boy. . . . There was a big gulf between his life and their lives. . . . The difference . . . lay in values and purposes. It was in what he thought and what they thought. It was in what he did and what they did" (pp. 31, 100, 348).

49 "Streets Still Studded with Studses," p. 9.

50 In the early 1920s after the Caron family moved into the neighborhood, Paul Caron became Jim Farrell's best friend. Paul was handsome, unusually attractive to girls, a fearless fighter, and had literary inclinations. The family lived near 57th Street and Prairie Avenue, and later near 58th and Calumet. As young men, the two hitchhiked to New York together in 1927.

"In 1928, following a party at which "Maxwell Bodenheim had been thrown into a bathtub" by celebrating university students and Bohemians, Farrell, Paul Caron, Nick Matsoukas, the black poet Donald Jeffrey Hayes [Joseph Howard Dickson], three Chinese students, Dorothy Butler and several other girls went to a Greek restaurant at 63rd Street and Ellis Avenue. "Some Irish yelled at us, calling us lovers of blacks, and using the insulting word that is so often used." Paul Caron and Jim Farrell successfully vanquished them outside the restaurant before an appreciative audience ("The World Is Today," *Park East*, 5 [19 Sept. 1968], pp. 6, 8). In *My Days of Anger* (pp. 290-91) Ed Lanson easily intimidates Tommy Doyle and Studs Lonigan who were threatening Danny O'Neill in the Greek's 58th Street restaurant.

On July 1, 1931, while Jim and Dorothy Farrell were in Paris, Paul Caron died of a cancerous brain tumor, the illness foreshadowed in Farrell's depiction of Ed Lanson in the final pages of *Boarding House Blues*.

Chapter Three: The Grid and the Garden

DURING THEIR LATE PRETEENS AND TEENS, Studs Lonigan, Danny O'Neill, and their future creator Jimmy Farrell all grew up in a neighborhood which included the greenery, lagoons, and open spaces of Washington Park and the gray pavement, apartment buildings, "L" tracks, and fenced-in often dusty back yards of the streets and alleys immediately to the west. From its beginnings, serious Farrell criticism has repeatedly examined Farrell's use in his Chicago fiction of city streets and city parks (the gray and the green, the grid and the garden) and the behavior these contrasting milieus generate in his characters. This was done in order to show how Farrell develops and demarcates his characters, especially his male characters living in the Studs Lonigan neighborhood, and within that group, Studs Lonigan in particular.[1]

Speaking very generally of the two boys, Studs and Danny, Studs is acknowledged to be fatally vulnerable to the destructive elements in the street culture and relatively unresponsive to the redemptive features available both in the man-made urban environment and what passes for nature in the city—the parks; whereas Danny, although handicapped in some respects and prone to stumbles and false starts, is able to transcend his limitations and to constantly grow by tapping the resources of his expanding environment. This chapter will touch only briefly on such matters, even though the subject continues to invite discussion. Instead, the focus will be upon Farrell's characterization in his nonfictional writing of the "gray" neighborhood—who knew it better than he?—and upon relevant information about the "green" neighborhood of the park itself, with some attention given to Farrell's feelings about these surroundings and what they meant to him.

Looking back in 1970 to his move into the Studs Lonigan neighborhood in 1915, Farrell wrote that the area "runs from Garfield Boulevard, which is 55th Street, to 61st Street, and from South Park Avenue to Wabash Avenue, which is five blocks."[2] In the neighborhood, he continued, "There were many three story brick apartment buildings, with six apartments to the building. And apartments did not go long for rent. When we moved to 5704 Indiana Avenue in May, 1915, there were very very few vacancies in the neighborhood." It was mostly built up, and few "For Rent" signs were visible. The apartment buildings were solidly built, well kept up, and usually painted once a year. Many of the flats, from six to eight rooms, rented for more than $50 a month. Each of the blocks running north and south, he estimated, "averaged over fifty families a block. And there were homes and apartment buildings in the numbered streets which ran east and west. It was a well populated neighborhood" and the residents "were generally considered to be of a good class of people, as the saying goes."[3]

This neighborhood, Farrell cautioned, should not be thought of in narrowly religious or ethnic terms. "What was it like? The Catholic world in which I grew up? Strictly speaking, it was not a Catholic world—it was a Chicago world, an American world—even a historic world."[4] Nor was it "predominantly Irish . . . The public school had many more pupils than St. Anselm's. In *Young Lonigan*—Helen Shires isn't Catholic. Davey Cohen.[5] Iris. Jew Percentage. Nate. Charlie Bathcellar. In YMSL a large number aren't. Slug Mason—Hink Weber—Slew Weber—Mose Levinsky—Phil Rolfe[6]—Nate Klein. And I picked the characters, you know. There were Jews—Protestants. . . . In South Shore, there were as many, or more, Irish than there were around 58th St."[7] This diversity, Farrell wrote, made the neighborhood heterogeneous. Where he lived was not a neighborhood "as 'back of the yards,' that is, the stockyards was a neighborhood. When you get apartment buildings, you do not have neighborhoods in the sense that you do when there are individual houses. The Church held the Irish together, and the parochial schools brought most of the Catholic kids together."[8] Elsewhere, Farrell wrote that it was "not a neighborhood that was closely knit together. The adults in this section of Chicago did not mix very much."[9] Families only rarely exchanged visits at their homes—Farrell remembered no families not related by blood being invited to dinner by other families—but they met in friendly, casual fashion on the street or at church.

Nevertheless, Farrell believed that the presence of ethnic groups in the area made centers of cohesion possible within a neighborhood whose moderate size encouraged a certain overall intimacy. It and other "neighborhoods of Chicago in which I grew up," he wrote, "possessed something of the character of a small town. They were little worlds of their own. Many of the people living in them knew one another. There was a certain amount of gossip of the character that one finds in small towns. One of the largest nationality and religious groups in those neighborhoods was Irish-American and Catholic. I attended a parochial school. Through the school and Sunday mass, the life of these neighborhoods was rendered somewhat more cohesive. My grandmother was always a neighborhood character, well known. I became known, too, the way a boy would be in a small town. With many other boys, it was the same."[10]

Many of the neighborhood men worked in downtown businesses and used the "L" to go back and forth. Others owned small family stores, usually but not always located on one of the "store streets," and especially on 58th Street at the neighborhood's center. In Farrell's day the north side of 58th was solidly built up with stores between Indiana and Calumet Avenues. On the south side of 58th Street there were stores from the alley between Indiana and Prairie Avenues to the elevated station, which crossed 58th Street over the alley between Calumet and Prairie Avenues. With an occasional chain store mixed in, here were the local grocery stores, butcher shops, drugstores, ice cream parlors, delicatessens, tailor shops, restaurants, dry goods stores, candy stores, cigar stores, and shoe repair shops—most of them known by the name of the owner— regularly patronized by local housewives, including Farrell's mother and grandmother. Some of these small entrepreneurs provided home delivery. Others, like Mr. Savois, the owner of the drugstore at 58th Street and Calumet Avenue, sponsored and outfitted neighborhood baseball and football teams that played in Washington Park.

For indoor recreation neighborhood residents looked to several nearby movie theaters, and Jimmy Farrell went to all of them. "The Prairie Theater was located at 58th Street and Prairie Avenue. It had been built in 1915, and Earl and Helen Shearer and I had played and eaten marshmallows on the foundation. There was the Vernon, located at 61st and Vernon Avenue [just outside the neighborhood's 'official' boundary] and, of course, the Michigan Theater, which had also been built about 1915. The Palm Theater, on 58th Street, between Prairie and Indiana Avenue, had gone under by 1918."[11] The poolroom attracted its special clientele, who sometimes also went to the poolroom on Garfield Boulevard operated for a time by Buck Weaver, the great White Sox third baseman. Studs and other men who went to brothels appear to have found most of them in Burnham, far to the south, or in neighborhoods to the north.

On Sundays families flocked to the churches of their denomination. Three churches were clustered near 57th Street and Indiana Avenue, where Jimmy Farrell first lived in the neighborhood: St. Edmund's Episcopal Church, a block-and-a-half south on Indiana; the white-tiled Methodist Episcopal Church, a block north on Indiana; and the Crerar Memorial Presbyterian Church, a short block away at 57th Street and Prairie Avenue. At 61st and Michigan, across the street from St. Anselm's Church was the imposing SS. Constantine and Helen Greek Orthodox Church and School. It drew parishioners and pupils from miles around. During Farrell's years in grammar school, its pastor, a friend of Father Gilmartin, was a cosmopolitan, scholarly priest known to all the boys as "Old fox-in-the-bush" because of his full flowing beard. Down the street near Michigan and 59th was the South Side Hebrew Temple and Community House. Farrell liked to mention that well-known professionals had lived in this respectable and established neighborhood: Ring Lardner at 60th and Prairie, the actress Mercedes McCambridge at 57th and Prairie, George Lott, Jr., a block away from Farrell's South Park Avenue apartment building, and the White Sox manager Clarence Rowland[12] in the 5900 block of Michigan Avenue.

"The neighborhood was not a tough one," Farrell wrote. "It was comfortable and included a large percentage of home owners, and/or of families which owned apartment buildings. . . . It was also a quiet neighborhood, unexciting in the sense of anything spectacular or dramatic happening." He recalled only one shooting. A young policeman, a distant relative on his grandmother's side "named something like O'Neill was shot dead on 57th Street, near Indiana Avenue" in the summer of 1915. Two policemen were neighborhood characters much talked about. "There was a cop named McNamara, who was rough on kids," who learned to give him a wide berth, and "a detective called Diamond Tooth, who had a reputation that inspired awe." But "there was very little crime in the neighborhood, and of what little there was, that was mostly very petty, for instance, robbing ice boxes. Ice boxes were usually on the back porch. Sometimes at night, an ice box would be robbed."[13] Adults and kids felt safe on the streets at any time. Typically, the neighborhood boys did not become criminals.[14]

For the kids, both boys and girls, the wide streets were an open invitation to play. Farrell recalled that his 5700 block on Indiana drew the kids in the evenings (especially after daylight saving time began in 1918) to play tin-tin, or run-sheep-run, or hide-and-seek, or baseball. There were few automobiles to watch out for, and traffic disappeared almost entirely on the gasless Sundays of World War I. Good hiding places abounded in alleys, backyards, and passageways. School and church playgrounds were close by, too. The kids also had fun at two nearby amusement parks: Sans Souci at the Midway and Cottage Grove Avenue, and the larger White City at 63rd Street and South Park Avenue.

"In 1915," Farrell wrote, "when I began living in what is now the so-called *Studs Lonigan* neighborhood, it was a relatively settled section of Chicago. I use the phrase, 'relatively settled,' because few Chicago neighborhoods have ever been settled for long. . . . The signs of change," however, were not apparent to "the ordinary citizen . . . It seemed as though a good life had been found, and by many, and the future was safe for those who had gained a position of some comfort. . . . They were settling into life, and becoming used to themselves in the position in life which they occupied." Faith in the neighborhood's long-term stability, though mistaken, was widespread. "I never heard anyone speak of the neighborhood's going to pot and decaying until after the war, around the mid-twenties. A street might go, or a block, but it was just about unthinkable that the whole area would decay."[15] For this reason Farrell objected to Frederic Thrasher's statement in his introduction to the first edition of *Young Lonigan* —whose action occurs in 1916—that the neighborhood portrayed there was "interstitial." That word, Farrell explained, was a sociological term "used to categorize and characterize certain kinds of neighborhoods that were in the process of change and decay. And the neighborhood of *Young Lonigan* . . . changes and decays, but not until the story gets into *The Young Manhood of Studs Lonigan*."[16]

The residents of this neighborhood, Farrell wrote, "the people with incomes of $5,000 or $10,000 a year [substantial sums in those days] . . . believed that 'Today was better than yesterday, and tomorrow would be an improvement on today'. . . Many of the men in this South Side area came in on a backwash of a high tide of capitalism. Many, if not most, of them believed that they were truly self-made, and that if anyone didn't do well, it was his own fault. There was a certain pride, confidence, and vanity which served their gratification. They were making the grade."[17]

Paddy Lonigan, Al O'Flaherty, and Johnny O'Brien's father, the coal yard owner, fit this pattern, each in his own way. These men, and their kind, Farrell continued, "had achieved enough of a place or position in the world, so that they did not have to feel ashamed of themselves, especially in public, because of the character of their work. Most of them did not go out to earn their daily bread, wearing old clothes, or overalls, and blue or black cotton shirts. Nor did they carry a lunch pail, or a lunch wrapped in the pages of a newspaper. Nor did they leave home, often in darkness, at five or six or seven in the morning. . . . A working man was often regarded as a failure. He was doing physical labor because he couldn't get any better, more remunerative, and, in some cases, a more refined type of employment."[18]

The change in the neighborhood—the massive racial shift—that Paddy Lonigan did not foresee in 1916 was inching forward during Farrell's grade school years at St. Anselm's. At that time, he recalled, "A few poor Negro families lived on Wabash Avenue or State Street, and were within the district of those who went to Carter Practice School, but they were not many. I recall only one black boy playing with the white kids. His name was Murphy. The kids called him 'Murph,' and all seemed to like him. I never heard any prejudiced or racial remarks about 'Murph,' who continued to play with his white friends during the Chicago race riots of July 1919."[19]

During the period of the riots, as well as in the previous summer, Farrell's uncle Tom Daly took him and his sister Helen to a summer resort, the Silver Saddle Farm at Grand Junction, Michigan [Silver Michigan Farm at Silver, Michigan]. "We returned, after our two week stay, with the riots calmed down and quelled, and with the South Side under martial law."[20] The riots had occurred in neighborhoods to the west and north, but racial fears intensified everywhere in the city. Farrell remembered that in 1920, as a member of the Carter School wrestling team which was entered in the city tournament, he, like his teammates, worried about the possibility of being matched with a Negro. "I shared the prejudices of the other boys."[21]

During the 1920s, Farrell continued, "There was a slow advance [of the black population], further south, as well as eastward, and to some extent westward, . . . until about 1927 the neighborhood around 58th Street just west of Washington Park, was considerably and noticeably black."[22] In July of that year, Farrell hitchhiked to New York, remaining there for six months. On August 14 his friend and next door neighbor Joe Cody wrote him that "The neighborhood seems to be getting blacker daily. Indiana Avenue between 58th and 59th has almost as many blacks as whites—perhaps more. So it looks like curtains for the old neighborhood as far as the whites are concerned." In a later undated letter, Joe wrote about landlords advertising for colored tenants on Prairie and Calumet Avenues, the dwindling church congregation, the increasing number of black parishioners, black whores moving in—all interesting sociologically, he admitted, but "almost heartbreaking. As I walk along the streets and think of all the happy times I used to have—as a kid—playing around them—and then realize that soon nothing but black faces will be seen there—I grow quite sad."[23] Like most of the other whites, Jim Farrell and Joe Cody would soon relocate further south in Chicago.

How has Farrell characterized the evolution of his personal feelings about the Studs Lonigan neighborhood and what it meant to him since he first came to it in 1915? When living in his former neighborhood, he wrote, "I had become ashamed because of my aunt's drinking. I had grown slack in school, also, and feared I would not pass." His feelings, like Danny's, were clear: "I was glad of our moving. For in a new neighborhood I was not known, and would get a new start."[24] During his four years at St. Anselm's until his graduation in June 1919, he was immersed in the life of his new boyhood community, as defined largely by his friends, his school, and his church. The key word here should be acceptance—often his unquestioning acceptance—of an environment that permitted him to achieve much happiness and success but that also provoked new tensions and rekindled old frustrations and shames. During these four years he strongly identified with the neighborhood, which became, as it were, part of himself.[25]

After his graduation, Jimmy Farrell's four years of high school scholastics and athletics in a different neighborhood, his labor as a clerk for the Express Company and as a service station attendant for oil companies, and his pre-law night school courses at De Paul [St. Vincent's] University broadened his horizons beyond the confines of the neighborhood.[26] But it was his liberal arts education at the University of Chicago beginning in the summer of 1925 that gave him the perspective on his neighborhood and on his future which he needed at that time. When he became an atheist in March of 1926, he felt an immediate release from fetters that had restrained his emotional and intellectual freedom. As he wrote to H. L. Mencken, he suddenly was able to surmount "barriers to growth and development [that] were erected in faith in the Catholic Church. . . . I mean that belief in the dogma of the Church, and most especially, acceptance of the idea of God constituted the barrier to my beginning to become more aware of the world and of myself and to cast aside, as if in one fell swoop, the confusing and contradictory thoughts I had, which made judgment and decision difficult. I seem to have developed a bit after losing my religion, and experienced a period of somewhat bitter and violent youthful rebellion."[27]

A direct and ironic consequence of his new freedom was that his neighborhood seemed no longer to be all-important but merely a tiny, meaningless human constellation within a vast soulless universe.[28] While at the university, he recalled, "my thoughts were on myself, not on any imaginary, or real Studs Lonigan, and my thoughts were also on the world, on life, on time, on death, on history. My thoughts were not, then, solely on a few blocks on the South Side of Chicago. Actually, I was liberated from the neighborhood, and I spent little time around it, once I had begun to attend the University of Chicago." In a university notebook of uncertain date he wrote without passion: "Mine is a bourgeois neighborhood, with all the deadness that comfort loving middle-classnesss implies. It is, I believe, an unhappy neighborhood."[29] He focused his attention in that notebook on the writings of Dewey, Whitehead, Mead, Veblen, Joyce, Dreiser, Dos Passos, Mencken, and Emerson among others, authors whose works he devoured in Harper Library and at home.[30] In his notebook he also composed such articles as "The Social and Aesthetic Values of Literature" and one on the need for ceaseless criticism of American culture by the younger generation.

Before he quit the university, Farrell wrote, "I had . . . rejected the values of my time, and had become a rebel. I was angry"—angry at man's existential predicament in a heedless universe and angry at the behemoth of America's materialistic culture. This anger, he noted, may bring to mind the passage in *The Young Manhood of Studs Lonigan* in which Danny O'Neill's anger focuses on the neighborhood. There Danny wants to drive the neighborhood out of his consciousness, to purge himself completely of the world of 58th Street, with its God, its lies, its frustrations, and the hatreds it had generated in him. But in reality, Farrell wrote in recollection, "this feeling grew out of the writing of the novels." It was not "an originating motivation" of them.[31] The act of composing *Studs Lonigan* crystallized his buried aversion for the neighborhood and floated it to the surface in the fiction. Thinking back to his year in Paris in 1931-32, he recalled in 1951 that the "beauty of Paris had overwhelmed me." The experience of Paris had contributed to his depiction of his Chicago in *Studs Lonigan* as "doubly ugly."[32]

Three years later, in 1954, Farrell concluded that "when I wrote of it [the Studs Lonigan neighborhood] and tried to re-create it, I was trying to do something different from the aim of driving this neighborhood out of my consciousness. I was trying to fix memories of it, to re-create them, and preserve them. In that way I was trying to see more and to understand."[33] Just as Farrell often returned in person to the neighborhood to indulge nostalgic memories of boyhood, to renew the sense of the mystery of life and of human development, and to reassure himself that he had overcome the ghosts of his past, so, he now believed, he had returned to his boyhood neighborhood in *Studs Lonigan* the better to understand and not to blame it.

When explaining his purpose as a novelist to explore the nature of experience and to see it directly and unflinchingly, Farrell liked to quote Maxim Gorky's distillation of what Chekhov's writing said to his countrymen: "You live badly, my friends. It is shameful to live like that." He also often cited Spinoza's aphorism: "It is not to weep, not to laugh, but to understand," and he endorsed Chekhov's statement: "Man will only become better when you make him see what he is like."

If we take Farrell's portrayal, in his fiction, of Catholic doctrine and education (major components of the neighborhood's ethos as he knew it), was he really seeking, perhaps unconsciously, understanding and not condemnation? Was a deeply buried basic motive his need to understand? In much of the relevant fiction and in a good portion of his adult life, it is the angry or satiric condemnation that stands out.[34] Yet we should remember that he believed great literature sought to achieve understanding. We should remember too his affirmation of his Catholic training made in 1963. It had given him the understanding (1) that "it's possible to think of the world in terms of order"; (2) that belief in the concept of truth, however defined, is important; (3) that he lived in a continuity of experience of great depth, of "something before me and something after me . . . where there was an idea of greatness and grandeur and also of mystery and reality"; and (4) that "there are things so important in this world that it's your duty to die for them if necessary, and that the values are more important than you."[35] Farrell's works, early and late, directly and indirectly, and in varying degrees in the characters and plots, do indeed reflect the presence of these principles of understanding in the mind of the author.

WASHINGTON PARK

Using a design by the landscape architect Frederick Law Olmsted, Chicago's South Park Commissioners began laying out Washington Park in 1873 on 371 acres outside the city limits. The park and surrounding attractions soon became a nearby resort area for city dwellers. Lying directly east of what would become the Grand Boulevard and Washington Park neighborhoods, the park extended from 51st Street to 60th Street between Cottage Grove and South Park Avenues. When Patrick and Mary Lonigan first visit the sparsely settled area around 1900, they use a horse-drawn carriage. When their son Studs graduates from St. Patrick's grade school in 1916, direct public access to the park is provided by the Jackson Park and Englewood "L" lines and the Cottage Grove and Indiana Avenue-51st Street streetcar lines. During that decade-and-a-half the Washington Park neighborhood (containing the Studs Lonigan neighborhood) built up quickly, and park development kept pace. Washington Park and Jackson Park, connected by the Midway Plaisance, became the jewels in Chicago's widespread South Park system.

By 1915, when Danny began living at Indiana Avenue and 57th Street, five miles of drives, many miles of walks, and three miles of bridle paths wove through and across the park. A year earlier, four water jets throwing spray fifty feet in the air had been installed in the park lagoon and pools. Major buildings for carrying on the business of Chicago's South Park system were located in Washington Park. Just off Cottage Grove Avenue south of 56th Street were the central Administration Building and two small greenhouses. Still further south for two blocks were the stables housing fifty-five team, buggy, and cart horses; the power house, the park's heating plant; and the pumping station which supplied unlimited water to Washington and Jackson parks, the Midway, and Drexel Boulevard; the central laundry for all the parks; the machine shop; and the storage shops for horse-drawn vehicles, automobiles, trucks, tractors, motorcycles, mowers and steam rollers.

Washington Park—Terrace at Adminstration Building, above. *Fly Casters' Pool*, below. (Photos Courtesy of Chicago Park District.)

At 56th Street and Cottage Grove Avenue was the popular Conservatory, with an elaborate flower garden in front and the rose garden to its north. Still further north was Chicago's large and busy Armory Building. On the lagoon shore were the boathouse, doubling as the skating-house in winter, the flycasters' log cabin, and the building housing three ice alleys for curling. Baseball, football, and soccer players used the shelter and its lunch counter near 51st Street. The public was served in the dining room or the soda fountain of the refectory—flanked by a spectacular flower garden—near South Park Avenue at 56th Street.

In the spring and summer baseball teams played hardball on the eleven diamonds and softball on fifteen other fields. Football took over in the fall. The park maintained twenty-five tennis courts, clay and grass, as well as horseshoe, croquet and roque courts. Field hockey, lawn bowling, and archery also flourished in the summer, and ice sktaing, tobaganning, and ice hockey in the winter. The youngest children fed the ducks in the duck pond and played in sand courts and a large wading pool. Along with children up to high school age, they flocked to the well-equipped playground on the park's west side about on a line with 56th Street. It was the largest playground in the park system, big enough to enclose a small softball field as well as the usual slides, swings, and ladders for the small fry. A trained director and a park policeman—both well-known to Studs, Danny, and Jim Farrell—supervised the activity there. Fifteen other cops—nine by day and six by night—patrolled the park outside the playground.

The park hosted large picnics, such as the one given for Chicago's newspaper boys. Three thousand folding chairs were available for the ten or twelve band and orchestral summer concerts. A large vegetable garden and a small "backyard" garden were planted in the spring to instruct the public about vegetable growing. Drinking fountains were located throughout the park for the many warm weather visitors.

The famous Bug Club, located in a hilly section near Cottage Grove Avenue and 56th Street, attracted a noisy, contentious audience willing to hear and bait anyone (including Ned O'Flaherty [*Farrell's Uncle Bill Daly*]) who wanted to stand on a soapbox and speak his mind. There Farrell heard believers of every stripe: spokesmen for Jesus Christ, atheists, founders of new religions, socialists, communists, single taxers, feminists, and, Farrell wrote, "retired business men who tried to think, talk, and look like, at least, United States Senators."[36] He heard the old Wobbly and powerful speaker John Loughman [John Connolly; Wallie Brockton; Larry Norton], the King of the Soapboxers; Boales, the tireless religious fanatic; Dr. Ben Lewis Reitman [Dr. Adam Bergman; Dr. Dan Eisenberg]—the former anarchist and the lover and traveling companion of Emma Goldman—known in Chicago as the King of the Hoboes and as the founder of the Hobo College on Chicago's West Madison Street;[37] Bishop Burke [Bishop Boyle; Bishop John O'Toole], and many others.

Washington Park—Central Pool, above. Lily Pool, below. (Photos Courtesy Chicago Park District.)

When returning home through the park, Farrell occasionally lingered at the Bug Club. "I listened to them often, and now and then even participated in arguments. I learned simple but valuable lessons from the Bugs, and for these I shall always be grateful. The Bug Club helped me to realize that it is not ridiculous to think and that one need not be ashamed of seriously trying to know and express oneself. And I came to understand more properly the virtues and values of tolerance. For with all of the haggling, the insulting, the brittle tempers and the sharp exchanges, the prevailing tone of the Bug Club was one of tolerance and of freedom.

"Everyone was generally granted the right to his opinion, and the chance—did he want it—to express that opinion. Underlying the sadness, the pathos, the maladjustment, the comedy, the little tragedies at the Bug Club, there were certain decencies that prevailed."[38]

A large maintenance force was required to support the park's activities: park policemen (a separate corps from the city police), engineers, carpenters, gardeners, mechanics, animal-handlers, shop-workers, and many laborers to spread manure on the meadow and to apply sod in the early spring, to clear seaweed from the lagoon, to apply cinders to the bridal path and crushed stone to the walks, and to remove snow in the winter. A shepherd tended a flock of 154 Shropshire sheep on the grassy areas of Wooded Island, where they were penned at night. It is reasonable to conclude that in Farrell's early days in the Studs Lonigan neighborhood the ambitious enterprise known as Washington Park was one of the city's "most humanly useful parks."[39]

Not surprisingly, in his autobiographical writings Farrell's memories of his boyhood in the park turn mostly to baseball. During the good weather of 1915 and 1916 he played indoor ball almost daily in the park playground, usually at second base, with Studs Cunningham sometimes at third. Miss Dyson, the popular playground director, often joined in enthusiastically, sliding into third or home with bloomers showing. Outgrowing the playground, Jim Farrell played hardball for years on many teams, and often with experienced adult players, in the park's regulation ball fields. At times his Washington Park team made it into the city-wide playground tournaments. He recalled with delight his six-base hit made in the 1917 tournament in a game with Sherman Park which his team won. Jim walloped the ball over the outfielder's head but failed to touch second base. He dashed back to second, tagged up, and high-tailed it for home plate arriving there just in time to be tagged out.

Ice skating was another park sport he enjoyed, especially during the winter of 1916-17. His incentive then was to be near Gladys Le Barr, a sixth grader who loved to skate and who had replaced Helen Shannon in his dreams and affection. He was a twelve year old small

Washington Park—Flower Garden, above; sheep grazing, below. (Photos Courtesy Chicago Park District.)

for his age, and Gladys was a tall, beautiful girl who skated much better than he did. Undeterred, he used every trick to meet her on the ice or at the skating-house, and then, at dusk, to walk her home. "We would walk slowly, and I would carry her skates, along with my own, and we would talk about school, or skating, or other kids. We would just talk." He desperately wanted her for his partner at the coming surprise party for his sister Helen. One afternoon as they walked home at twilight, "the world seemed to be as still as the snow that was spread and crusted all over the park . . . The darkness and the almost dark winter sky was like an encompassing mood. In a vague way, I felt that the sky and the world was part of my mood."[40] He told Gladys he wanted her as his partner. Always kind, Gladys promised nothing, but a few days later she told him she could not go to the surprise party because it was being given during Lent. Before very long, the young boy's unspoken affection turned to Dorothy McPartlin, another St. Anselm classmate.

During the summer of 1919 Farrell also took great pleasure in playing in the park with his third dog, Lib (for Liberty), as he had done with his dog Gerry. "Uncle Tom and I went to Washington Park before breakfast, and we walked barefooted in the grass, with the dew still on it. We took Liberty with us and . . . would take her off of the leash by the lagoon, and she would go in for a swim. She would swim part of the way out, about or almost about half way across the lagoon, but then she would turn around and come back to shore. We used sometimes to throw a tennis ball or a stick in the water. She would retrieve them for us.

"There was a flock of sheep in Washington Park. They were kept in pens on the Wooded Island and taken out to graze twice a day by the shepherd who herded them. Liberty—after all she was an airedale and a good sheep dog—would round up the sheep whenever she saw them, and if she happened to be off of the leash. She would cause some havoc for the shepherd. She managed the sheep as though she were an expert who had spent all of her life rounding up and managing sheep."[41]

Scenes in which Farrell pictured Danny in psychological turmoil or spiritual crisis are often laid in Washington Park. Because they convey a compelling sense of Danny's authenticity as an "autobiographical image" of the author, they suggest the park's importance in Farrell's life too. The many scenes of Danny as a boy and a young man in Washington Park, in fact, parallel and flesh out what we know of Farrell's experiences in the park at the same times.

The natural yet mysterious beauty of the park stimulated the thought and stirred the imagination of both Danny and Jimmy Farrell. In 1951 Farrell remembered that when he was a boy living on South Park Avenue, "I would look out of the window, across at Washington Park, at the trees, the grass, the lagoon in the distance. Sometimes in the summer, I would nap or leave the window open, and I would hear the wind in the trees. In winter, I would gaze out and see the bare park, the bare trees under dreary skies. I would dream of the future. . . . To me this park had once been the world of nature. It was where I located dreams and hopes."[42] Danny, too, remembers how the park "had become the source and stimulation" for his brooding: "he had so often stood by the parlor window, brooding as he stared out at the park; in those days he had lacked confidence in himself. He had seen Washington Park in all seasons, when it was green and when it was dreary" ("Kilroy Was Here," *Vicious*, pp. 80-81).

For Danny as a young boy, the park is not only a source of sensuous enjoyment where he can run, shout, and play; it is where he goes when he is lonely, sad, misunderstood, rejected.[43] For no matter what his mood, the park becomes for him a magical world that shares and understands his feelings. So it is a place where he also can freely release his deepest wishes and fantasies, always within an ambience of sympathy and hopefulness for the future. The park is where Danny realizes that life offers wondrous possibilities for him, where he experiences a never-ending emergence of novelty.

The same is true for Danny the young man. The park has a way of becoming an actor in the dramas of his intellectual and spiritual growth. Thus in August 1925, during his first quarter at the University of Chicago, Danny lies on the park grass and reads Swinburne's "Garden of Proserpine." The poem promises "that the end of life was merely the end of weariness" and that death brings "Only the sleep eternal / In an eternal night." But Danny is still a devout Catholic. His faith tells him that "The purpose of life was death" and that for all his sins "he was sliding into Hell, . . . that "time was rolling inexorably onward to the horrors of eternity." At that moment "The soft grass of the park rested his eyes." If Swinburne's "sleep eternal" was impossible, then at least Washington Park was a blessed oasis, "a Paradise set on the path of one's life as one journeyed toward the terrible storms, the winter rages . . . He wanted to arrest this moment in the park and hold it as it was forever" (*Anger*, pp. 122-24). Washington Park enables Danny to achieve a temporary stasis in the wrenching conflict between the Catholic believer and the natural man.

Seven months later, in March 1926, Danny becomes an atheist.[44] No longer is he wrapped in his protective blanket of an absolute faith. Instead, he believes he is merely a chance resident of "a second-rate planet which was spinning dizzily in . . . [an] empty universe."[45] It is fitting that when he first reveals this spiritual earthquake to another, he is walking in Washington Park toward the University of Chicago with his friend and university student Jim Gogarty.[46] As Danny unburdens himself to Jim (who also has just lost his Catholic faith), he feels a cold wind sweeping over the park and sees the desolate gray lagoon. He looks back over the bare park trees to see the buildings on South Park Avenue. "Those buildings bounded his neighbor-

Washington Park—The Bridle Path, above. The *Bridle Path Bridge,* below. (Photos Courtesy Chicago Park District.)

hood.... That world and its God had become his enemy." Danny knows that he must tell this to his family and that the telling will hurt them—part of the price he must pay for his new freedom[47] (*Anger*, pp. 215-17).

Twenty years later Farrell pursued this theme in *The Silence of History*. Danny and Jim Gogarty are now named Eddie Ryan and Peter Moore. In the bright spring of 1926 the first shock of their loss of faith has passed. One morning as they walk across the "green and shining" park to their university classes, Eddie is sensitive to his fresh responsibilities: he knows that his new freedom "demanded knowledge, and this he must acquire, and acquire, and acquire." At the same time the park's beauty reminds him and Peter of their innocent boyhood days, of playing by the lagoon with their dogs, of their joy at being in the park when the sun was rising. "That wonder of the sun, then, had also been the promise of life, and it was as though the world belonged to them and they would live in the sun forever."

But Eddie's nostalgic thoughts of those boyhood years of "innocence and ... the perpetual wonder of life" are weighted with a heaviness of spirit, for his new faith proclaims "the dark meanings of impermanence": that the universe is "empty" of God and that everything in it is the fleeting product of "chance and chaos." But as he and Peter continue to walk, "The chirp and song of birds, the croak of a frog, the bark of a dog in the distance somewhere behind them, the fresh smell of the spring morning, sky, and sun, all the greenness, and their own beating pulses, all seemed to press a cry upon them, but they did not cry out. They wanted to cry out, speak out to the sky, and the sun ... and to be spoken to ... and they wanted to feel that this ... wonderful something and they themselves, were part of a plan and purpose. They had the habit of God and of God's design." But God was silent. There was "only the voiceless voice of the universe." So with "a painful dolor in their minds ... they walked on, and the world was the same world, the sky the same kind of sky, but theirs was the sadness of seeing that same old sameness with new outbursts, with new and old feelings" (*Silence*, pp. 271-76). In this way, not long before Eddie (like Farrell) moves out of the old neighborhood, Washington Park reasserts its magical control over the complexities of his mind and spirit.

[1] See, for example, Edgar M. Branch, "*Studs Lonigan*: Symbolism and Theme," *College English*, 23 (December 1961), pp. 191-96, and Edgar M. Branch, *James T. Farrell* (New York: Twayne, 1971), pp. 67-73; Donald Pizer, *Twentieth Century American Literary Naturalism* (Carbondale: Southern Illinois University Press, 1982), pp. 17-38; Robert Butler, "Parks, Parties, and Pragmatism," *Essays in Literature*, 10 (Fall 1983), pp. 241-55, and "Farrell's Ethnic Neighborhood and Wright's Urban Ghetto: Two Visions of Chicago's South Side," *Melus*, 18 (Spring 1993), pp. 103-11; and Charles Fanning and Ellen Skerrett, "James T. Farrell and Washington Park: The Novel as Social History," *Chicago History*, 8 (Summer 1979), pp. 80-91.

[2] "Since I Began," completed 29 August 1970, pp. 339-40. State Street, not Wabash Avenue, is sometimes considered to be the western boundary of the Studs Lonigan neighborhood. Aware that State Street was a busy commercial thoroughfare and served as a dividing line between predominantly middle class and poorer working class families to the west, Farrell here has pushed the western boundary of his residential neighborhood one block east to Wabash Avenue. Most of his friends in the area lived east of Wabash.

[3] Ibid; "Dut," p. 38.

[4] "Chicago's South Side: The World I Grew Up In," *Commonweal*, 83 (25 Feb. 1966), p. 606.

[5] No major black characters are in *Studs Lonigan*. But several Jewish characters are important in the plot and also serve as sounding boards for the intolerance and intellectual limitations of many residents of the 58th Street neighborhood. Davey Cohen and Phil Rolfe are the most prominent Jews in the story. Davey's father owns the tailor shop at 58th Street and Indiana Avenue. Davey is first seen making trouble at Studs's graduation exercises. He wants to be one of the gang. He acts and talks tough, smokes discarded cigarette butts, plays up to the Irish. He joins them in forays into the park to sock the Jews and to throw pepper in their eyes. But underneath this facade, he is proud to be a Jew. When an opportunity comes his way, he likes to read poetry, identifying with poets as different as Walter Scott and Heinrich Heine. He can carry on an intelligent discussion with Christy, the educated radical waiter in Gus the Greek's restaurant. But Davey is rejected by all. To Helen Shires he is a louse. In the gang-shag episode, Iris throws him out of her house before his turn comes up. He learns to hate Studs. He runs off and for ten years wanders the United States, returning in 1926, a consumptive, impoverished, tormented Jew.

[6] Phil Rolfe [*Louis Lederer*] first appears in an August 1919 episode when he is squirted by some young punks using a Washington Park drinking fountain. Like Davey, Phil is a prime target for the gang's prejudice. Studs, for example, thinks of him as "that snotty, loud-mouth little hebe," calls him a "kike," a "goddamn Jew," and a "fish peddler," and asks him if he is a fag, a pansy (*YMSL*, 66, 166, 171, 242). But Phil has a resilience and a street wisdom Davey lacks. He knows when to assert himself, how to ingratiate himself with others, and when to simply withdraw—as when he walks away from Studs's challenge to box in the park. In 1926 he is working in a clothing store on Adams Street in the Chicago Loop. He holds his own in the poolroom give-and-take, makes no apologies for being a well-dressed cake-eater exuding a "talcum-powdered, stacombed charm" (*YMSL*, 214), and knows how to please the girls. By the mid-1920s he is dating Studs's sister Loretta—in the face of Studs's warning both to him and to her—and makes steady progress. They marry in a few years. By 1931 Phil is a prosperous racetrack bookie, protected by city hall politicians and the police in return for favors, and lives with Loretta in an attractive apartment overlooking Lake Michigan. He can now patronize Studs, who is rapidly going broke in the Depression and who is known to new acquaintances as Phil Rolfe's brother-in-law. Phil is a survivor, well on his way to a successful career. Louis Lederer's son, William L. Lederer, has stated that his father was a bookie, as in *Studs Lonigan*, and was one of the first organizers of Las Vegas (Letter to Branch, 13 Dec. 1994).

In an April 3, 1936, letter Farrell informed James Henle that Louis Lederer, Patrick Cunningham's son-in-law "has left the bookie business, and started a bakery." Farrell's sister Helen remembered somewhat tentatively that Lederer owned a fur business. In 1946 Farrell spelled out his early feelings toward Lederer, the man who succeeded—where he had failed—in winning the affection of Loretta Cunningham: "He was a cakeeater, had girls like him, could dance well, and I was envious of him as a boy in the jazz age. . . . He is superior to me as of those days in getting dates, and he is inferior in terms of the mores. He is Jewish. He became a Catholic. I rejected the Church. At the wake [Studs's wake], he thanked every one for coming, and I felt he didn't belong in the family" (Letter, Farrell to James Henle, 15 January 1946).

[7] Letter, Farrell to Branch, 26 Sept. 1961. Cf. Farrell in 1970: The neighborhood "was not all Irish, nor was it even predominantly Irish. There were many Irish, many Jews, many Nordic Protestants" ("Since I Began," completed 29 August 1970, p. 338). Charles Fanning and Ellen Skerrett have underscored Farrell's point: "The area's first residents had been mostly Protestants of English or German descent, with a few Irish families along the western border. They were followed in the 1880s and 1890s by Jewish and more Irish families." See "James T. Farrell and Washington Park: The Novel as Social History," *Chicago History*, 8 (Summer 1979), p. 84. In 1975 Farrell reiterated that the ill-informed belief "that I lived in and have principally written about ethnically Irish and religiously Catholic neighborhoods" was untrue. "There were many Irish-Americans and Catholics in the 58th Street neighborhood . . . but there definitely was not a majority of them" ("Since I Began," completed 17 July 1975, pp. 2827-28, misnumbered for pp. 2287-88). Farrell was proud that *Studs Lonigan* and the O'Neill-O'Flaherty novels introduced, in a big way, the urban Irish into modern American literature. But when he bore in mind the totality of his writings and the diversity of his subjects and settings, he strenuously objected to being pigeonholed as an ethnic author focusing on Chicago's South Side Irish. On November 10, 1976, he noted: "Now, I am being tagged as an ethnic writer. I have never considered myself as such, and it is a new way of tagging me" (Letter, Farrell to Branch, 10 Nov. 1976).

[8] From an undated, untitled autobiographical fragment, p. 37. Farrell explained the misapprehension that the neighborhoods he wrote about were ethnically Irish-Catholic: "When I came to writing my books and stories, I chose or invented a number of characters who were Irish-American and Catholic, and included among them a great many who attended parochial schools. It was simply a matter of course that the associations of these characters would be largely among their own kind. This is particularly true of the boys and girls who attended parochial schools. Thus, many of my books and stories set in this neighborhood, or in similar ones, include many with Irish names, and persons who were practicing members of the Catholic religion." Consequently, he added, critics and readers "unfamiliar with the character, racial and religious composition, and history of the South Side of Chicago . . . have acquired the impression that I grew up in, and that I have written about neighborhoods, areas of Chicago that were ethnically Irish" ("Since I Began," completed 17 July 1975, pp. 2282-86).

On 17 May 1948, in the court proceedings brought by Farrell and the Vanguard Press to restrain the Philadelphia police from interfering with the sale of *Studs Lonigan*, the author testified on the neighborhood's diversity: "It was a district racially composed largely of Irish and Irish-Americans, with a considerable proportion of Jewish families, and on the fringes of it some colored and some Polish and other Slavic families. The neighborhood had no clearly defined composition, it was a neighborhood of homeowners, of small businessmen, or workingmen, part of the workingmen who were considered to be the labor aristocracy, and then a number of poor families. It was also a neighborhood in which you had a number of first- and second-generation American boys. You had a sufficient composition on the basis of race and of color and of creed to have an exacerbation based upon senses of differences, which is a very common American phenomenon" ("The Author as Plaintiff: Testimony in a Censorship Case," *RAF*, p. 192).

[9] "Since I Began," completed 29 Aug. 1970, p. 338. Catholics, Protestants, and Jews played on Jim Farrell's 1918 baseball team, the Hirsches, outfitted by Morris Hirsch, the owner of the grocery store on 58th Street near Calumet. Farrell noted that "When morale and good will deteriorated among us, bigotry came out. . . . Suspicion, dislike and nasty insults were exchanged. Words like 'dirty kikes' and 'dirty Irish' came out. The Hirsches broke up. Or rather there were some kids who quit. I led the quitting by doing so myself" ("Autobiography," completed 15 Jan. 1973, pp. 2425-26). On Farrell's next team, the Rowlands, the Irish and Jewish boys learned to play together without hostility.

[10] "A Memoir on Sherwood Anderson," *Perspective*, 7 (Summer 1954), p. 83. Reprinted in part in "A Note on Sherwood Anderson," *RAF*, p. 164. One way Jimmy Farrell may have become "known" is suggested in this passage: "Since I really had learned to read, I had read the sports pages of the Chicago newspapers. I would go to the newsstand at 58th Street and the elevated station, and get the box edition, and then, I'd walk along 58th Street with my nose almost in the newspaper, reading the box score, the play-by-play account of the Chicago White Sox ball games, and, sometimes, of the Chicago Cubs, as well. There were jokes about my reading along 58th Street, lost to the world, and reading the box score and other baseball news" (Undated and untitled autobiographical fragment, p. 20).

[11] "Since I Began," undated but written in Jan. 1971, pp. 1878-80.

[12] Clarence ("Pants") Rowland was a prominent baseball man. Manager of the Chicago White Sox from 1915 to 1918, he also during his career was an American League umpire, the President of the Pacific Coast League, and Vice President of the Chicago Cubs. He and Farrell became good friends and spent time together during Farrell's visits to Chicago.

[13] "Dut," pp. 26-27; "Since I Began," begun 29 August 1970, pp. 641-46.

[14] In an undated note to Farrell written in the mid-1930s, James Henle commented that "despite your eminently sound contention that Studs is merely a normal guy, he seems (to a number of the so-called intelligentsia) hardly better than a gorilla." In a letter of 4 September 1942 Farrell wrote to Henle: "Even the neighborhood is not a really tough neighborhood. Normally, strange young men and kids could come in it, and leave with their teeth all in place. There were exceptions, and on occasions, a little toughness burst loose: you really see that it isn't too tough by reading the story 'The Merry Clouters'; you see how merry they are, and what clouters they are. You will further note that the neighborhood is not described as one in which there are many robberies: people are not afraid to walk around at night in the neighborhood; girls are not afraid to [go] out alone at night and to come home alone. If it were a tough neighborhood, would this be the case? If it were really tough, would I have missed at least one scene in which the Lonigan parents talked of their fear of the girls being out, and asked Studs to see to it that they come home? Boys who are not really tough do a normal amount of fighting, you know. Further in the tough scenes, what happens is that it is a sudden social compulsion: fighting in groups, a wave of toughness as it were, a contagious feeling excites them. In election times in this neighborhood, there was never any slugging either."

[15] "Dut," pp. 32-36. Compare Farrell in 1954: "In these neighborhoods on the South Side of Chicago, life seemed settled. Parents and elders had found their place in the world. A fair number of them were home

owners. A fair number were neither go-getters nor Babbitts" ("A Memoir on Sherwood Anderson," p. 83).

16 "Introduction to Studs Lonigan," completed 16 Feb. 1972, pp.27-29. Professor Frederic Milton Thrasher taught at New York University, Washington Square Branch. Formerly he had been a member of the Sociology Department at the University of Chicago. He was Professor Robert Morss Lovett's second choice, as proposed to James Henle, to write the introduction to *Young Lonigan*.

Farrell noticed two signs of neighborhood change before the inundation of blacks in the mid-1920s. The first sign came at the end of World War I when "an increasing number of single men came into the neighborhood and were able to rent rooms. There was an increase in the number of such boarders." The second sign was the early exodus of well-fixed white families, mainly to the South Shore district (the area south of East 67th Street and east of Stony Island Avenue). In the early 1920s the family of Ed Kenny, a friend of Farrell's on Indiana Avenue, moved there as did Dorothy McPartlin's family—into the highly respectable 7000 block of Oglesby Avenue. So did Morris Hirsch, the grocer who lived in the Daly's South Park Avenue apartment building. Farrell's Indiana Avenue friend Billy Maurer moved with his family to the north side, near Loyola University, in 1919. ("Since I Began," completed 17 July 1975, pp. 2268-81.)

17 In 1938 Farrell wrote of these men: "They rose socially and economically. Ultimately many of them owned buildings and conducted their own small business enterprises. They became politicians, straw bosses, salesmen, boss craftsmen and the like. And they became tired. Their spiritual resources were meager. They believed in the American myth of success and advancement. They believed in the teachings and dogma of their faith. They believed that with homilies, platitudes about faith and work, and little fables about good example, they could educate their children . . . and that their children would advance so much the farther, so many more rungs on the economic and social ladder" ("Introduction" to *Studs Lonigan*, Modern Library edition [New York: Random House, 1938], pp. xii-xiii).

18 "Dut," pp. 38-42.

19 "Since I Began," completed 25 Feb. 1973, pp. 387-88.

20 Ibid., p. 391. Farrell knew Clackey Metz, the prototype for Clackey Merton in *The Young Manhood of Studs Lonigan* and for Morty Aiken in the Chicago race riot tale "The Fastest Runner on Sixty-first Street." Out of the city when Clackey was murdered, he wrote his story some thirty years later, based on written and oral accounts. According to the reports, Farrell stated, Clackey was one of a white mob inflamed with racist hatred and out for blood. Farrell played down this aspect of Clackey's character in his portrayal of Morty Aiken by having Morty pulled somewhat innocently into the mob action and by linking his death to his much admired speed as a runner.

21 Ibid., p. 385. In 1912 when Farrell's parents lived at 25th Street and La Salle, he and his brother Earl, eight and twelve respectively, wandered into the nearby black belt and were saved by a white telephone repair man from being beaten up by a gang of black boys. Farrell noted that it was just as dangerous for black boys who wandered into the white district.

22 Ibid., p. 426.

23 Department of Special Collections, University of Pennsylvania Libraries.

24 "Dut," p. 26.

25 The O'Neill-O'Flaherty novels allot surprisingly little space to Danny's four years at St. Patrick's [*St. Anselm's*] : altogether 138 pages out of thousands in the pentalogy, and, in terms of time, about eight months out of forty-eight. *No Star Is Lost* concludes in May 1915 as the O'Flahertys and Danny move into the neighborhood. *Father and Son* begins in October 1918. At the end of Chapter Eleven of Section One, Danny graduates from St. Patrick's in June 1919.

26 Farrell attended St. Cyril's High School from 1919 to 1923. In September 1922 during his senior year, his father suffered a first and partially disabling stroke and died in November 1923. From May 1923 until March 1925 Farrell worked in the Wagon Call Department of the Express Company. For three nights a week from September 1924 until March 1925 he attended night school at De Paul University in Chicago's Loop. In March 1925 he withdrew from De Paul, quit his job at the Express Company, and began as a service station attendant with the Sinclair Oil Company.

27 Letter, Farrell to H. L. Mencken, 21 March 1946.

28 In portraying Danny O'Neill's conversion to atheism at this time, Farrell chose to highlight Danny's hostility toward his neighborhood. See *Anger*, pp. 215-17.

29 Undated fragment from Farrell's Dutton typescript on *Studs Lonigan*, p. 74; untitled notebook, badly burned, with no front cover (Department of Special Collections, University of Pennsylvania Libraries.)

30 Joe Cody remembered that Farrell "went through a period at the University of intense and sustained reading in the library. He was there all the time, tremendous plugging, day and night." Cody believed that with the aid of Professor Linn, Farrell received a scholarship, but that he forfeited it by cutting classes and giving all his time to reading and writing. Cody may have been thinking of the tuition remission Farrell received for the Spring quarter 1928, quickly followed by his withdrawal from all his courses (Interview, Joseph Cody, 3 April 1956).

31 Undated fragment from Farrell's Dutton typescript on *Studs Lonigan*, pp. 73, 75.

32 "Hometown Revisited," *Tomorrow*, 10 (Jan. 1951), p. 25.

33 "Farrell Revisits Studs Lonigan's Neighborhood," *New York Times Book Review*, 20 June 1954, p. 4.

34 This is evident in his depiction of the Catholic Church. Yet his mature view of the Church, as forcibly expressed in 1957, was that it is a "wise and flexible and dangerous" institution. Wise and flexible because it recognizes the need of men and women for confession, relief of guilt, and the assurance that permits renewed activity and strength; because it adapts its practices to the facts of human nature, builds upon them, refuses to insist upon an impossible ideal in this life, and offers compassion and forgiveness when required. With great delight Farrell liked to tell the Catholic wheeze about the Confessional: All the girls of the parish confessed they had fornicated with Reilley. They were given their penances, which they accepted. When Reilley came and confessed, he was given an unusually harsh penance, which he cockily refused as an unheard-of punishment. For Reilley had a weapon more potent than the priest's: he threatened to take his prick out of the parish.

But the Church's authoritarian dogmatism, Farrell believed,

restricts and endangers free human development to the degree that he would have destroyed the Church if he could have done so. He affirmed, though, that he came to the wisdom that it could not be battered down (Interview, 16 March 1957).

35 "A Novelist's Reflections on Writing and His World," *Catholic Messenger*, 31 Oct. 1963, p. 5. Farrell, the atheist and rationalist, realized early that his Catholicism had contributed significantly to his perceptions and his value system. "I'm still a left-handed Catholic," he wrote in his 1933 diary (p.94). In an autobiographical fragment Farrell wrote: "I have had my bouts with Catholicism, but I have always believed that I gained a flying start because I was raised a Catholic and attended parochial school. I absorbed as part of my orientation a sense of a world where there is order in relationship, and truth is an orderly system. I lived the facts of meaning, meaning everyday. Sin and goodness. Truth and evil—the currents of a world in movement" ("Section II," undated, but probably written in the early 1970s). Compare his statement made the year of his death: "'Altogether, I attended three parochial schools. I used to call that a miseducation, but if I lost my faith, I learned moral values. And they never left me.'" (Interview by Stefan Kanfer, "As 'Studs Lonigan' Goes on TV, James T. Farrell Still Sings of the City with the Big Shoulders," *People*, 11 [12 Mar. 1979], p. 44.)

36 Farrell's typescript on the Bug Club titled "Chapter Seven."

37 Dr. Reitman published two books: *The Second Oldest Profession: A Study of the Prostitute's "Business Manager"* (1931) and *Sisters of the Road* (1937). Vanguard Press, Farrell's publisher, put out his first book.

38 "Jim Farrell Fondly Recalls Hectic Hours with 'Bug' Club," *Chicago Daily News*, 1 Dec. 1943.

39 South Park Commissioners, *Report for a Period of Twelve Months from March 1, 1915, to February 29, 1916* (Chicago: W. J. Hartman Co.), p. 40.

40 "Autobiography," completed 19 Sept. 1972, pp. 1557-58, 1563-65.

41 "Autobiography," completed 28 Feb. 1973, pp. 542-45.

42 "Hometown Revisited," pp. 23-24. To Eddie Ryan in 1925, "Washington Park was the landscape of many associations, many memories, many dreams that never came true, many brooding boyhood sadnesses, many recollections of running, shouting boyhood play.... His own moods were as one with the park" (*The Silence of History*, p. 53).

43 Farrell wrote an untitled poem, dated March 18, 1930, in his "Notebook and Diary for 1930," pp. 104-105:

> He was a boy alone in the Park
> That chilled
> With all November's gathering dessication.
> He walked
> Brooding over the hurts
> Other boys had inflicted on him.
> Refusing to play with him
> And afraid to fight him.
> He walked,
> And watched the wandering leaves
> Cracking
> Crunching
> Whirling
> Swirling
> On tips of wind.
> And he said
> That the leaves
> Were souls of the dead,
> Traveling Purgatory,
> Wailing for God's grace
> To cap their race.
> And he walked.
> The leaves
> He told himself,
> Were the souls of the boys
> Who had hurt him,
> And he was God
> Who would get even.
> And he crunched them,
> Leaves and leaves,
> Under his boots,
> And he walked on
> Brooding
> Amidst November dessication,
> Watching
> And watching
> The wandering leaves.

Farrell expanded the image of the lonely, brooding boy in Washington Park in his tales "Helen, I Love You" and "Autumn Afternoon."

44 Farrell's notebooks and his novels *My Days of Anger* and *The Silence of History* make plain that his university studies in the social sciences destroyed his overt acceptance of the Catholic faith and eased him into a secular view of human existence. They gave him a new perspective on his own past, present, and future. Of particular importance in this respect were the instructors of his three history courses (121, 131, and 141, covering European history from early Medieval times to World War I) taken before March 1926 during his first two quarters at the university. They were, respectively, Professor Einar Joranson [Prof. Cotton; Prof. Kraft], Mr. John Wesley Hoffmann [Mr. Thornton], and Professor Walter Louis Dorn [Prof. Dorfman; Prof. Bertram Carleton]. Farrell received grades of "A," "B," and "A" in those courses.

Also of signal importance to Jimmy Farrell's evolving views were Professors Rodney Loomer Mott [Prof. Donald W. Torman], his instructor in Political Science 101, Introduction to American Government (Winter 1926 quarter) and Mr.—later, Professor—Harold Dwight Lasswell [Dr. Pearson; Mr. Torman—erroneously repeating the fictional name given Professor Mott], his instructor in Political Science 103, Comparative Government, courses taken respectively during the Winter and Spring 1926 quarters. Farrell received a grade of "A" in each course. He took the courses as part of his pre-law training, but they awoke in him a desire "to go from law to politics" in order "to participate in the changing of the world, the solving of problems, and the righting of wrongs." Sometimes, Farrell wrote, he "would look at Rodney L. Mott, and think of him," as well as his other instructors, as men who were preparing "a whole generation to go out into the world" to make it "more reasonable and just" ("Since I Began," completed 22 Oct. 1975, pp. 2672-73, 2685).

For Professor Mott Farrell wrote two long "field work" papers: one on the work of his precinct captain, and the other on the Harrison Street Police Station. For Professor Lasswell he wrote an exceptionally good paper on Benito Mussolini and Italian Fascism. After Farrell became a prominent writer, Lasswell wrote to him that he regretted Farrell had not become a political scientist, but that he recognized that the novelist *was* a political scientist in the broadest sense of that term.

Eyler Newton Simpson, Jim Farrell's instructor in his single Sociology course, 110, Introduction to the Study of Society, taken during the Autumn 1926 quarter, made a lasting impression on him. Farrell wrote a long term paper for Simpson, "The Sociology of the Service Station Attendant." It was based on the only available sources— his personal experience, observation of fellow workers and bosses, and bulletins and work orders distributed by the Sinclair Oil and Standard Oil companies to their employees. He received an "A" in the course. He did less well, and was less interested, in his two Political Economy courses (grades of "B"), his two Economics courses (grades of "B" and "C"), and Introductory Psychology 101 (grade of "C").

45 Farrell codified his atheism in a section of his 1933 notebook dated April 30 and headed "What I Believe?"—the question mark presumably suggesting a lingering doubt:

"1. Life, in the cosmic sense, is purposeless & without order.

"2. Man's hold onto life is precarious. As far as he is concerned, his destiny is preponderantly a matter of chance.

"3. There is no certainty except—death.

"4. No system can be a satisfactory ordering of the universe.

"5. People always tend to make a religion of their needs. Then they absolutize the expression of that religion of their needs. The Communists do this. A denial of the absolutization of needs is not a denial of the efficacy of a solution of those needs" ("Notebook—Novel—Am. Ex. Company," pp. 34-35).

46 Farrell writes of this memorable experience in his unpublished autobiography: "One Saturday afternoon in March, 1926, I was off from work, and I took a walk in Washington Park with Joe Cody. We were both moody, and thoughtful, and as our conversation quickly revealed, we had much on our minds.

"It was a gray and windy day, and as I recall we walked, for a few minutes, in silence. We still were planning one day to become law partners . . . What we both had on our minds was breaking with our pasts. This meant the rejection of the values, attitudes, mores, and even the faith in our respective families. This, each of us saw coming, although neither of us knew that the other had been coming to this change . . . Much of what passed as truth in our respective homes was largely untruth, and even bias and bigotry. The world in which we had grown up believing it to be the real world, was tissued with many lies. Much that we had learned . . . was, to be blunt, nothing but lies. . . . We had begun to discover this since we had started our college studies.

"There was hurt and pain in our discoveries. . . . And on that afternoon, walking randomly in Washington Park, which was dreary of prospect, because of the dirty patches of snow, the dark grayness of the sky, and the bareness of the trees, I became indignant. . . . Yes, we had been lied to. And this, I believe, was the source, or the major source, of my indignation.

"Since I had previously been educated in parochial schools, I had always had an idea of truth. . . . The Church, I had been taught, was the repository of the most important truths in life. And these truths came from God. . . . On the final Day of Judgment . . . the souls of everyone who had ever lived, or who would ever live, would know all of the truth.

"Now, . . . my altered sense of truth was not as clearly definable, as really logical, as the one that I had learned of as . . . a good young Catholic. . . . Nor was it crowned with certainty. . . .

"As Joe and I talked, he seemed to be more sad than I. . . . But my rising indignation was swallowing some of my sadness. . . . After we had talked for only a few minutes . . . I knew, definitely and instantly that I no longer believed in the faith in which I had been raised and educated. I knew, at the same time, that I no longer believed in the existence of God. . . . The winds of ideas of some relatively few books, plus what I heard in classroom lectures, plus my own observations were enough to tumble the principles of a whole system like a child's house of cards" ("Since I Began," begun 22 Oct. 1975, pp. 2702, 2730-2751).

47 In contrast to Jim Farrell's vigorous embrace of atheism, Joe Cody settled for becoming an agnostic, according to Farrell. To avoid hurting his family's feelings, Joe kept his doubts to himself and continued to attend mass. Within a week Jim announced to his family that he no longer believed in God or the dogmas of the Roman Catholic Church. "My announcement," he wrote, "came as a shock, but less of a one than might have been anticipated." His Uncle Tom wanted him to continue attending mass and not to let others know how he felt. But he refused. He felt he had to live by his convictions. "My grandmother was scandalized, and did not like this news. She went into huddles with my Mother about it. But she was not at all broken up or hurt as I had feared she might be" (Ibid., pp. 2792-95).

Chapter Four: Jimmy Farrell in the Neighborhood

BEFORE LOOKING AT JIMMY FARRELL as a young impressionable grammar-school boy in the Studs Lonigan neighborhood, we would do well to first briefly consider the origin and composition of *Young Lonigan* and *The Young Manhood of Studs Lonigan*. The action of these two novels (in contrast with that of *Judgment Day* which occurs outside the neighborhood) projects important cultural features of the boy's surroundings and underscores their effect on him. Farrell wrote the first draft of both novels between June 1929 and February 1931, and he completed his final version of *The Young Manhood* in September 1933. By focusing on the writer at work on these novels, we gain insight not only into the creative process animating their composition but also into the author's preoccupation with the Studs Lonigan neighborhood, a preoccupation which had at its core Farrell's profound boyhood memories of these thirty-six square city blocks. First, we will turn to the contemporary historical record of the actual composition of the two novels; then, to its fictional counterpart found in several unpublished novels: Farrell's self-portrayal as the young artist struggling to shape and complete his manuscript. Finally, we will look at the life Farrell led as a young boy in the neighborhood.

1923 St. Cyril yearbook photo of James T. Farrell. (Courtesy of Father Leander Troy, O. Carm.)

THE CONTEMPORARY RECORD

James T. Farrell's own thoughts and ideas about the Studs Lonigan neighborhood began to take significant shape once he had left it. In May 1928 Julia Brown Daly, her three grown children and her grandson, Jim Farrell, moved from their South Park Avenue apartment to 7136 East End Avenue in the South Shore District, where the Cunninghams also then lived. Jim had completed six quarters of work at the university, and he had spent almost six months in New York City hoping to support himself by his writing. Within the next two years he and the Dalys moved twice to two other South Shore District addresses: 7046 Euclid Avenue, where they occupied a five-room flat on the second floor of a three story building, and 2023 East 72nd Street. The Dalys were hard-pressed financially. Only Jim's Uncle Tom was working, at a reduced income. From time to time Jim earned a little money—doing night work in a funeral parlor on 67th Street (for a room and three dollars a week), writing class papers for other students, and distributing handbills. For seven months beginning in January 1929 he earned about twenty-five dollars a week as campus reporter for the *Chicago Herald-Examiner* [Chicago Questioner; Chicago Scope; Chicago Chronicle].[1] But mostly, when not with Dorothy Butler or his friends, he sat at a table reading or writing.

William ("Studs") Cunningham died on March 10, 1929, and was waked the following evening. At the time, Jim Farrell was in his last quarter of work at the university. He was taking "Teddy" Linn's Advanced Composition 211 and Philosophy 208, Aesthetics, taught by Charles Hartshorne [Herbert Caldwell], substituting for James Tufts. About two years earlier he had vowed to become a writer. He wanted to write a novel about his experience within his family. But instead, he was producing many short stories, most of them about his acquaintances in the 58th Street neighborhood or other persons he knew from his past work for the Express Company and in service stations. He was discovering that writing about his intimate family past was difficult and did not meet self-imposed standards of objectivity.

Among the stories Jim Farrell wrote for his composition teacher was "Studs," an effort undertaken one day in his friend Mary Hunter's apartment in the Coudich Culture Center. Linn's response was enthusiastic, and Jim discovered that he could not forget the feelings aroused by the tale. "After writing this story in the spring of 1929, before I had published any fiction, the impressions here recorded remained with me so vividly that I could not let them rest."[2] Jim's first published story, "Slob," appeared in the June number of the little magazine *Blues* as the spring term ended. On June 19 Clifton Fadiman [Tommy Stock], an editor with Simon and Schuster [Wallingford and Wyndfall], wrote Farrell stating that he had read "Slob" with great pleasure and interest. He invited the author to submit any longer fiction underway. "So there I was, asked by a publisher if I had a long manuscript after the publication of my very first piece of fiction" ("Reflections at Fifty," *RAF*, p. 59).

Jim immediately took the manuscript of "Studs" to Professor Robert Morss Lovett [Lloyd Dunning Sheldon] of the English Department. Lovett encouraged him to develop the story and its milieu in greater detail and assured him that Fadiman was known for his ability to pick writers. Probably on Monday, June 24, Jim sat with Mary Hunter on "the grass near the Botany pond"[3] and the university commons, while "hatless lads and girls in their summer dresses" passed by. There, Farrell later wrote, "The first outline of the book was made. . . . I talked with Mary and got her advice on the letter I would write to Fadiman. . . . I spoke of possible scenes, of how my book would lead to Studs's death, of a character who later became Weary Reilley. Mary took what I said very seriously and made comments. In a sense, *Studs Lonigan* was born that afternoon" (Reflections at Fifty," *RAF*, p. 59).

That evening Farrell replied to Fadiman: "At present, I have no long work completed, but I have been working on two novels. One is a realistic story of a corner gang at Fifty Eighth and Prairie Avenue of this city. The neighborhood background is that of a middle class community which slowly disintegrates into a rooming house section, finally succumbing to the advance of the negro. I shall send you shortly, a draft of a story which suggests the method of handling, and the types of characters to be described.

"The other novel is a tale of a boy in a Catholic high school of this city during the early part of the jazz age. It will deal with the innumerable conflicts resulting from the development of an adolescent sexualism, and the failing struggle to conform these impulses to the athlete type idealized in this particular environment."

Fadiman immediately replied that he welcomed material from either or both of the two manuscripts. Two weeks later, on July 10, Farrell responded. He explained that his manuscript of the Catholic high school boy was too disorganized to send. But he outlined his corner gang novel in broad detail. In the 58th Street and Prairie Avenue neighborhood, he wrote, "I intend to treat a number of boys who grow up, and who, mainly, drift to the poolroom and its complements as the only outlet of their impulses for the romantic and the adventurous. The characters form a vivid set of contrasts, and include such different types as George Lott, ranking Davis cup star, Frank Egan who was recently sentenced to Joliet for rape, after a spectacular trial, a young fellow who went up for violation of the Mann Act, a misguided young man who died from internal complications of gonorrhea, a Quixotic medievalist who has done everything from check-forging to elevator starting, sound substantial oil salesmen, small-time politicians, hoboes, poolroom loafers, nymphomaniacs, cab drivers, middle class virgins, high school athletes, and others.

"This diverse group is in a sense my old gang, the fellows I grew up with, whose stories I listened to, who I played ball with and later got drunk with. I know them intimately, and have absorbed the background out of which they came. Similarly, I have moved far enough away from it, to have developed something of a perspective; but am still close enough to it, to write the story with some degree of sympathy and comprehension.

"It seems a vital aspect of contemporary city life, and I am impelled to do it immediately." He added that he expected to be in New York in the summer or fall and wanted to discuss the novel with Fadiman. The editor's encouraging response on July 16 asked to see sample chapters, and early in August Farrell sent him a thirty-six page excerpt. Fadiman replied on August 9. "To tell the truth, I don't believe the method you have employed is capable of producing anything like a mature fictional effect. I know exactly what you are trying to do and I am in thorough sympathy with the insurgent movement of American letters but I think the prose is wordy, disorganized and a bit hysterical.

"In my opinion, it would be much more advisable for you to work on the other novel which sounds much more promising and put this script in the drawer for a couple of months." Characteristically, Jim Farrell did the opposite, such was the pull of the neighborhood and the attraction of the "old gang." For the next six years he shelved his autobiographical tale of the Catholic high school boy and forged ahead with the corner gang novel.

Late in August he hitchhiked to New York, hoping to support himself by finding a place in the city's literary establishment. Two meetings with Fadiman in early September proved inconclusive. When not reading books and writing low-paying book reviews, he revised his corner gang novel. He reported to Dorothy Butler in Chicago that he was improving the novel's beginning. In October, discouraged and broke, he returned to Chicago and the Dalys. From then until February 1931, twenty-one months after he had begun his "Studs Lonigan" manuscript, he doggedly wrote at home, the university, and the Chicago Public Library. He completed hundreds of manuscript pages in his long novel about Studs. During this time he also wrote additional short stories and sprayed them out to magazine editors. Rejection slips piled up, including one from *Modern Quarterly* turning down his tale "Studs" in June 1930.[4]

In February 1931 Farrell decided to divide his long manuscript into two as yet untitled divisions which eventually he would title *Young Lonigan* and *The Young Manhood of Studs Lonigan*. His friend Lloyd Stern, who had seen the undivided manuscript, had suggested the commercial and literary advantages to making that change. In one final try—ignoring the advice of Milton Peterson and Ed Levin, two university acquaintances—Jim sent the tyepscript of *Young Lonigan* to Fadiman. The editor replied: "I am afraid I cannot cotton to this. It seems to me rather crudely and over-emphatically written; you stress your irony too much for it to be very effective.

"You have got some really genuine material here but you seem to go at it with both hands."[5] Ultimately *Young Lonigan* was rejected by four other publishers: Brewer and Warren, Smith and Haas, Coward McCann, and Covici Friede. Their reasons were as diverse as fear of censorship and the failure of the novel to appeal to shop girls as they rode homeward on the subway.

Only Paris, where the seminal story "Studs" had been published in 1930, was a source of hope. He had sent several tales, including sections of what would become *Young Lonigan,* to Edward W. Titus's [Robinson's] Paris journal *This Quarter* [This Era]. On April 23, 1930, Samuel Putnam [Bert Falk], the associate editor, wrote Farrell: "I like your work very much. I think it's swell . . . but Mr. Titus is still a bit in doubt." Putnam urged Farrell to "fire something else back at us." Back came a folder of stories. From it Putnam selected "Studs" and, without consulting Titus, slipped it into the July-August-September 1930 number of *This Quarter*—Titus eventually paid Farrell twenty dollars for it. In March 1931 Sam Putnam, now the editor of his own journal, the *New Review* [This Age], forwarded to Farrell Ezra Pound's enthusiastic approval of Farrell's tales, along with Pound's recommendation that four of them be published in book form.[6] He promised Farrell a "spread in the near future" and followed through in the fall by publishing Farrell's tale "Jewboy" in the *New Review.*

Frustrated in Chicago and beset by personal problems, Farrell sensed that Paris offered him greater freedom and the opportunity to further explore—as he had written to Fadiman—the lives of the boys in the "corner gang at Fifty Eighth and Prairie Avenue" and their neighborhood, "the background out of which they came." For a considerable time both he and Dorothy had wanted to go to Paris anyway. Before they sailed on April 17, 1931, Farrell made last minute efforts to find a publisher in New York City. Failing to do that, he left the manuscript of *Young Lonigan* with Walt Carmon [Carl Warton], editor of the *New Masses,* who acted as his agent. Carmon knew Eva Ginn, the bookkeeper for the Vanguard Press, and through her he brought Farrell's mauscript to the attention of the firm's president, James Henle, who immediately liked it.

Once Jim and Dorothy were in Paris, Jim's career was on track. He accepted Henle's proffered contract for the publication of *Young Lonigan,* agreed to Henle's shrewd editorial suggestions while making his revisions, and then mailed the revised manuscript to Henle. Before returning from Paris in April 1932, he proceeded to write several short stories (which again centered his attention on the Studs Lonigan neghborhood) and a draft of *Gas-House McGinty,* his second novel. Chapter Four of the latter work, Farrell explained, "introduces the dreaming, sleeping life of my chief protagonist, Ambrose J. McGinty, into the novel. My idea for this came from the famous Nighttown scene in Dublin in James Joyce's *Ulysses.* And also, I looked upon this chapter about McGinty's dreams as a preparation for my writing the scene when Studs Lonigan would die." Since early 1932 Farrell had planned to end the unpublished part of his already completed Studs manuscript (what became *The Young Manhood*) with a narrative of Studs's "dying consciousness, and of the images and fantasies of that consciousness while he lay on his death bed." These "would be organized in terms of the Day of Judgment."[7]

Back in New York City in mid-April 1932, Farrell and Dorothy lived hand to mouth during the following year on income from his writing. He sold scores of book reviews as well as eight or nine short stories, did occasional editing for James Henle, and received a modest return from the publication and sale of *Young Lonigan* and *Gas-House McGinty.* In April 1933 Farrell went back to the bulky manuscript stack about Studs Lonigan that he had written between June 1929 and February 1931. The remaining part of that manuscript, which became *The Young Manhood of Studs Lonigan,* he wrote, was "virtually a novel in almost publishable condition. . . . But also, I was working carefully, going over what was already written line by line, adding new lines, and parts to the book."[8] In May he settled on "The Young Manhood of Studs Lonigan" as the title for his novel and began mailing revised sections of the typescript to Henle. He and Dorothy then spent a month in June and July at her mother's apartment in Chicago, where he continued his intense revision.

On August 1 Jim and Dorothy Farrell began their first stay at Yaddo, in Saratoga Springs. There, he wrote, "I was able to pitch into my work. . . . I would work for many hours during the day, and on many nights, after dinner, I would go back to my studio, and work for a few more hours. The strain on me became more harsh, and there were days that I did not know how I could go on. But I went on. I felt driven and possessed with the book. . . . I wrote to Jim Henle and said that I was so mentally fatigued that I did not know if I would be able to finish the book on time." But he did—after completing a third revision on his battered typewriter.

During this final period of revision, Farrell realized that the Day of Judgment scene narrating Studs's dying consciousness "would not do as the end of *The Young Manhood of Studs Lonigan,*" as he had orginally planned. "The death of Studs Lonigan," he concluded, "would have to be presented in powerful scenes. I had written the chapter which described the New Year's Eve party, the 'Walpurgis Nacht' chapter. It brought *The Young Manhood of Studs Lonigan* to a fitting end. The death of Studs Lonigan would have to be handled in a third volume."[9] Farrell had decided that for maximum impact his narrative of Studs must become a trilogy.[10]

On September 25 he mailed the final installment of *The Young Manhood of Studs Lonigan* to Henle. In November he read galleys. His novel was published on January 30, 1934, with an advance sale of 666 copies.

Farrell had completed the two novels in his trilogy which reveal the Studs Lonigan neighborhood from the perspective of Studs's consciousness. Because of his "stick-to-itiveness" and his own hard-won penetrating insights into the neighborhood and its people, his unfortgettable trilogy, *Studs Lonigan,* was well under way.

The Fictional Record in Unpublished Novels

In the late, unpublished novels "The Distance of Sadness," "The Call of Time" and "When Time Was Young," Farrell's imagination, directed by the guidance system of his remarkable memory, hones in on that period of his life when, in the person of his autobiographical character Eddie Ryan, he composes much of the long manuscript that eventually becomes the first two novels of the trilogy. Grace Hogan Dunne with her three grown children and her grandson Eddie Ryan now live in the South Shore District. Since 1928 Eddie has been writing short stories and sending the manuscripts out to magazines in a steady flow—as many as twenty in the hands of editors at one time in 1929, and thirty-four in mid-1930.

Eddie has long since vowed to become a writer, for he sees writing as his escape hatch to freedom. "There was anger in his spirit" because he feels himself still to be in a life-trap, both at home with the Dunnes and at large and vulnerable in a materialistic society. He is angry, too, because of his awareness of unfulfilled time rushing by him and lost forever. It is accompanied by a "consciousness of death as a total defeat imposed or to be imposed upon [him and] all of the living" ("Call," Vol. 1, p. 364). Increasingly he realizes that if he could make his way by writing, "he could freeze Time in words" and save what he had experienced from "the decaying and the passing away of time. This was why he wanted to write.... He must write to save yesterday, forever.... The living minute could be rescued only by recreating it and casting it into art.... He could live for others in the living minutes that now were alive for himself." Writing, he feels sure, can open a pathway to the only kind of personal immortality he can believe in ("Call," Vol. 1, pp. 159, 364; "Distance," p. 99).

Most of Eddie's stories are not about himself, but about others. Because he is filled with a "sense of sadness about the Dunnes," his adopted family, and recognizes that "their lives were hopeless, . . . the book of fiction that he really wants to write is the story of their lives, and of his own life" ("Young," p. 819). Eventually he intends "to write about himself, about his life, and even about his most intimate feelings" and to present them truly and objectively ("Call," Vol. 1, pp. 866-67, 896).

He enrolls in Professor Lyman's Advanced Composition class, perhaps reaching out blindly, unknowingly, for help he cannot foresee. In rapid succession come the death of Jud Jennings, Jud's wake the following night, the composition of his tale "Jud" in Joan Jackson's apartment, and the enthusiastic approval of his professors. Without at first knowing it, he has found his proper subject—one that plays off his most intimate personal past and is nourished by it but not confined to it. Increasingly he realizes that probably he is too close to his turbulent family experience to translate it into viable fiction. Still, for a time, he cannot decide what else to write on. "He was letting a chaos of mind prevent him from doing it" ("Call," Vol. 1, p. 434). But in June 1929 Eddie does decide. He begins working on a novel about Jud Jennings.

As he gets into his subject, "he thought back to younger days, when they had lived at Fifty-eighth and South Park Avenue. . . . he was getting nostalgic for these earlier days. Sometimes as he wrote, he would become possessed of the illusion that those days were not gone, they were not gone past all recall. They were stored away some place in the universe, and they could be, not brought back, but they could be, they could be something, somehow . . . . They could be written about" ("Young," p. 211). The more he writes the more he understands that "he had activated his past, the years when he had been growing up around 58th Street. His past, from 'the old days,' . . . had been coming alive ever since he had begun work on this novel, and he was re-seeing much of it with a greater objectivity than he had ever done before. . . . The old neighborhood . . . had become, in Eddie's perspective, a world, not a mere neighborhood. . . . He knew this without having to know" ("Call," Vol. 2, pp. 78-79). He also knows "that he could never regard this South Shore neighborhood the same as he could the old 58th Street one" ("Young," p. 815).

The days and weeks go by, and Eddie continues the daily grind of composition, whether at home, at the university, or at the public library. Working on his novel at his second floor Euclid Avenue apartment near 71st Street in the spring of 1930, he sits at the dining room table "with his back to the windows which looked out on a big vacant lot. During the winter, this was a bleak sight. His portable Royal typewriter, already much used, was set on the table usually on top of pieces of paper or over a newspaper. . . . Eddie would spread a pile of papers all around the typewriter. These were manuscripts that he was working on, letters, blank paper. Also on the table were books, pencils, fountain pens, a bottle of ink, ash trays, cigarettes. Much of the time there would be a coffee cup on the left of his typewriter. As he worked, Eddie would gradually take over the whole table" ("Young," p. 208). Often his invalid grandmother sits in her wheelchair in the same room, silent except for an occasional pungent remark.

What Eddie "didn't know of many of his characters, he had to imagine." He had to "imagine rightly, truly, consistently what he did not know. He had to make up life and render what he made up as though it were like life, as if it was actually life laid out and speaking on the printed page" ("Call," Vol. 2, pp. 172-73). Eddie had to place "Jud Jennings in situations common for a character like Jud, and he imagined what he would think and feel, and do, and say if he were Jud in such a situation" ("Young," p. 211).

"Once . . . he had thought or feared that he did not have any imagination, or at best, that he had very little imagination. Now, he believed that he had imagination, and he not only believed it, he knew it. If he hadn't any imagination, he wouldn't have been able to make as much progress in his writing as he had already made. . . . If God were God," he reflected, "what an artist He could be. The artist played God in lower case, knowing that he wasn't God, and sometimes, or maybe always writing as though he were. His imagination was a substitution for the difference of being artist and human being, and being God" ("Call," Vol. 2, pp. 7, 79).

Through the working of his imagination, "Some of the old days around 58th Street . . . had expanded for him in time and space, and in ideas, emotions and feelings. He was outside and beyond that world. His Jud Jennings was not outside. He was writing of Jud and of Jud's world as Jud saw and felt it . . . He was writing in a vocabulary that could be Jud Jennings' own, either his speaking vocabulary, or his broader, more understanding vocabulary. . . . He was making everything concrete . . . There were no signposts along the way in this work to tell the reader . . . of the author's meaning or intention. Jud revealed and exposed himself. . . .

"Jud's story unfolded in a situation of events of his life, and in the flow of his thoughts before, during and after these events. It was being worked out, thought out, and written as a story of what happens . . . presented from the standpoint of immediate experience, but written in the past tense. In each scene, the time was now, the present, the immediate and successive moments of the scene. Jud's character was a bundle, some kind of a complex complication, . . . a gestalt of tendencies, habits, reactions, day dreams, spoken words, physical movements, and actions taken or not taken. He was not a type. He was one person, living his own life, in his own way, by his own lights, and, insofar as Eddie himself was concerned, Jud Jennings represented no one but himself, nothing other than what he was" ("Call," Vol. 2, pp. 79a-80).

When Eddie's writing is going well, he finds it is "an adventure into the understanding of reality." It leads him down unexplored paths to new destinations. He finds that writing is "an adventure into yesterdays, and todays, and into his own mind and memory, and into the lives, and, in an imaginative way, into the minds of others." On a good day he feels that "there was an exhilaration in being able to write as he was doing. . . . He had a sense of *control* over himself, while at the same time, he seemed to be carried away. There was more fervor and force within than he had believed that there was, or even that there ever could be. There was a free-flow in his mind, and a satisfaction of flowing thoughts and expression that was like something new in experience. . . . When Eddie was able to work this way, he had no consciousness of time. . . . Time and place faded away" ("Call," Vol. 2, pp. 71, 78, 81). [The three manuscripts—as located among Farrell's papers—break off at this point in the story of Eddie's composition of Jud Jennings in America.]

THE YOUNG BOY IN THE NEIGHBORHOOD, 1915-1919

In his autobiographical memoirs and late letters Farrell characterized the inner story of the birth of his trilogy in a somewhat different fashion from the foregoing. "*Studs Lonigan*," he wrote, "was born from the creative womb of death. . . . I conceived it from the end, backwards, . . . from the standpoint of death . . . I determined that Studs should die at the end of the story I would tell. This was my starting point. . . . My primary interest and intention was the premature death of my character in his young manhood. I had the general pattern of events, an idea of the direction which these were to take, and the end which they would reach. Also, I had in mind many scenes . . . as well as words, phrases, bits of dialogue, incidents . . . and other characters to include. . . . Hour by hour, day by day, I created the events and circumstances that were part of his journey to his grave. [I recorded] the physical condition in that small area of the South Side in Chicago as well as the attitudes and beliefs. . . . Each detail of his surroundings was created as part of a bigger scene, a tragic scene. That is why the details of his neighborhood are important. . . . What was important about Studs, as my chief protagonist . . . was that he dies, and that his death would constitute the reflector, the mirror of meanings, as the end toward which the characters and events of the book were moving."[11]

In those words Farrell revealed what was in his mind when he began writing his trilogy. Studs's destiny was a given for the author. Selected events, scenes, dialogue, attitudes and beliefs, and characters—all judged by the author to contribute meaningfully to the pre-determined end—would meld into the social world through which Studs journeys to his early death. They would, in fact, constitute the building blocks of Studs Lonigan's neighborhood as Farrell pictured Studs experiencing it. For most of Studs's life that neighborhood would be the few blocks centered around 58th Street and Prairie Avenue.

If, in retrospect, the Studs Lonigan neighborhood turns out to have been doom-laden for the kind of person Studs Lonigan was, what was it like for Jim Farrell during his formative years there? And what kind of a boy was he, whose destiny was so different from that of Studs? Farrell knew the district from the inside and became our greatest authority on it. From 1915 to 1919 the boy Jimmy Farrell, between the ages of eleven and fifteen, progressed from the fifth through the eighth grade at St. Anselm's parochial school. Increasingly after the fall of 1919 when he entered high school, his life took him out of the neighborhood.[12] Drawing heavily on Farrell's memoirs, we will look at what kind of boy he was, and at some of the experiences he had in the neighborhood during those final four grade school years, when that neighborhood seemed to him almost like a self-projection, "as real as I was real to myself."[13]

Jimmy Farrell was older than most of his classmates at St. Anselm's because he had not entered first grade until he was seven and a half. He was among the smaller boys, weighing about seventy-five pounds when in the fifth grade. He wore glasses and was called "Four Eyes" in boyhood disputes.[14] Unquestionably intelligent, he had quick, sensitive impressions, and under the right conditions was capable of strong initiatives. But he was shy, self-absorbed, and given to daydreaming, a habit he hugged to himself for years.[15] He carried with him burdens of shame and humiliation—heaped on him because of family troubles—that he wanted to keep hidden. He was far more interested in sports of all kinds than in his school work. His grades at St. Anselm's Parochial School were average until he excelled under Sister Magdalen in the eighth grade. Referring to the Studs Lonigan neighborhood in 1954, Farrell wrote: "This was a milieu conducive to naiveté . . . And I, personally, was quite a naive boy. I was slow to mature emotionally, bewildered, dreamy and alienated. My lack of confidence in myself produced a sense of shame about my own feelings and emotions. These I kept very much to myself, locked up in my thoughts, my dreams, my fantasies."[16]

In his brooding, introspective moments, Jimmy was sometimes lonely, feeling cut off from others.[17] In writing about his early story "Helen, I Love You" in 1951, Farrell explicitly identified himself with his character Danny, the boy who had lost out with Helen, the girl he loved and whom he had imagined saying to him, "Dan, I love you, and I'll always love you." Feeling forsaken, Danny wanders into Washington Park. Farrell wrote: "The park. The boy going to the park—this is connected with an earlier story, 'Autumn Afternoon.' Sometimes, in unhappy moments, I wandered and brooded in Washington Park. . . . there were my unexpressed boyhood feelings and sensibilities expressed here, as in 'Autumn Afternoon.' My loneliness. I used to feel that if I were only understood by someone, loved as I wanted to be (this is my phrasing of now)—life could be different. Here was idyllicism and romanticism. Then, the darkness, going home alone . . . to the unhappy Daly home." Jimmy had had these feelings for years. "Ever since my first grade year at Corpus Christi," Farrell wrote, "I had had these daydreams and yearnings. I had wanted a girl. I had wanted a girl, whom I could call 'my girl,' 'my sweetheart.' I had wanted a girl to kiss and who would kiss me."[18] Most important to Jimmy the boy and Farrell the man was unquestioning love and loyalty from the one he loved.

As a child, Farrell also craved public adulation, and he secretly believed that someday he would deservedly get it. "As early as seven or eight, I somehow acquired a sense of destiny. I have never lost it. It is a belief that is rooted in my nature, and has long since become an ineradicable part of myself. I am sufficiently well aware that there are no laws, no stars, no forces unseen, that work for me. I depend and must depend upon myself. But the belief is in me, nonetheless. It is the source of my confidence, which never deserts me, except only in moments, now and then. It is the source, I believe, of a refusal on my part to place any but far off limits on the impossible. I wanted to be a hero, and a great man. I wanted to be Somebody, upper case. . . . I had believed that it would happen, that I would stand out in greatness, and that I would become famous."[19]

As a boy and through his teens, he believed that athletics was his road to fame and greatness. "For me, through boyhood," he wrote, "athletics was something of a way of life. . . . Needless to say, baseball was at the center of my entirely absorbing interest in athletics, and it took precedence over other sports." As a child, he grew up in the oral traditions of baseball by listening to his uncles, his father, and his brother Earl discuss players and games. "Before I ever saw Ty Cobb play I almost believed that I knew him. . . . I knew the names of almost every player in the big leagues before I could so much as read one word." At an early age he read *Touching Second* by Johnny Evers and Bill Klem, and *Inside Baseball* by Christy Mathewson. These books helped him to see "players as heroes. . . . A home run, a squeeze play, a stolen base could, in my mind, take on the character of an immortal deed. Eddie Collins, Ty Cobb, Stuffy McInnis, Hal Chase, Ray Schalk were greater and more important to me than the President of the United States. . . . My brother Earl once found one box seat ticket. It was on the sidewalk on Wentworth Avenue, on a Sunday morning, Aug. 27, 1911. The two of us got into Comiskey Park on it, and sat in the grandstand. Big Ed Walsh, a handsome and powerful spitball pitcher, hurled a no-hit game against the Boston Red Sox. That was history to me."[20]

Baseball was not his only love. In 1915-16 he also became an ardent boxing fan. "In fact," he later wrote, "I almost brought my knowledge of prize fighting lore up to my knowledge of baseball. I had my heroes and favorites of the past and present."[21] Among them were heavyweight champion Jess Willard, light heavyweight champion Battling Levinsky, middleweight champion Mike O'Donald, and the Chicago welterweight Packy McFarland. Heading his panoply of heroes, which included such fighters as Ad Wolgast, Battling Nelson, and Joe Gans, was William Kelly, who became known as the Original Jack Dempsey, the Nonpareil, the first recognized middleweight champion of the world. Instructed by newspaper articles, Jimmy began training himself to box, practicing before his bedroom mirror.

At this time, too, one of Farrell's sports heroes was heavyweight wrestling champion Frank Gotch. He began to practice wrestling. Coming home from school, he would wrestle with his friends. He discovered he could throw almost all of them, even the larger boys. He persuaded his Uncle Tom to buy him the Farmer Burns mail-order wrestling course. Eventually his practice paid off. In February 1920 as a member of coach Galoin's Carter Public School wrestling team, Farrell won the gold medal in the 105 pound division of the South Side Playground and Public School Wrestling Tournament. Later that winter, still at 105 pounds, he won the silver medal in the City Playground and Public School Wrestling Tournament. Football was another enthusiasm. His football hero at this time was the "triple-threat man" Paddy Driscoll, who played for Northwestern University, the Great Lakes Training Station team, and the Chicago Cardinals. Sports gave Jimmy Farrell many transporting moments.

Writing to H. L. Mencken on March 21, 1946, Farrell probed some of the hidden sources of his boyhood nature. He recognized that as a boy, he was "maybe . . . a bit of a misfit" and "perhaps too serious," a condition he traced to chronic bewilderment and its accompanying frustrations. "At the age of three, I went to live with my grandmother, my uncle and my aunt, instead of at home with my father and mother and brothers and sisters. . . . On the one hand, I had presented to me glimpses of what the normal 'social normal' family is, and on the other hand, I was not living a socially normal life. . . . I had a dual focus on family life, a focus based on my own childhood home, and on that of my parents and of others whose family life was (in the sense I use the word here) socially normal. This seems to have caused great bewilderment in my boyhood." On the one hand he felt like an outsider, different from his socially normal friends who lived with their parents. "I had," he wrote, "a spectatorial attitude towards things around me, and at times, even towards myself." On the other hand, he was a sensitive insider, deeply involved with an aberrant family racked by familial tensions and conflicts. To Mencken he expressed an important long-term consequence of his dual focus: "My having become a writer is related to early frustrations and bewilderments, and to the anxieties which accompany these."

The boy felt the unsettling contrast between the two families years before he moved to the Studs Lonigan neighborhood. When he was seven or eight, Farrell recalled, "I'd visit my real mother and sit in front of the oven to get warm, get up from the kitchen table still hungry, fight bedbugs all night long. Back at my grandmother's, the apartment was kept clean and orderly. There was heat and a bathroom indoors. A colored girl washed and ironed for us, and I was sent to school with a fresh, clean white waist every day."[22] Even when his parents moved in 1918 to their modern apartment on Calumet Avenue, Jimmy resisted taking meals with them. He tried to avoid staying overnight.

Farrell often insisted that he was not a deprived child. Rather, he said, he was spoiled by the Dalys and especially by his grandmother Julia—and he loved her for it. In his grandmother's home, he was "cock of the walk." Uncle Tom, who was a traveling shoe salesman for Upham Brothers of Stoughton, Massachusetts, earned at least $10,000 a year.[23] When he worked, Uncle Bill's earnings swelled the family income, and Aunt Ella, who was a cashier in the Loop, brought in perhaps $1,800.[24] Julia Daly managed the household money carefully but generously. There was always money to spare for Jimmy—for a ticket to a White Sox game, or a baseball bat, or boxing gloves. But for most of Jimmy's boyhood, the Farrells—his parents and their four children living with them—existed skimpily from paycheck to paycheck. His mother's compulsive donations to the Church were a constant drain on the family's domestic funds.[25]

The boy's bewilderment and anxieties were compounded because he was not at one with either family. He knew his mother loved him, but he was ashamed of her slovenly dress and housekeeping, her unkempt hair, the rag she wore around her neck to prevent wrinkles, her fighting, her coarseness and religiosity. He was proud of his father as a fighter and respected his independent nature, but he did not want his friends to know that he was a "working man"—a teamster or a scripper (a record keeper) at the Express Company. "My father was hot-tempered," Farrell recalled, "and I was afraid of him.

... Toward me, he did not show particular affection or any particular interest. There was a cold distance between my father and me, and this distance was from his end as much as it was from mine, if not even more."[26] The boy was troubled by his father's binge drinking. And the last time the two had gone out together was in 1911 to Comiskey Park to see a City Series game between the White Sox and the Cubs.

Jimmy felt a steadfast love for his grandmother Julia Daly. She fed him, pampered him, understood him, and supported him in his boy's life. He felt a milder affection and respect for his well-intentioned surrogate father, Uncle Tom Daly. Tom tried to look after Jimmy. Moreover, he was a baseball buff, and the game linked the man and the boy from the time the two played catch in Washington Park before Jimmy was in school. Tom knew some Major Leaguers. In 1916 he introduced Jimmy to Stuffy McInnis, the first baseman of the Philadelphia Athletics, and Stuffy and Farrell became friends. But Tom was often away from home. His cultural pretentions, his arbitrary and occasionally explosive discipline, and his imperious advice pressed heavily on his nephew.[27]

In the Daly apartments Jimmy and his sister Helen got along exceptionally well. She remembered that "Jimmy in his early teens was a very congenial brother, always treating me friendly and helping me with homework, teaching me to play marbles, which he was an expert at. When I visited at 5704 Indiana [before she moved in permanently] Aunt Ella would read to us—Grimm's Fairy Tales and all the Billy Whiskers books. She also took us both to the circus, movies and shopping and bought us many clothes for use. Of course he was my Grandmother's favorite. Jimmy and my Grandmother had a real good relationship."[28]

Like Jimmy's grandmother, Aunt Ella Daly mothered the boy, but it was she who kept the family in unpredictable turmoil. Ignored by the man she loved and refused to give up, she became "the center of unhappiness in the Daly family."[29] The boy was shamed and humiliated by her drunken rages directed at her brothers and mother, her screaming and cursing, her prolonged binges. In 1912 these had caused the Dalys' landlord to refuse to renew their apartment lease. In the Studs Lonigan neighborhood Jimmy's next-door friend Ralph von Borries was pressured by his mother not to play with Jimmy because of Aunt Ella's actions. For the same reason Walter Rogan, a boy from a wealthy neighborhood family, refused to let Jimmy play touch football in his large back yard. Mothers of other neighborhood boys were also concerned. Jimmy's feelings of shame and insecurity flowing from family discord intensified his need to win the respect of his gang through athletic prowess, and to win the reassuring affection of a girl.[30]

The boys Jimmy ran with after moving to Indiana Avenue in 1915 were, as Farrell noted, not a gang in the sense of being marauding delinquents but rather in the sense of the word as used in the song title "That Old Gang of Mine." He had many happy times with his bunch, playing games in the street or in Washington Park. On Halloween their pranks, their taunting of neighborhood "grouches," and their breathless escapes from "Bushwah," an irate janitor, mirrored the actions of juvenile boys all over the city. His bunch included Ralph von Borries, whose father was a plastic surgeon noted for having reshaped the face of the prizefighter Battling Nelson, and whose mother taught in the public school system; Dick Buckley, whose father was a telephone lineman and who, like Jimmy, lived with his grandmother; Billy Maurer, a year ahead of Jimmy in school; Andy Dugar, whose father was a waiter at the Hotel La Salle; Stewart Dollard, later to become a Jesuit and the Dean at Loyola University; Joe Squibbs, from a wealthy Protestant family and the cousin of Dorothy McPartlin, who later became Jimmy's dream girl; John McDonough, a smart, mild-mannered boy and a future Rhodes Scholar, who astonished Jimmy in class one day by telling him he was writing a novel; Walter Rogan, a big, surly boy who disliked Jimmy and came from a wealthy home; Jim ("Fat") Martin, sometimes the butt of the gang's jokes; and the Irish Protestant Paul O'Dea, the finest baseball player in the neighborhood. Paul and his family moved in across the hall from the Dalys in May 1916. He died in a car crash while still in his twenties.

In this bunch, as in all groups, there were cliques, rivalries, and jealousies, and the moody, serious-minded Jimmy Farrell from a suspect family had much to live down. But he won general acceptance because of the intensity with which he played, coupled with his athletic ability. Most important, perhaps, was his dominance as a fighter.[31] In his memoirs Farrell chronicled his early boyhood fights in detail, sometimes almost blow by blow. The boy's skill at boxing made up for his small size and his short reach. He always felt ready to remove his glasses and fight, if necessary. Among eight fights that he described, he recorded only one loss—to Ralph von Borries. There were epical juvenile fights under the "L" tracks, fights against bullies, and fights bareknuckled or with boxing gloves. Studs Cunningham recognized his ability and "sponsored" him by egging him on several times.[32] Jimmy, it appears, became a "designated fighter" for his gang—when trouble broke out with a rival bunch on Halloween night, or with the schoolboys across the street from St. Anselm's at the Greek Orthodox Church.[33]

In 1917 when Jimmy was in the seventh grade, Father Stanton [Father Shannon] of the Oblate Fathers in

Buffalo, New York, came to St. Anselm's to conduct his bi-annual mission. Father Stanton was well-known to Catholic congregations across the country. He was a famous, self-assured orator. Farrell takes up the story: "He paid a surprise visit to our class room. Looking toward the . . . seventh grade pupils [seventh and eighth grade boys were in the same classroom, taught by the feared "Battling Bertha"], he asked: 'Who's the best fighter in the class?'

"'Jimmy Farrell,' Billy Maurer called out.

"'Farrell, stand up,' Father Stanton said, with sudden sternness.

"I stood up, but I was very uneasy and inwardly nervous. He stared at me for a second or two, and then he said: 'Congratulations, Farrell.' That was recognition."[34]

Jimmy was less successful with the girls. His first love in the Studs Lonigan neighborhood was Helen Shannon, a ten year old in the fifth grade at St. Anselm's. Helen had long red hair flowing down her back. She was the young sister of Lucy Shannon and she lived just down the block on Indiana from Jimmy. In the summer of 1915 Jimmy and Helen, along with Roy Legarland and Marion Shearer, two Protestant friends attending Carter Public School, rode on the tailgate of the horse-drawn Ebert's Grocery wagon, driven by George, a kindly humpbacked man who was making home deliveries of grocery orders. They rode for two or three idyllic hand-holding hours, up and down the neighborhood alleys. The boys sometimes made the deliveries up the back steps of the apartment buildings. A few weeks later, Farrell recalled, "a group of the kids were all going to Washington Park. We were more or less paired off, and I was paired with her. I didn't go. Either my grandmother wouldn't let me, or else, I just didn't—out of shyness. The kids had a good time. I'd wanted to go and sit in a tree with Helen [the origin[35] of the Wooded Island tree scene with Studs and Lucy Scanlan, which never happened]." Later, egged on by Studs Cunningham, Jimmy beat up Dick Buckley, "a kind of a rival for Helen," in front of Helen's house. Farrell wrote: "I recall my having had the wish that Helen Shannon had seen me win from her parlor window."[36] Then one day at dinner Jimmy's grandmother scolded him for foolishly spending money he had earned. He sulked indoors. Helen came around to play, and a friend called through the window: "'Jim, Helen Shannon's here,' meaning outside. I, sulky, said: 'I don't care if she is.' That seemed the end of my possibility of success with Helen.'"[37] For a brief time his thoughts turned to Loretta Cunningham, Helen's friend and Studs Cunningham's younger sister. But his boyish affair with Loretta had to wait until after he graduated from St. Anselm's.

Gladys Le Barr, the girl who loved ice-skating, immediately replaced Helen in his affections. After Gladys came Dorothy McPartlin, whom Jimmy met in 1916 during a short-lived series of dancing lessons given in the basement of St. Anselm's.[38] Early in 1917 at his sister Helen's surprise party, Jimmy was elated that he and Dorothy were named partners (that is, they were to sit next to each other at the refreshment table). Farrell remembered that at his own thirteenth birthday party the following Saturday, he and Dorothy exchanged winks, and he called her into the "post office" and delivered a kiss to her cheek. But some of the neighborhood mothers complained to the nuns that kissing games had been played at Helen's and Jimmy's parties. The day after his party, Jimmy came down with a bad cold and missed two weeks of school. "When I returned to school, Sister Cyrilla told me that God had punished me by making me sick because of the two parties held in Lent. But I didn't believe her."[39] Jimmy was not invited to Dorothy's party later on. The other kids were.

In his memoirs Farrell described the neighborhood parties he attended in almost as much detail as he described his fights. The fights gave him status and respect in his boy's world. The parties—the main occasions when the boys and girls got together—did not bring him the affection he desired from a girl.[40]

For at least five years Dorothy McPartlin was the one he loved, remotely and silently. With rare and brief exceptions his social life with girls remained barren. He remembered himself as he was during his junior year at St. Cyril's High School in 1921: "Socially, I was shy, awkward, a cipher or a minus sign. At the time I was seventeen, and I had never gone out on a date with a girl. Of course, I could not dance. I did not know what to say to girls. I was utterly at a loss as to what to say to girls. I still thought that I was in love with Dorothy McPartlin, but if I saw her, which was rare, I wasn't able as much as to say 'Hello' to her." Later that year he joined the high school fraternity, the Alpha chapter of Alpha Eta Beta, hoping thereby to meet girls and acquire an easy social manner. But it did not work.[41] He remained "naive, shy and innocent . . . I was full of simple-minded yearnings for girls. I daydreamed of them almost daily. It was still Dorothy McPartlin."[42]

Jimmy, however, came to the attention of the girls at St. Anselm's in January, 1917, during a Friday afternoon spelling bee. The match pitted the fifth grade boys and girls against the sixth grade boys and girls. "All of the sixth grade boys, except myself, were spelled down in the first few rounds—all except myself. There were about fifteen girls standing and myself. The spelling match got exciting: it became dramatic. But I was not thinking of that. I was [concentrating] on the words to be spelled as

Sister Bernadette Marie, the pretty Mother Superior, pronounced the words . . . I was using my ears more than my eyes.

"I was still something of a newcomer in the school and parish. I was a little kid, curly haired, and with gold-rimmed glasses, and thick lenses. And one by one, in round after round, I spelled the word given me, correctly. Ever so often, a girl would go down. I would get her word and spell it correctly. . . . There were about five girls still standing when I finally went down. . . . Anyway, I had upheld the spelling honor of the sixth grade class."[43] Jimmy was happy when his sister Helen came home from school the next week and said the girls were talking about his good showing in the spelling bee.

On May 1, 1917, Jimmy and his sister Helen moved with the Dalys to their new, larger apartment on South Park Avenue. He now had easy access to Washington Park. There were new kids to play with—more than on Indiana Avenue, and most of them from Carter School. That spring and summer were happy times for him. In the spring Jimmy began playing hard ball in the park, with swift pitching. He put together his own boys' team, for which he pitched. One afternoon he, his brother Earl, Paul O'Dea and Studs Cunningham were asked by a group of men to fill in on their team. Jimmy played in right field and Studs at third. Baseball in the park became a daily habit. More and more for Jimmy and his friends, Washington Park was becoming "a little island of baseball comradeship" (*Baseball*, p. 80).

With Earl or his Uncle Tom, he went repeatedly to see the White Sox play. One of his many memories of the 1917 season is of Babe Ruth, then still a southpaw pitcher with the Boston Red Sox, striking out the White Sox stars Joe Jackson and Happy Felsch with the bases loaded. Two years later Jimmy saw the Babe hit a home run over the Comiskey Park right field bleachers. The great White Sox team of 1917 won the American League pennant and defeated the New York Giants in the World Series. Using money orders mailed to him by his Uncle Tom, and after setting the alarm for 4 A.M. to get a good place in the ticket line at Comiskey Park, he and Earl watched the first game from seats half way up in the bleachers. They went again to see game five. To Jimmy's satisfaction, the White Sox won both games, and he saw sparkling performances by Joe Jackson, Eddie Cicotte, Eddie Collins, Ray Schalk, Happy Felsch, and the spitballer Red Faber, who would win his third game in the series when the teams returned to New York. After the fifth game the two boys went under the grandstand to watch the White Sox players come out of the clubhouse in their street clothes. They followed Buck Weaver down 35th Street while he was being pestered by a persistent drunken fan.

Many years later in *My Baseball Diary*, Farrell spelled out what Major League baseball meant to him as a boy: "It was no mere game. It was an extension of my inner feelings and hopes. My favorite players were like my ambassadors to the world. They were doing what I was too small to do." And the poetry of baseball was a unique appeal. "The spectacle, the movements, the sounds, the crack of the bat, the swift changes from routine dullness to sudden and dramatic excitement, all of this is part of that appeal. But the drama of victory and defeat, the playing out of a boy's unformed sense of grandeur, of hope, is also bound up with this poetry of baseball" (pp. 192-93).

The summer was also memorable for Jimmy because he got Gerry, the first of his three dogs. Gerry was a female Airedale shipped to him from Boston by his Uncle Tom. She quickly became a much loved family member and an ever willing playmate in Washington Park. A severe loss came while Jimmy was watching the first World Series game: Gerry ran away through an open gate in the back yard. Fearing that God had taken Gerry from him as a punishment for his sins, Jimmy examined his conscience, went to confession, and the next day received Holy Communion at Mass, offering up his faith and repentance in the hope that Gerry would return. But Gerry was never found, in spite of the family's frantic searches and newspaper advertisements.

For Jimmy, the summer of 1917 was a time of patriotic war fever. Even before the declaration of war against Imperial Germany on Good Friday, he had read newspaper war reports with avid interest. He idolized Woodrow Wilson as the greatest president after George Washington and Abraham Lincoln. In his mind he honored American war dead as Christian martyrs. He shared the universal admiration of the "doughboys" and the "devil dogs." He thrilled to Guy Empey's *Over the Top*. Like boys all over the city, he ridiculed the Kaiser and the "Clown Prince" in ribald rhymes. He sang "Over There" and "America, Here's My Boy." He believed that the war effort was a payment on his country's debt to the Marquis de LaFayette and that the war was waged to avenge "the rape of little Belgium," to end all wars, and to make the world safe for democracy. He felt personally shamed until his Uncle Tom bought war bonds and hung the war bond sign in the window. He also read the newspaper accounts of the Russian revolution—the advent of the Kerensky government followed later in the year by the "Bolsheviki" Lenin and Trotsky. The newspapers predicted the Bolsheviks would not remain in power for long.

"The war," Jimmy remembered, "became a source of daydreams for me. . . . I would imagine myself as a soldier and as a hero who would win medals, and have my name in the history books."[44] He and his friends dug trenches in the vacant lot on the Indiana Avenue block near his former home, tossed tin can hand grenades back and forth, and went "over the top."[45] In the meantime, the war had favored both the Farrells and the Dalys financially. Uncle Tom's income went up, and so did Big Jim Farrell's. Following the government takeover of the railroads and its amalgamation of the competing express companies into the American Express Company, Mickey Hanrahan [Patsy McLaughlin], cousin to Jimmy's dad, became superintendent of the wagon department. He promoted James Francis Farrell from teamster to wagon dispatcher. His father's salary, Farrell believed, immediately jumped from something under $100 to $175 a month, and in the fall of 1918 the family was able to move to their new home, a five-room flat at 5939 Calumet Avenue near the Dalys. Earl, the oldest boy, took a job at the express company. Joe, Jack, and Mary enrolled in St. Anselm's, making a total of five Farrells taking instruction there.

Entering seventh grade in the fall, Jimmy began his worst year at St. Anselm's. His teacher was the dreaded Sister Bertha, known by all the students as "Battling" Bertha and described years later in Farrell's bitter tale "The Bride of Christ." Farrell's memoirs picture her as a religious fanatic convinced of her closeness to Christ and her rightness in all things. She was a stern and humorless disciplinarian who taught by rote and hated boys. She screamed at them, hit them, and punished them severely. So relentlessly did she torment Jimmy's friend Johnny Johnson, who was a year ahead of Jimmy in school, that he hit her back—an offense against a nun that Jimmy at the time found unimaginable even if justified. Johnny was not expelled because, Farrell believed, of his father's wealth and standing as a Catholic.

After Father Stanton visited Sister Bertha's class and recognized Jimmy as a fighter, the nun singled Jimmy out for punishment. "She kept at me, and socked me fairly often," he remembered. "'James Farrell, kneel in front of the class. The only thing you're good for is fighting,' she would sometimes say. . . . My interest in school dropped. My records likewise dropped. My general monthly average fell from over 80 to between 75 and 70. Each school morning became something that I dreaded . . . my confidence in my ability to learn much also slipped. . . . I simply didn't care about school, and thought of it as a prison."[46] By the end of the school year, he believed he would not pass into eighth grade.

That same year, on June 21, Jimmy's youngest brother, "Frankie," four year old Francis Edward Farrell [Arty O'Neill; Vincent Ryan], died of diphtheria in his mother's arms after several days' illness. Frankie's parents had been unable to get Dr. James Roach [Dr. Mike Geraghty; Dr. Ralph Jameson], the Dalys' family doctor, to make a house call. The day before, he had sent Helen Farrell, seriously ill with the same disease, from the Daly household to the Municipal Contagious Disease Hospital. He then injected Jimmy and the Daly adults with an antitoxin.

"My youngest brother Frankie," Farrell wrote, "was a beautiful, light and curly-haired boy. His charm and a beauty of young childhood and of boyhood were infectious, and we all loved Frankie. He was born in 1914. . . . I was thirteen and fourteen when Frankie began to grow on me, and became a little friend. I wasn't interested in little kids. It was Frankie's charm."[47] Jimmy last saw Frankie in March, when the Farrell family visited the Dalys, and he remembered Frankie riding horseback there on the big collie named Jim that Jimmy had found and brought home after losing Gerry. The evening of the day Frankie died, Big Jim Farrell, bitter and grieving and accompanied by his son Earl and daughter Mary, took the body in an inexpensive coffin to Calvary Cemetery in Evanston for burial in the family plot. That evening Mary Daly Farrell gave birth at home to a stillborn child.

It now became evident that the other children—Earl, Joe, John, and Mary—had also contracted the disease. Dr. Roach (sometimes spelled "Roche" by Farrell) had them taken to join Helen in the Municipal Contagious Disease Hospital for their eventual recovery. Among the children, only Jimmy escaped the disease. In one day, Mary and Jim Farrell saw two of their children dead and five others in the hospital.[48]

Jimmy's fear of going to school evaporated the first day in his eighth grade class, for in Battling Bertha's chair was a new teacher. She was Sister Magdalen [Sister Josephine], a tall, sallow, middle-aged nun, who turned out to be the best and most influential teacher James Farrell ever had. Jimmy and his classmates were won over by her kindness, her controlled firmness, and the unmistakable personal interest she took in each of them as individuals. "Sister Magdalen," he wrote, "in the eighth grade had redeemed me from being a mere tough guy, and trouble maker, to be studious, polite, loyal. She had a fine technique. She picked out the boys she thought had possibilities, and kept telling them that they were smart, loyal, mannerly, religious. Her reiteration eventually convinced them, and they strove to justify her conceptions of them. She had done that with me."[49] Jimmy's interest and self-confidence exploded. His first month's grades shot up.

Because he liked his teacher he often stayed after class to clean the blackboards, beat the chalk dust out of the erasers, and perform other simple chores. He discovered that Sister Magdalen was aware of his fear and dislike of Sister Bertha, and he was able to talk to her about those feelings. She offered him a prominent office in the snow brigade she formed—a group of older boys prepared to shovel school sidewalks after snowfalls. When the students held a bazaar in the basement, Jimmy brought a cake baked by his Aunt Ella. Sister Magdalen divined his secret wish and suggested he donate it to Dorothy McPartlin's booth. He did, but was tongue-tied in the presence of Dorothy.

In their talks together during the school year, Sister Magdalen told Jimmy his character was marked by loyalty and stick-to-it-iveness. She also said, "James Farrell, you have the germ of destructiveness in you."[50] This remark puzzled him. Her manner suggested she meant it kindly and half-way as flattery and not as criticism, but at the time he thought she had in mind his bad habits of chewing pencils and nervously squirming in his seat.

Not only could Sister Magdalen be personal when talking face to face with a boy, she was personal in her way of teaching. At St. Anselm's the students did not read the Bible but learned about it by studying a book of glorified Biblical history. Consequently, Farrell recalled, Bible characters had become "super human, extra human figures in the life of Jesus and/or in the designs of God." Sister Magdalen knew how to humanize them. "The way . . . Sister Magdalen spoke of . . . Biblical figures . . . struck us, held our attention, kept the images in our mind, and touched off streams of our own thoughts and associations." She spoke of St. Peter, for example, "as though he were or had been some one whom she had known. She also spoke of him as though he . . . could have been like me. Or to reverse the association, I got the feeling that I was someone who could . . . [be] like St. Peter."[51] She vividly explained that St. Peter's three denials of Christ, which Christ understood and forgave, were due to his fear and to his impulsive nature which led him to err—weaknesses that every boy identified with.

Sister Magdalen also had her pupils write. Jimmy turned in an exceptionally long paper on Andrew Jackson's fight against the Bank of the United States. She deplored his handwriting, but apparently liked his writing and intelligence enough to enlist him among eighth-graders who were assigned to correct and grade the homework of seventh-grade boys. At the end of the school year, to Jimmy's astonishment, she helped him win a Palmer Method diploma. She had asked all of her students to submit a carefully fashioned set of the twenty-six exercises in the Palmer Method textbook. Jimmy worked on it and turned his papers in even though he had no expectation of success. Many of his exercises, Farrell remembered, looked like "a remote foreign language. I doubt that there was a boy in class whose handwriting was poorer, more illegible, or sloppier than mine was."

But he got his diploma. "After the announcement of the winners in class, she told me why I had been successful. Sister Magdalen had sat up until late one night, cleaning up and improving the looks of my exercise papers."[52]

In eighth grade, Jimmy's aspirations were still limited to Major League stardom, acceptance by Dorothy McPartlin, and saving his soul and going to heaven. Looking back, Farrell credited Sister Magdalen with opening the door a crack to other aspirations—to moral and intellectual development and to "becoming a better, and to some degree, as well, another kind of person."[53] In class she read Catholic boys' stories, such as Father Finn's *Tom Playfair*, and she encouraged her students to read. *Tom Sawyer*, *Huckleberry Finn*, *Penrod*, *Penrod and Sam*, and Burt Standish's Frank Merriwell books were already some of Jimmy's long-standing favorites. At this time he began reading more of the books his uncles Tom and Bill brought home from their travels. Many of these were popular or sentimental novels by such authors as Lew Wallace, Maurice Thompson, Rex Beach, and William Henry Drummond.[54] He also read Kipling's *Barrack Room Ballads* and O. Henry, and Ring Lardner's *You Know Me, Al*, which ran in the *Saturday Evening Post*. Among Shakespeare's plays he particularly liked "Julius Caesar," "The Merchant of Venice," and "The Taming of the Shrew." For everyday reading, the living room tables were stacked with daily and Sunday Chicago newspapers. In them Farrell first met Finley Peter Dunne, George Ade, Ring Lardner, H. L. Mencken, and James Weber Linn. The magazines that Farrell remembered his uncles and aunt subscribing to or buying at the newsstand were *Colliers*, *Readers Digest*, *Cosmopolitan*, *Red Book*, *American Magazine*, *Popular Magazine*, *Blue Book*, *National Geographic*, *Popular Mechanics*, *Baseball Magazine*, *Nautillus* (a New Thought magazine) and *New World* (the weekly paper of the Chicago diocese). Jimmy continued going to the nearby branch of the Chicago Public Library where in 1918 he had drawn out books on German war atrocities. During these years, his reading, he later confessed, was mostly "motivated by interest and the desire for enjoyment and excitement, not by a desire to learn."[55]

During his second month in the eighth grade, Spanish influenza swept the neighborhood. While his uncles Tom and Bill were on the road, Jimmy's grandmother Julia, aunt Ella, and sister Helen all caught it. They were barely able to totter from their beds to the bathroom. Julia and Helen were hardest hit, Helen still feeling the after-effects of her diphtheria. In a darkened apartment and a gloomy, disrupted household, Jimmy found himself the sole, but inept, nurse and provider. "It was a home," he wrote, "in which there was an invisible intruder, who was full of the most evil of menaces."[56] For more than a week he worried, he prayed, and he did what he could. All three patients eventually picked up strength and were well by November.

Farrell also remembered his celebration of the False Armistice in World War I that November. Newsboys running down the street and shouting "Extra Paper!" broke the news, and Sister Magdalen dismissed the class. "We let out a shout and piled out of the classroom and the building, yelling at the top of our lungs. Outside, we milled, yelled, ran about, scrambled and wrestled . . . The war was over. . . . America had won the war. . . . Old Glory had been victorious one more time."[57] Standing on the landing at the top of the long flight of steps leading to the side entrance of St. Anselm's Church, Jimmy Farrell, showing off, jumped to the cement sidewalk below. He landed on his knees and face, and for two weeks showed scabs and bruises. When the armistice was signed on November 11, school was let out. His grandmother forbade him to go to the big celebration in the Loop. That day, with most of his friends gone, he wandered disconsolately in Washington Park and daydreamed about Dorothy McPartlin. Farrell relied on his friends' stories, newspaper accounts, and his imagination to reconstruct the Loop celebration scene in *The Young Manhood of Studs Lonigan*.

"It was very much due to the influence of Sister," Farrell wrote, "that I was more religious and more pious during my eighth grade year than I had been during any other year of my grammar school life. I went to Mass almost every morning during Lent. I received Holy Communion on the nine first Fridays of the month. Sister approved of this, and I prized her approval."[58] In a 1971 notebook, however, Farrell revealed that he had inadvertently lingered too long over a morning cup of coffee and had missed making the seventh or eighth Friday, reaching church after the eight o'clock mass was over. "I went to the parish house, or the residence of the priests. . . . Father Gilmartin was having breakfast when I was brought into the dining room of the parish house. I was perturbed. I told him what I had done, and asked him if he could give me Holy Communion, anyway. I knew that he couldn't. I do not know why I asked him this question. He told me that he could not give me Holy Communion. He was friendly and kind. He always was friendly to me, and to our family as a whole."[59]

Jimmy's religious fervor peaked in the eighth grade. "I believed everything I was told about the Catholic religion," he later wrote. "I never had any doubts about the dogma of the Roman Catholic Church, or about any of the matters that related to my religion, and to its history. I also performed my religious duties, or obligations. I never missed Mass. . . . I knew the catechism well; in consequence I was conscious of sin. . . . When I sinned, I knew it. . . . I could, without doubt or other difficulty, distinguish between what was a mortal or a venial sin." Certain that he had committed mortal sins of thought or desire, he worried lest his soul should go to Hell. "Hell," he believed, "was dark, black, pitch black, probably, except for the red of the flames from the pits of Hell. It was full of gleeful Devils, and they all had horns. The souls of the damned burned." Having heard "that those who wore the scapular of the Blessed Virgin would not die with their souls in a state of mortal sin, and with the deprivation of the last Sacrament," he wore his scapular at all times except when he bathed.

Jimmy was haunted by the fear that the confession he made when he took his first Holy Communion was tainted by mortal sin. He had been afraid to confess that he had eaten some candy his brother Earl had bought with stolen change. The mortal sin was his failure to have confessed the venial sin. He could repress the fear, but it remained "in a dark closet of my mind, and sometimes the door to this closet would fly open, and then, I would see the skeleton like a shadow of some evil substance, visible as a frightening shape in the chimerical darkness of this closet."[60] Entering the confessional at any time was difficult for him. It added another layer of shame and fear to his burden, for he knew he could not attain the state of mind of perfect contrition, which signified genuine sorrow and repentance for some of his sins.

Utterly serious about his religion and committed to trying to live up to what he believed to be its truths, Jimmy Farrell in the eighth grade foreshadowed the writer whose commitment to write the truth as he had known it was a cardinal principle of the art he embraced. The depth of his faith in Catholic teaching was a measure of the strength he eventually would summon to deny the doctrine the Church had taught him.

Holding fast to his religion, encouraged by Sister Magdalen to search his soul to see if he had a vocation, and yet desperately desiring baseball stardom and success in love, the eighth grader intermittently suffered the pangs of lonely, internal conflict. Finally Jimmy told his teacher that he believed he had a vocation. According to the man, the boy reasoned that "the risk to my immortal soul would be very great if I ignored the call . . . [and] if I were to become a priest, I would have special power. I would be able to change bread and wine into the body and blood of Jesus Christ, Our Lord. I would be able to absolve sinners from their sins. I would be able to save souls from the eternal shame, disgrace, and pains of Hell. At the same time, I would be able to help souls win eternal salvation. This was a strong appeal. It amounted to the gaining of some of the powers of God."

But his decision also meant the sacrifice of his dream to be another Ty Cobb or Eddie Collins, and to win the love of Dorothy McPartlin. "I would have to abandon my dreams. . . . The future, with my dreams abandoned, loomed as one in which sacrifices would take the place of fulfillment. The sacrifices were of the things of this world in order to do God's work for the things of the Next World. The things of this world were temporary, and of far less importance than the things of the Next World. But I did not want to give up the things of this world. . . . This prospect did not make me happy."[61] Nor did it make his uncles Tom and Bill or his aunt Ella happy. They argued strenuously against his decision. Uncle Tom vigorously pointed up the commercial advantages of being a salesman.

As for Jimmy, the boy's worldly heart won out over his otherworldly head. He continued to lead the active life of a healthy boy. As Farrell later put it, "I did a lot of praying, and I tried not to sin. But for the rest, I did and I dreamed as I had been doing."[62] His belief that he had a vocation was "more superficial than the simple and instinctive forces of growth in me" ("Sister," p. 362). At graduation time he gave in to his Uncle Tom. He would become a salesman and not a priest. The remnants of his priestly inclinations suffered a death blow during a class picnic in Jackson Park a few days after graduation. Dorothy McPartlin was not there, but he kissed Loretta Cunningham, Studs's sister, who *was* there. She was the prettiest seventh grader at St. Anselm's. "Her lips were red and sweet. That kiss was more powerful than all of the words of Sister during the entire school year. . . . One could have more kisses. Life was wonderful" ("Sister," p. 362).[63]

In many ways Jimmy's final year at St. Anselm's was the happiest and most fulfilling of his grammar school days. "I had finally conquered," he wrote. "For several years, I had been the class goof, generally tolerated because I could fight nearly everyone else in the gang. Then, Sister Magdalen came along to teach us in the final year. Under her tutelage, things changed. I was one of the leading lights of the class, smart in school, good in fighting, wrestling, baseball."[64]

He raised his grades, he recalled, to around 95. He was one of five boys selected by Sister Magdalen to take the parochial high school scholarship examinations—only one, his friend Ed Drumm, won a scholarship.[65] He played the part of Lord Heathcote in the May production of the boys' class play, a melodrama pitting a Handy Andy stage Irishman against the English nobility. Stronger, heavier, and noted as a fighter, he was one of the "big kids," proudly wearing his blue and yellow class ribbon. He stayed in shape by regularly jogging through Washington Park to Stagg Field on the university campus, and back; just as, a few years later before leaving for work in the Express Company, he would jog to the Washington Park boathouse, circle the lagoon in a rowboat, and jog back home. This year, too, he began to play basketball, practicing on a court behind the Episcopal Church on Indiana Avenue and in the Carter School gymnasium. He felt the pull of coming good times in high school. "There was a sadness in leaving grammar school, and in leaving Sister. But the possibilities of the future, the joy of growing up . . . outweighed my moments of sadness" ("Sister," p. 362).

Looking back on his boyhood, Farrell occasionally raised the question of his youthful happiness. For example, in 1967, at a time of low ebb in his adult life, he stated: "I was not a happy boy. But that does not matter. I have not lived a happy life. . . . Happiness is a matter of moments."[66] We have already seen that in 1973 Farrell rejected the notion that his life in the Studs Lonigan neighborhood had been "a lower class Hell on the order of Dante's Inferno." That same year he wrote: "There have been times in my life when I have remembered my entire boyhood as though it had been an unhappy and even a wretched one. There have been times, also, when I have remembered [it] as having been a hard boyhood, one in which I had been the victim of unjust and unfair treatment, and I have filled, to the point of swelling, with resentment. I do not think so now. As I have been writing of my boyhood in these pages, and over the past year or so, it comes back to me in a different, and in a happier light than it has in earlier years of my life."[67] Farrell recognized that the quicksands underlying memories of his boyhood could engulf the truth he sought. In his memoirs he tried to avoid oversimplifying the complexities of his past experience, which he re-examined time after time. His boyhood, in fact, reveals extremes of happiness and unhappiness, but a preponderance of day-by-day satisfying involvement with others. It also reveals a pervasive innocence and idealism and a constant and urgent need to find acceptance by others.

As a child of two family groups, Jimmy was burdened by an uncertain identity and by family turmoil. He knew what it was to be socially unacceptable because of family associations. It made him feel ashamed and "different." He was burdened by his inability to "get his girl," and by the sharp inner struggle between his religious and secular ambitions. He reacted variously to these burdens. He sought lonely isolation—but only temporarily. He daydreamed, he steamed with resentment, he planned to somehow, sometime, "show them." More important for this intense boy who harbored a still undefined sense of "destiny," he acquired new and enviable habits and skills, forged new identities, and learned how to turn negative experiences to positive account. He broadened his interests, acquired additional circles of friends, and welcomed new experience. For fundamentally, he was an active, outgoing boy looking to the future.

Speaking of some of his burdens in "Sister," he wrote: "I think I should add here that most children are not burdened with problems and inner conflicts as adults are. Boys can more easily forget their burdens than men can. There were many hours of play, of baseball, and of fun when these burdens did not lay on my mind in any conscious sense. I did not drag them with me, minute by minute through my school days and the times when I would be playing. But I came back to them" (pp. 360-61). Perhaps it is this and similar mature analytic memories of his childhood days that provide the best clues to what kind of boy Jimmy Farrell was, what his experience of the Studs Lonigan neighborhood was like, and what kind of a man he would become.

[1] Farrell worked under city desk editor George Morganstern [Bill Judson; Jack Henry], the brother of William V. Morganstern [Bobby Wallace; Thomas Holmes], the university's Director of Publicity from 1927-42. Bill Morganstern strenuously objected to some of Farrell's more frivolous items: the mustache-growing race between George Lott the tennis star and Pat Kelly, captain of the football team; or the co-eds' shapely leg contest; or his hoax about a four-legged duck found in an off-campus kosher delicatessen. At the other extreme, Farrell was sometimes given serious assignments, as when he was asked to investigate the activities of Jake Guzik, the treasurer of the Al Capone mob, following the St. Valentine's Day massacre of 1929.

[2] "Author's Note" prefacing "Studs" in *SS*, p. 348. On July 12, 1942, referring to "Studs," Farrell suggested the importance of that tale to his career thus far: "A strong reaction to the patterns of experience with which I had been familiar since my boyhood was here a starting point: it was a guiding chart (so to speak) directing me into certain avenues of the American way of life as that life is lived concretely by a great number of Americans. From this beginning I was led forward in a search for what this particular way of life meant to those who have lived it"("Why he selected STUDS," *This Is My Best*, ed. Whit Burnett [New York: Dial Press, 1942], p. 440).

[3] Letter, Farrell to Ralph Marcus, 25 Aug. 1943.

[4] Letter, W.J. Wescott to Farrell, 2 June 1930. "I had sent 'Studs' out to a number of magazines since it was completed in the spring of 1929. The *Modern Quarterly*, edited by the late V.F. Calverton (F.C. Valic), and the late Samuel Schmalhausen had advertised a short story contest. I sent 'Studs' in to this contest, and, in fact, I was hopeful that it would win the contest. It came back. And I read an announcement that no story, submitted to the contest, had been of sufficient merit to win the short story contest. It was called off by default" (Farrell in "Introduction to *Studs Lonigan*," a manuscript dated Feb. 16, 1972, renumbered pp. 12-14).

[5] Letter, Clifton Fadiman to Farrell, 4 Feb. 1931.

[6] For this purpose Pound selected "Looking 'Em Over," "The Scarecrow," "Honey, We'll Be Brave," and "Meet the Girls."

[7] "Introduction to *Studs Lonigan*," renumbered pp. 65, 68-70.

[8] This quotation and those in the following paragraph are from "Introduction to *Studs Lonigan*," renumbered pp. 32-33, 46-47, 49-50, and 51-52.

[9] "Introduction to *Studs Lonigan*," renumbered pp. 72-73.

[10] In his manuscript "The History of Studs' Death Consciousness," Farrell explained "how *Studs Lonigan* became a trilogy." "My starting point, when I began to write the work which became *Studs Lonigan*, was the death of my intended chief protagonist." After *Young Lonigan* was published, he continued, "I had a long stack of manuscript about Studs Lonigan, and this contained very much of the substance of what became the second novel of the Studs Lonigan trilogy. I had all but my ending, ... that is the scene of Studs' death. I planned to write this as the conclusion of the second volume about Studs Lonigan. I did not, then, envisage a third novel about Studs Lonigan.

"My intention had been to follow the wild New Year's Eve party scene (now the last chapter of *The Young Manhood of Studs Lonigan*) with the death dreams and death of Studs himself. However, when I had completed the party scene, I knew that *The Young Manhood of Studs Lonigan* could take no more.

"I planned the final novel of this series of novels, *Judgment Day*, to be a fantasy of the content of Studs' mind, as he lies upon his death bed"—a plan Farrell would radically revise.

[11] Farrell's statement to Branch in New York City, 10 June 1957; "Dutton. How I Wrote Studs," p. 2; "Dutton Final," p. 17; an untitled fragment on the Studs Lonigan neighborhood.

[12] "From the time I started to high school, on, I spent less time around 58th St. than I did away from it, with the boys from St. Cyril... Between 1925 and 1929 I recall having seen Studs Cunningham only twice" (Letter, Farrell to Branch, 29 Jan. 1978). During the six years following his graduation from St. Cyril High School, Farrell split his time between university studies and low level business employment. He experienced the conditions and rewards of money-making as opposed to those of acquiring a general education. His work for "the Express Company, and for Sinclair Oil and Refining Co., and then, the Standard Oil Company of Illinois [taught me], relatively speaking, about the way a big business corporation functioned, and something practically of economics and of working life" (Letter, Farrell to Branch, 14 Jan. 1976).

[13] "Dut," p. 42.

[14] Jimmy began wearing glasses at the age of nine. Joe Cody recalled that he had a habit of peering over his glasses, giving him a quizzical look. The gang would seize on this as a peculiarity (Interview, Joseph Cody, 3 Apr. 1956).

[15] Jimmy's sister Helen remembered the boy as "shy, very honest" and "smart." "He always seemed to obey my Grandmother who adored him. ... He helped me a lot especially in composition. He could write very well back then. At St. Anselm's [Helen was three years behind Jimmy] we all had to learn Irish History and when we graduated, received an Irish History Diploma. Jimmy helped me a lot when I had to write my essay on it. He was always kind to me. Taught me how to play marbles. He was an expert on marbles" (Letter, Helen Farrell Dillon to Branch, 9 Aug. 1994).

[16] "A Memoir on Sherwood Anderson," *Perspective*, 7 (Summer 1954),

pp. 83-84.

17 "I was an intense and rather lonely boy, except that I was able to cope with loneliness. I played games by myself, daydreamed, invented a whole variety of new games with cards, and golf or tennis balls, rubber balls, and tops" ("Biography, Note," received from Farrell 8 Oct. 1962).

18 "Origin of 'Helen, I Love You,'" pp. 7-9 (Department of Special Collections, University of Pennsylvania Libraries). "Autobiography," completed 19 Sept. 1972, pp. 1609-10.

19 Farrell's incomplete typescript, "A Catholic High School Education," pp. 25-26 (Department of Special Collections, University of Pennsylvania Libraries); an undated autobiographical fragment, p. 18. Farrell once explained that his use of the term "destiny" implied nothing mystical or predestined. He meant by it the full realization of one's potentialities, of one's true self. For him it signified a theology of self-realization, an ethics of self-development to be pursued at all costs and with a willingness to accept the consequences if the pursuit infringed upon others, as it did, he said, when he used his family in writing the O'Neill-O'Flaherty books. He sharply distinguished playing for high stakes in achieving one's destiny from the conscious manipulation of others for one's own ends, something to be avoided at all costs. (Interview, 16 March 1957).

20 "Autobiography," completed 30 Sept. 1974, pp. 1327-29; "Memories of the Hot-Stove League," *Saturday Review of Literature*, 32 (10 June 1950), pp. 18-19; "It's a Long Way from the Sandlots," *New York Times*, 12 Apr. 1969, p. 34. During his four years at St. Cyril High School, Farrell believed that he earned seven major "C's" in baseball, basketball, and football and, he added, not nine, as he correctly recalled was indicated in the school's annual, the *Oriflamme*, for his senior year (*St. Cyril High School Yearbook*, June 1923, p. 19). In 1976 he became a charter member of the St. Cyril-Mount Carmel Athletic Hall of Fame. Jim Farrell's last participation in organized sports was as a member of the University of Chicago freshman basketball squad. Injury to a cartilage in the right knee, previously torn in high school football games, forced his early retirement from the squad.

21 "Since I Began," begun 29 Aug. 1970, p. 564.

22 "Section II," an undated autobiographical fragment, p. 3.

23 During the Depression era, early in the 1930s, Tom and Bill Daly lost their jobs with Upham Brothers as shoe salesmen. In January 1933 Tom was selling the expensive Sister Superior line of shoes but making virtually nothing (Letter, Ella Daly to Farrell, 1 Feb. 1933). In a letter of July 11, 1933, written from Chicago, Farrell asked James Henle for twenty-five dollars for his destitute Uncle Tom, who had lost everything—job, stocks, money—and was getting evicted. "It's one of the most miserable experiences of my life, having had to see him and learn of the way he's gone down. It's really distressing. Several times already, I've had to quit in the midst of my work to bring him money to eat, and Jesus Christ it's terrible. It's a story in real life to rival Hurstwood's." Farrell noted in 1935 that his uncle made five to ten dollars a week peddling eggs (Letter, Farrell to James Henle, 14 Mar. 1935). Thereafter Tom, Bill, and Ella Daly subsisted on a very low income. Farrell helped them out as best he could.

24 Ella began work at age fifteen. She worked at one time or another as a cashier in the fashionable Alleghretti's Ice Cream Parlor, the Grand Pacific Hotel, the La Salle Hotel, and the Stevens Hotel (now the Hilton). Her sponsor and boss at the two last named hotels was the prominent Chicagoan Ernest James Stevens, president and manager of both those hotel companies.

25 Joe Cody remembered Farrell's mother as "a religious fanatic" who often went to church missions miles away (Interview, Joseph Cody, 3 April 1956).

26 "Since I Began," completed 30 Dec. 1970, pp. 1340-41, 1348-49. Joe Cody remembered Farrell's father as a very hard worker (Interview, Joseph Cody, 3 Apr. 1956). Farrell's sister Helen had great affection for him: "He was a wonderful father. Took us many places when we were little and was so proud of us. When we lived at 45th Place, Joe, Jack, Mary, sometimes Frankie & myself would go to meet him when he got off the street car. He would carry Frankie, & Mary & the other three of us all talking & kissing him would go the short block home. We would all sit on the curb and wait for the street car to bring our Papa home. No other kids did that" (Letter, Helen Farrell Dillon to Branch, 9 Aug. 1994).

27 Something of Farrell's mixed feelings about Uncle Tom and his home environment in the late 1920s is revealed in a diary passage dated March 15, 1928: "Home continues irritating and (to me) a tragedy. Uncle Tom seems in many ways a sad man, buffeted by life. He wants (I imagine) to escape these, in books. He likes to talk to me. I'll be reading or thinking and show signs of being peeved. And he cannot get away from his habit of correcting you. Mother, too, is sad. If I can ever get the home into proper words, it will be a masterpiece.... And another day. So many minutes, hours, vaulting out of nowhere into oblivion. The dullness and tragedy of life hit you and what can you do?" (Department of Special Collections, University of Pennsylvania Libraries.).

28 Helen Farrell Dillon to Branch, 7 July 1994. Early in the 1870s Julia Daly had lost an infant son named James.

29 Farrell, untitled autobiographical fragment, p. 21. In his memoirs, Farrell recorded that before the Dalys moved to Indiana Avenue, Ella, an alcoholic, became the mistress of Wirt H. Cook [Lorry Robinson], a wealthy Minnesota lumberman. Cook was a partner-owner of the Virginia & Rainy Lake Lumber Company. His testimony in 1911 before the Helm Committee of the Illinois Senate and, in 1912, before the Dillingham Committee of the U. S. Senate helped to convict William Lorimer, formerly the Republican Boss of Chicago, of buying his seat in the U. S. Senate, a position he had won in 1909. The Senate ousted Lorimer on July 13, 1912. During the hearings, in an effort to discredit Cook, supporters of Lorimer hired detectives to follow Ella. See Joel Arthur Tarr, *A Study in Boss Politics: William Lorimer of Chicago* (Urbana: University of Illinois Press, 1971), passim. For years Ella continued to pursue the elusive Cook, who had tired of her. "Slob," Farrell's 1929 tale published in *Blues*, is based on one or more of Ella's drunken sprees.

30 Likewise, Eddie Ryan's desire as a freshman at the University of Chicago to be accepted in "the world of those who were something" on campus is accentuated because he belongs to "the world of those who weren't much." He wants this "because he had been ashamed of so much, of his grandmother smoking a pipe and not being able to read or write, of his mother dressing like the scrubwoman's cousin and his father driving a horse-and-wagon and not being a businessman, and dying like a sick pauper, of his aunt's drinking and cursing, of his having had to graduate from high school without paying his senior year's tuition, of the times he had not been wanted, had been ditched by other kids, not invited to parties, turned down when he phoned girls for dates, and of all the pretending that he and his family were more than they were, and were just like those who were better off." Eddie cannot dispel this feeling, even though he recognizes the element of snobbery in it. (*The Silence of History*, pp. 130-31.)

31 He recalled: "I was anything but a sissie. I was a good fighter, boxer, wrestler, and I never saw a boy fight or box more than one or two minutes, but that I knew how I'd fight him, if I should have to do so. . . . I didn't realize it, but I hit hard. . . . I had stamina, and could box five, six, seven kids in an afternoon, after school, or fight a half hour or more, without being winded, or tired. The way I fought was me, and there was something deadly about my fighting. . . . And something deceptive" ("Biography, Note," received from Farrell, 8 Oct. 1962).

32 Studs and his friends used to hang out at Henry the Tailor's Shop just north of Levin's drugstore at 58th and Indiana Avenue. Early in 1917 Studs promoted a fight there between Jimmy and the bigger Joe Baron, Henry's delivery boy. Jimmy's uncle Bill came along and broke the fight up, but Farrell recalled that his good showing in the fight added to his reputation as a boxer. Farrell's sister Helen recalled that despite Jimmy's shyness and sometimes withdrawn nature, "He was a good fighter and in those days boys had fist fights to settle arguments and Jimmy was about the best so the older boys respected that" (Letter, Helen Farrell Dillon to Branch, 9 Aug. 1994). In Washington Park Farrell outboxed—and showed up—the older and heavier Harold ("Red") O'Keefe [Harold "Red" Kelly], giving him a bloody nose. From then on, O'Keefe's dislike of Farrell became a confirmed enmity.

33 In his letter of 3 January 1973 to William L. Lederer, Farrell noted that "You were measured for being tough around the neighborhood if you beat up a kid named Andy Dugar. Only three of us did, Paul [Caron], a kid named Bus Stern, and I." Both Caron and Lloyd ("Bus") Stern were exceptional athletes and fighters. Stern, a friend of Farrell's since their childhood, became a "tramp athlete" who attended Butler University during the 1928-29 academic year and again in the 1930 Spring semester. Farrell revised and edited Stern's novel, *Stars Road*, for James Henle. The book was published by Vanguard Press in 1932. Lederer, in his 13 January 1973 response to Farrell, wrote that his Uncle Martin Cunningham recalled that Farrell had good athletic ability and was tough, without being a bully.

Referring to this period of his life, Farrell wrote: "I guess I can say that I was tough. But not a tough guy. I didn't pick on smaller kids, but often protected them, and had a reputation beyond my immediate circle. Kids, whom I didn't know, knew about me. For awhile I had the reputation of being the kid who couldn't be hurt—I wouldn't show it. But I wasn't tested much. I took on kids bigger than I, up to fifteen or twenty pounds, and one or two of them saved me many fights" ("Biography, Note," received from Farrell 8 Oct. 1962).

34 "Autobiography," completed 2 Nov. 1972, pp. 1843-44.

35 Dorothy Farrell told Branch on 10 June 1957, that Farrell had been afraid to sit in the tree with Helen Shannon but that he had sat in a Jackson Park tree with Dorothy after their meeting in 1928. Farrell, who was present at this time, did not dispute her statement. Dorothy's implication was that her rendezvous with Farrell had inspired the Wooded Island scene with Studs and Lucy. When speaking with Branch in October 1992, Dorothy made the connection explicit. However, in his account of the origin of "Helen, I Love You," written August 9, 1955, Farrell stated: "I wanted to sit in a tree with Helen. (This is the origin of the scene describing Studs and Lucy in the tree in *Young Lonigan*.)" (Department of Special Collections, University of Pennsylvania Libraries.) Farrell repeated this claim elsewhere.

36 "Origin of 'Helen, I Love You,'" pp. 1-6. Farrell commented: "Roughly, this fight took place at the same spot as the fight between Studs and Weary in *Young Lonigan*. In 'Helen, I Love You,' I didn't have Danny fight and win. This may have been because I was at work, creating another image of myself as a boy—dividing myself into Danny, and giving a part of myself to Studs—which I was writing when I wrote 'Helen I Love You'" (pp. 6-7). (Department of Special Collections, University of Pennsylvania Libraries.)

37 Ibid., pp. 3-4.

38 Farrell's sister Helen wrote: "I remember Dorothy McPartlin. She was on the lighter side. Not exactly a blond, a real pretty girl. Quite a favorite of the nuns who taught us. . . . Jimmy had a crush on her" (Letter, Helen Farrell Dillon to Branch, 7 July 1994).

39 "Since I Began," completed 19 Sept. 1972, pp. 1621-22.

40 Farrell's semi-autobiographical character Bernard Carr, a promising young writer in 1932, prepares to join a party with his New York friends. He wants to have a good time but is still haunted by memories of boyhood parties. "He remembered Billy Tannehill's party when he'd been in seventh grade. The kids had cracked jokes, but he hadn't been able to think of one. They'd danced, but he couldn't dance. They'd played post office, but he'd been called in only now and then out of pity. Elsie Cavanagh had ignored him during the whole party" (*The Road Between*, p. 48.).

41 Farrell's story "Senior Prom" reflects his state of mind resulting from continuing "girl troubles" during his senior year in high school. Unable for weeks to get a date for the prom, Danny O'Neill feels despair "creeping through him. He believed that almost no one in his class seemed to have poorer prospects in life than he. He couldn't go to college and he had lost interest in study . . . girls just didn't want to go with him." When he does get a date for the prom with pretty Sis Hansen, she is cold and indifferent to him all evening. Trudging home down South Park Avenue, he thinks: "What was the matter with him? What was wrong with him? He looked at the sky and the shrubbery of the park across the street, and he was just hurt with a sense of defeat. His dreams of Sis and of love were dust" (*ADW*, pp. 69, 79).

42 "Since I Began," completed 30 Sept. 1974, pp. 1392-93, 1407. According to Farrell, between his Junior year (1921-22) in high school and his matriculation at the University of Chicago in 1925 he dated a variety of girls, but apparently he formed a satisfying relationship with none of them. Some of his dates were Edith Powers (his very first date, coming in June 1922), Loretta Cunningham, Natalie O'Reilley, Helen Bridges, Frances Skeffington, Ruth Jackson, Bea Harmon, Cecille Golden, Frances Golden, Geraldine Shea, Marcella McVeay, Clarisse Taylor, and Mary Kelly, his cousin ("Biography, Note," received 8 Oct. 1962 from Farrell). During his first year at the university the time spent on his studies and his job eliminated virtually all dating. After seeing Rudolph Valentino dance at the Trianon Ballroom at 62nd and Cottage Grove Avenue in Chicago, Farrell taught himself the tango and became especially proficient in that dance.

43 "Since I Began," begun 29 Aug. 1970, pp. 704-11.

44 "Since I Began," completed 2 Nov. 1972, p. 1893.

45 The account of Eddie Ryan's life in 1917-18 in *The Silence of History* (pp. 291-311) reprises numerous elements in Farrell's life during those years.

46 Ibid., pp. 1845, 1849-51, 1922.

47 From an undated, untitled autobiographical fragment, p. 42 (Department of Special Collections, University of Pennsylvania Libraries). In *No Star Is Lost*, Arty O'Neill [*Frankie Farrell*] dies in April 1915 before the Dalys move to Indiana Avenue and 57th Street.

48 Mrs. Helen Farrell Dillon provided some of the details of this tragedy.

49 "A Catholic High School Education," p. 3. Farrell's sister Helen remembered Sister Magdalen as "strict but also a kind loveable nun, and fair. You know, I think some nuns had favorites" (Letter, Helen Farrell Dillon to Branch, 9 Aug. 1994).

50 "Since I Began," completed 8 Jan. 1973, p. 2155. Farrell's story "Sister" is about Sister Magdalen. It is included in *Judith and Other Stories* (Garden City, N. Y.: Doubleday, 1973), pp. 339-63.

51 "Since I Began," completed 5 Jan. 1973, pp. 2108, 2109-10, 2111-12.

52 "Since I Began," completed 10 Feb. 1973, pp. 3078-80.

53 "Since I Began," completed 8 Jan. 1973, pp. 2154-55. The year in which this other kind of person began to emerge with some clear certainty was 1925, when Farrell matriculated at the University of Chicago. As he stated, "From 1925, on, ideas play an increasing role in my life, and much of it was concerned with the writing of others" (Letter, Farrell to Branch, 4 Sept. 1976). After he became a college student, Farrell rapidly developed his insatiable lifelong appetite for reading books covering a broad range of human thought. This sea change in Farrell's life was confirmed and more narrowly defined on March 16, 1927, the day Professor Linn published Farrell's classroom sketch, "Pie Juggling in the Loop," in his newspaper column. On that day, Farrell decided to become a writer. He stated, "I decided to quit college. . . . It was the column . . . that was the precipitant" (Letter, Farrell to Branch, 15 Aug. 1976).

54 In "The Story of *Studs Lonigan*" Farrell wrote: "The only significant [novels] I had read before my entry into the University in June 1925, were *Ivanhoe* by Sir Walter Scott, *A Tale of Two Cities* by Dickens, *Lord Jim* by Joseph Conrad, *The Adventures of Tom Sawyer* and *The Adventures of Huckleberry Finn* by Mark Twain, *The Way of All Flesh* by Samuel Butler, *You Know Me Al* by Ring Lardner, and *Casuals of the Sea* by William McFee" (p. 5, the Department of Special Collections, University of Pennsylvania Libraries).

55 "Since I Began," completed 19 Jan. 1973, p. 2626.

56 "Since I Began," completed 18 Jan. 1973, pp. 2563-64.

57 "Since I Began," completed 15 Jan. 1973, pp. 2297-98.

58 "Sister," p. 356. Farrell explained in his memoirs that "to receive Holy Communion on the nine first Fridays of nine successive months . . . was sometimes a difficult thing to do because usually confessions were not heard on Thursdays. This meant that usually when making the nine first Fridays, we had to go to confessions on a Saturday afternoon or a Saturday night and then stay in a state of grace, that is, free from mortal sins, until the next Friday" (Ibid., pp. 2388-89).

59 "Since I Began . . . New Autobiography," undated, pp. 1656-59.

60 "Since I Began," completed 11 Jan. 1971, pp. 1606-08, 1615-16; "Since I Began," completed 15 Jan. 1973, pp. 2349-50, 2355-58, 2365. Joe Cody remembered the intensity and public ardor of Jimmy's religious faith as a youth. Jimmy would hail him on the street, "asking if he wouldn't go to confession" (Interview, Joseph Cody, 3 Apr. 1956).

61 "Since I Began . . . New Autobiography," undated, pp. 1886, 1887-89; "Since I Began," completed 19 Jan. 1973, pp. 2639-41.

62 "Since I Began . . . New Autobiography," undated, p. 1892.

63 Farrell's sister Helen remembered Loretta Cunningham as a pretty and popular girl a grade or two ahead of her in St. Anselm's, a brunette of medium build and about five feet two or three inches (Letter, Helen Farrell Dillon to Branch, 7 July 1994). In his letter of 15 January 1946 to James Henle, Farrell wrote that after Helen Shannon lost interest in him, his thoughts turned to Loretta Cunningham, Helen's friend. "Loretta was smaller than she. As I knew them, Loretta grew in my mind, and I felt a liking for her. She was smaller than Helen, smaller than I, and a kid, seeming like a kid too small for a boy to love." Several years later Farrell "went to a picnic after graduation. We played kissing games. Loretta had been eating candy. I kissed her in the games. In post office, I had always kissed girls on the cheeks. She kissed me on the lips, at her initiative, and her lips seemed very sweet. It was the first time in my life that a girl had kissed me on the lips. I was very happy and very guilty, because I was going to be a priest, and I couldn't kiss girls. Later on, I took Loretta out twice. There was significance to me in this. In those days, almost no girl would go out with me a second time. . . . I wanted to go out with her more than twice, but she didn't give me dates." In his short story "Studs" Farrell wrote "I know that Studs' family, particularly his two sisters [Frances and Loretta] were appalled at his actions" (*This Quarter*, 3 [July-August-September 1930], p. 190). He recorded that he had loved Loretta "in an adolescently romantic and unsuccessful manner." As he left Studs's wake, he remembered, "I saw Loretta, Studs' sister. She was crying so pitifully that she was unable to recognize me. It must have been fun for her. She never could have been affectionate toward Studs. He was so outside of her understanding. I knew she never mentioned him, the few times I took her out. But she cried pitifully" (p. 194). When Farrell revised "Studs" for publication in *Guillotine Party and Other Stories*, he omitted Loretta's name and deleted the sardonic sentence "It must have been fun for her." In *Studs Lonigan*, Loretta marries Phil Rolfe [Louis Lederer. See Chapter Three, footnote 6].

64 "A Catholic High School Education," p. 5.

65 St. Cyril's Scholarship Entrance Examination given May 17, 1919, included four questions under "Grammar" (e.g., "What is the difference in meaning between 'I feel bad' and 'I feel badly'?"), four under "Arithmetic" (e.g. "In how many days will a dollar amount to $1.13 at 5.5%?"), and a composition on the topic "My Aeroplane Flight across the Atlantic."

66 Untitled autobiographical typescript.

67 "Autobiography," completed 17 Jan. 1973, pp. 2544-45, and "Autobiography," completed 18 Jan. 1973, p. 2546. Farrell noted that "Our memory of our past, and of our past happinesses and sorrows is variable, not invariant. . . . It depends upon remembered feelings as well as remembered events, and we often recall or bring back past times, events and experiences without regaining or restoring the quality of our feeling at the time" ("Autobiography," completed 17 Jan. 1973, pp. 2542-44).

Chapter Five: Coda—*Young Lonigan* on 58th Street

WE HAVE SEEN HOW JIM FARRELL AND STUDS LONIGAN came into being and developed in a historic Chicago neighborhood. But how did the neighborhood itself respond toward the young author and his work—to the metamorphosis of Jimmy Farrell into James T. Farrell, author, and to his portrayal of the world in which Studs, a son of 58th Street, is shown to live and move? Also, what did James Farrell's family, friends and his university associates think of what he had created?

In June 1925 when Studs Cunningham, a high school dropout and Jim Farrell's fellow Irish-Catholic believer, was still making the corner of 58th Street and Prairie Avenue a center of his existence, Farrell enrolled at the University of Chicago. He did this buoyed by the encouraging understanding of neighborhood friends Joe Cody, Paul Caron, and Takiss Georgis; repulsed by the prospect of spending his life as an expressman like his father and his brothers Earl and Joe; in response to an appetite for learning and training whetted by night school work at De Paul [St. Vincent's] University; and driven by a relentless sense of destiny. When his enrollment became known in the neighborhood, no doubt a good many who knew him either were indifferent to it or approved, silently or otherwise.[1]

James T. Farrell at Yaddo, early 1930s. (Photo Courtesy of the University of Pennsylvania Library.)

Yet, in Jim Farrell's neighborhood, there was widespread suspicion of the University of Chicago, and some hated it. Certain members of the 58th Street gang were particularly outspoken in their hostility to the university and to Jim. They labeled him goofy, too smart for his own good, radical, book-crazy, or atheistic. Harold ("Red") O'Keefe, for example, told him that he, Farrell, believed himself to be too good for the human race. Jim Barnes, Joe Cody's cousin, "was angry and a little insulting to me once or twice," Farrell wrote. "He raised his voice, in fact he almost yelled at me, asking me who the hell I thought I was, and what the hell I thought I was doing, going to the University of Chicago."[2]

Farrell understood that these attitudes arose from the background of oppression and suffering of Irish Catholics in Ireland and their feeling that the Church and its doctrine were all they had. He also understood that Catholics of limited education were probably more suspicious of what they regarded as an A. P. A. (American Protective Association) university than were their Jewish or Protestant counterparts. Farrell's friend Joe Cody, a graduate of Englewood High School [Sherman High School] and a pre-law student at the university, tried deadpan humor to dispel his family's misconceptions about the university. He would assure his Aunt Lizzie Barnes [Kate Moore Nolan; Kate Dolan; Margaret ("Maggie") Doyle], a devout Catholic who believed the institution was "rife with anti-Catholicism and atheism," that "a student at the University of Chicago was locked up in a tower . . . and held there until he admitted he was an atheist."[3]

When "the boys" learned of his decision to become a writer, Farrell wrote, "I was sometimes laughed at. In the old neighborhood around Fifty-Eighth Street, the boys thought I was even crazier than they [thought I was] . . . when I had merely been a student at the University. And one of the most repeated remarks I heard directed at me was the familiar one: 'Where will it ever get you?' . . . I was told that I would never make any money."[4] "The background from which I came was one in which many people, not understanding better, thought that if you wanted to write you must be something of a freak."[5] Several of the young men in *Studs Lonigan* continue their education beyond high school, but their intent is to excel in a conventionally acceptable and utilitarian profession.

News of the coming publication of Farrell's first book spread rapidly in the Studs Lonigan neighborhood in the late summer and fall of 1931 when Jim and Dorothy Farrell were in Paris. In an undated letter Joe Cody informed them that Wilson Gilligan, a mutual acquaintance, had told him about it and that Lloyd ("Bus") Stern, Farrell's friend since early childhood, and Farrell's brother Jack were talking it up. Bus Stern wrote to Dorothy and Jim in Paris in August 1931: "Told all the boys about 'Studs' Lonnergrin—told 'em it's a take-off on Studs. All are keen to read it." In several later letters Stern expanded his information: "All the boys are eating their heart out until that book of yours comes out." "Every guy on Fifty eighth is after it. Gillegan, the town gossip and cryer is taking up the question, 'have you heard of Farrell's book? . . . It's so good he won't come back to this country. All the guys will beat him up' . . . that's the story." "Your book will sell, Farrell, as I tell you the whole south side is waiting for it . . . I hope you make three thousand bucks or more."[6] Even Harold ("Red") O'Keefe, no friend of Jim's, was reminiscing about incidents that he felt might appear in the book.

In *The Dunne Family* Farrell imaginatively represented the feelings of the Dalys at the news. Eddie Ryan's grandmother, Grace Hogan Dunne, to whom the book was dedicated, celebrates by wearing her red blouse. Eddie's Uncle Larry and Aunt Jenny are excited at the prospect of Eddie becoming famous and rich; but Larry darkly adds that if Eddie wants to make money, he must write "what people want to read." Eddie's Uncle Dick feels that "if Eddie wanted to become a writer, that was as good as being a lawyer or an M.D.... Dick Dunne was deeply moved. He was close to tears.... He had often wished that Eddie were his own son" (pp. 110-111).

Following publication,[7] Farrell learned that Dorothy McPartlin, whom Danny O'Neill adores from afar, had asked Catherine ("Cabby") Devine [Cabby Devlin], a mutual friend, if she might borrow her copy. Jim reported to Richard Parker, a high school friend, that Frances Metevier, one of their classmates at St. Cyril's, lamented Farrell having gone astray in such fashion, for he had been such a good football player.

Again, in *The Dunne Family*, Jim projected the feelings of his family, this time after they read *Young Lonigan* [Young Jud Jennings]. All of the Dunnes are shocked by it. Uncle Larry and Aunt Jenny feel that the book brings shame and disgrace down upon Eddie and them. Uncle Dick wishes Eddie had written a different kind of book, one without vulgarity and "in the language of *belles lettres*." But he understands that Eddie "was trying to write about things the way that they were," and he maintains that "'Eddie's book is literature.' As he said it, he felt a tremendous pride in his nephew." Eddie's mother, Nora Ryan, listens to her brothers and sister discussing the book. "She was afraid that it might be a sinful book. She would have to say prayers and offer up a novena and holy candles for her son Eddie and his soul. But she was proud, too. They had had to sit up and take notice of her boy. He had shown them" (pp. 256-58).

In New York City on 26 April 1933, Farrell received a letter from his brother Jack. He wrote in his notebook: "*Young Lonigan* caused Helen Von Borries' husband to threaten murder and divorce. The goddamn fool. He must have had some gripe or suspicion on hand before this.... I realized that I was sooner or later destined to be an exile from Chicago, and felt in the mood of one exiled. If not already, it is merely a matter of one or two books and it will be, to say the least, exceedingly trying to go there."[8] Yet Farrell returned to Chicago in December, 1933. There he met his St. Cyril friend Paul ("Fat") O'Brien who told him: "'That was an awful thing you did, Jim, writing that book.'"[9]

While visiting in Chicago in March 1936, Farrell picked up more about the reaction of former friends and acquaintances to *Studs Lonigan*. He wrote to James Henle on April 1: "You know Jim what hurts in relation to *Studs*. The portraits of the people are, in so many cases, so damn accurate.... It is the accuracy of some of these portraits that makes people detest me so." Farrell's observation is borne out by William L. Lederer and by Farrell's sister, Helen Farrell Dillon. In his letter to Farrell dated 13 January 1972, Lederer, the son of Louis Lederer [Phil Rolfe] and of Loretta Cunningham Lederer, remarked that Farrell's portrayal of Phil Rolfe's gestures and one of Rolfe's statements about the desirability of not fighting when challenged reminded him of the gestures and attitude of someone he implied was his father. Mrs. Dillon, presumably having in mind Farrell's Chicago-based fiction, observed "that Jimmy had a remarkable memory and writes so true of people's characters." But his books, she added, also contain "some fiction."[10]

Farrell wrote to Henle on April 3, 1936, that "the Cunninghams are sore as all hell at me. People in general are sore, and at the same time proud. One fellow named Ed Kenny is always trying to prove that he is Kenny Kilarney in the books when he isn't. And he will always say—sore—goddamn it now I never [did] that, what the hell did he have me doing that for." Farrell further noted that Jawbones Levinsky, a minor poolroom character then working in the advertising department of the *Chicago Times*, took on "the job of telling people who everybody is in *Studs*. In fact the guessing of who is who in *Studs* is a kind of Chicago sport it seems."[11] Farrell also recorded that Joel Caron [Roger Raymond], the younger brother of Farrell's close friend Paul Caron, told him he believed Farrell had used "some of that putrid material in my books to make money, and since I had done it to make money, he felt it was justified. A comment on the moral sense of Americans. Or of the savages out here."

In 1933, Jim and Dorothy Farrell were talking in her mother's Chicago apartment with Jim's brother Jack and two university friends. Harold O'Keefe, then a bailiff carrying a gun, arrived and drunkenly challenged Farrell for insulting him by his characterization of Red Kelly in *Studs Lonigan*. Farrell and his brother took him outside and subdued him.[12] Following this episode, when Farrell visited Chicago, Felix Kolodziej, Farrell's big and loyal friend since their university days, sometimes followed him around as a self-appointed bodyguard.

In May 1957 Dorothy Farrell attended a reunion of neighborhood boys portrayed in *Studs Lonigan*. Many of them had turned out well. They pridefully called themselves "the Studs Lonigan Boys."[13] William Lederer, the nephew of William ("Studs") Cunningham and son of Loretta Cunningham Lederer, informed Farrell in a letter dated October 26, 1972, that his family was still bitter about *Studs Lonigan*, and still refused to read it, but that the trilogy spoke to his roots and moved him deeply.

Farrell's family members were proud of his success and the recognition he received following the publication of *Young Lonigan* in 1932.[14] Farrell's older brother Earl went on record that the novel "sure is a masterpiece, very understandable, as for me, all very true and it reached a definite point."[15] However, judging by Farrell's account in his unpublished novels "When Time Was Young" and "Equal to the Centuries," his two uncles had serious doubts about Eddie plugging away at the typewriter and about the subject matter and morality of his first novel. In the former manuscript, Uncle Larry aggressively discourages his nephew from entering on a career of writing. In the latter, Farrell wrote that Eddie Ryan's younger brother Steve Ryan reported to him that their Uncle Dick wished that Eddie had written a more elegant book, and that his Uncle Larry said Eddie would get nowhere writing books like that. Farrell's sister Helen remembered that "Uncle Bill said you had to wear mud boots to read it, so evidently he didn't like it."[16]

In an undated letter of about May 20, 1932, Joe Cody wrote to Jim and Dorothy Farrell that the Butlers, Dorothy's family whom he had visited, wanted *Young Lonigan* to be a success. But Mrs. Butler thought the novel itself was shocking. She worried about what her wealthy relatives would think. Dorothy's cousin, Isabel Simpson, the daughter of Dorothy's Aunt Annie Simpson and John Simpson, wrote to Farrell on May 20, 1932: "Jimmy, frankly, I don't like that kind of a story. I like a book that leaves a pleasant thought, something to think about afterwards and that leaves a little sweetness after it. 'Young Lonigan' does anything but that."

After the publication of *A World I Never Made* in 1936, Farrell suspected "it's quits between me and the family. I suspect also between me and Chicago. I shall be too much of a home town pariah then."[17] But apparently Farrell's immediate family, for the most part, learned to accept the inevitability of their serving as models for major characters in the O'Neill-O'Flaherty series and in other fiction. For them, Jimmy Farrell remained a close family member on whom they often relied for help. Yet as late as 1970 Farrell mentioned that some in his family were complaining that his books did not really give it "the way it was." With a grin he added that he was trying to avoid similar complaints about two novels then under way: the unfinished "Between Heaven and Hell" and *The Death of Nora Ryan* (1978).[18]

From Farrell's friends and professors on the University of Chicago campus—geographically so close to the Studs Lonigan neighborhood, but culturally so distant—came opinions of a different order. Professor James Weber ("Teddy") Linn, Farrell's teacher in English 210 and 211, Advanced Composition, was consistently proud of the success of such students as John Gunther, Glenway Westcott, George Dillon, Harry Barnard [Bill Hallsberg] and others. The first faculty member to read the proto-manuscript of *Young Lonigan*, he praised the published novel, even though he had strong reservations about what he considered to be Farrell's over-zealous and excessively frank realism. At the time *Young Lonigan* was published but before he had read it, Linn wrote that "Jimmy . . . was one of those here-now 'realists,' who tended to confuse fiction with organ pumping." We all know that there are garbage dumps, he said, but who wants to lie down on one? He facetiously remarked that when he read extracts from Farrell's work in the classroom, "now and then some nice young undergraduate would faint, and have to be carried out."[19] Even so, as early as 27 February 1927 his comment on Farrell's theme "Three O'Clock Fancies" read "It is impossible for me to believe that at your age either Sandburg or Ben Hecht did as good work as this. See me." "I kept assuring him," Linn wrote, "that some day he would be the nation's pride, as well as mine."[20] Later, Linn would publish his opinion that Farrell was one of two or three young American novelists most likely to achieve greatness.

Professor Robert Morss Lovett of the English Department who, like Linn, had read Farrell's 1929 manuscript, also praised the published book to campus colleagues and students. In a 1937 critical study of Farrell's writing, also published that year as the "Introduction" to Farrell's *Collected Stories*, Lovett placed Farrell "among the foremost in the group of younger writers who are taking the stage in succession to those we already think of as the old guard: Theodore Dreiser, Upton Sinclair, Sinclair Lewis, Sherwood Anderson, and Ernest Hemingway." What made Farrell an important writer, Lovett added, was "the richness of his material within sharply defined limits, the robust naturalism of his treatment, the social significance of his view of the American scene, and, it must be added, the strain of pity which humanizes while it never distorts the picture."[21] In later years the two men became increasingly friendly and together pursued several common interests.

Martin Joseph Freeman was another campus advocate. Freeman was then an instructor of English who had given Farrell a grade of "B" in English 202, Advanced English Composition, in the Summer 1928 quarter. Three years later he sent small gifts of money to the needy Farrells in Paris. Professor Harold D. Lasswell, whom Farrell knew from his course in Political Science 103, Comparative Government, taken in the spring of 1926 for a grade of "A," praised Farrell for *Young Lonigan* in a letter to the author, talked it up on campus, and tried to get the student newspaper, the *Phoenix*, to publish a review of it.[22] Frederick Schuman of the Political Science Department also championed *Young Lonigan*. Philosophy professor T. V. Smith, whom Farrell knew from his university days, read the proofs of *Young Lonigan*. In a letter to Farrell of April 9, 1932, he wrote that the novel's great truth to adolescence applied to the Texas prairies as well as to Chicago streets. In addition, he stated, "It presents shockingly the discrepancy between the intellectual triviality of adolescent thought and talk seen from the outside and the emotional substantiality of this same thought and talk seen from the inside."

Among Farrell's campus friends who thought highly of *Young Lonigan* were George Brodsky, an aspiring poet and fellow classmate in Professor Linn's English 211, and Edward Bastian [Alvin Dubrow and Bob Estrelle], who was also close to Farrell while the two were in Paris in 1931-32.[23] Perhaps Farrell's best friend at the university was Felix Kolodziej who, like Brodsky, was a classmate in Professor Linn's Advanced Composition course. Felix, Paul Caron, Mary Hunter, Vladimir Janowicz, Lloyd ("Bus") Stern, and, Farrell recalled, perhaps Ted Marvel and Jack Sullivan, had read portions of Farrell's "Young Lonigan" manuscript. They had offered their criticisms and in most instances their heartening encouragement.[24] On April 25, 1932, in a letter to Farrell, Felix wrote that the published novel was "superb." But he regretted in the published version "such subtle evasions of censorship as 'gang-shag' for the more usual 'gang-fuck,' the more obvious 'you know' for sexual intercourse etc., not forgetting the gentle reference to the phenomenon of tumescence." The book, he continued, was "unequalled as an exposition of the confusion resulting from the realism of the streets, set up against the pious puerilities of the Church and the Christian home." Ed Bastian reported to Farrell a rare negative appraisal of *Young Lonigan:* their mutual campus acquaintance John Bobbitt regarded the novel as "unfortunate."[25]

Apparently the news of Farrell's success with his first book evoked a lukewarm or highly qualified response among some of the residents of the 57th Street Hyde Park Artists' Colony. On March 20, 1932, Lloyd Stern wrote to Farrell in Paris shortly before Farrell's return to New York: "Saw Mary Hunter and Jack [Sullivan], & a few of the pinkreds over at the East 58th street school of artists—bullshit. They titter a bit at the name of Farrell, a good sign if you ask me." Ruth Jameson [Barbara Morgan; Janet Ross], the former Mrs. Vladimir Janowicz [Comrade Stanley; Stanley Gradek; Jan Varsky], an expatriate returned from Paris whom Farrell had known in the Hyde Park Artists' Colony, was a moralist of a radically different kind than Felix Kolodziej. Farrell had acted as the go-between in helping her try, with no success, to place her manuscripts: her novel with James Henle of the Vanguard Press, and her short stories with magazines. An active Communist, she was the first to voice what would become an intensified Stalinist refrain directed against Farrell's writing.

Some two weeks following the publication of *Young Lonigan*, Jameson warned Farrell that unless he joined his American comrades in the imminent Communist revolution, he would have no readers for his second book. "In your first book you describe a decaying bankrupt state of society in respect to youth (you do it better than anyone else has done it). We read your book . . . with a feeling that you had penetrated, artistically and socially, right down to the rotten roots, so to speak. But now we are going beyond that stage of rebellion and examination of things as they are, and are beginning to rebuild society as we would see it built. . . . We aren't interested in any mere examination of the old order no matter how artistic, any more. I think that if you don't go radically left, that you will be obliged to go radically right, and be a voice for the D.A.R. and the Legion. Those in betweens, those Paris people, those artists, those 'intellectuals' who felt vitally concerned with such men as Proust, and all the others, are interested in something different now. Before, we stood on the outside and scoffed, expatriated ourselves to Paris. Now we stand with the ranks of working men."[26] Farrell, an artist and an intellectual who recognized the greatness of Proust and loved his writing, and who knew at first hand what it was to be a working man and to have a father who struggled tirelessly as one, was amused and annoyed at such sterile and programmed pseudo-Marxist criticism. He already had begun developing the ideas that informed his book *A Note on Literary Criticism* (1936). He stated the crux of the matter in his 1933 notebook: "Literature if it is to mirror life is too wide in scope to submit to the constrictions of a system" (p. 36).[27] As a literary theoretician and political activist in coming decades, Farrell would remain an anti-Stalinist and an independent thinker on the political left, as well as a faithful adherent to his personal literary vision.

The hostility directed toward Farrell from some residents of his old neighborhood led him in 1935 to examine the question of the American writer's relation to his milieu. In an unpublished diary essay titled "The Writer and His Sources of Material," he disputed Albert Halper's [Henry Abelman's] contention that if the writer was to avoid being "doomed to rootlessness and creative poverty," he "must return to his people again and again for nourishment, even if he hates or despises them." To support his position, Farrell described in general terms his experience with residents of the Studs Lonigan neighborhood after the publication of *Young Lonigan*.

"The writer," Farrell wrote, "who has written of his own people is very often placed in the position that he cannot actually return to live with them, and then to find in them a source of fresh material. He has developed a sense of values, which remove him from it. And if he has written of them in terms of this sense of values, he cannot seek to explain them to his own people, because they treat him with suspicion, and the mere fact that he preaches to them a sense of different values results in their meeting it with hostility.

"This is precisely the situation in which I find myself. The last place in America where I could go and seek to explain to people a sense of values which I accept, and which they do not accept, is amongst the Chicago Irish with whom I grew up. I should, in fact, do more harm than good to the point of view I espouse, except in the case of certain individuals, and for every individual whom I could talk to with any rapport, there are from five to ten with whom I could establish no rapport. In other words, the young American writer who has written realistically of his people, his early associates, the types in the social milieu which he first knew often comes to be considered by persons in that milieu as a 'stool pigeon.'"

Those persons, Farrell continued, "are convinced that I have written about them, and that my only purposes . . . have been one, to make money by lying, and two, to 'get' them. It may not matter that many characters I have sought to establish in books are composites, or may have been completely imagined. . . . On many occasions when I have returned to Chicago, they have met me with suspicion, with condemnation, and in one case, one of them even set out to 'get' me. In some cases, there are those who are now married, and they are convinced . . . that I wrote specifically of them, and that in consequence I have told their wives things about them that their wives should never have known. There are others, whom I do not know at all, who have threatened divorces against girls on the sheer assumption that I have described these girls in earlier years.

"In other words, by utilizing certain environments, languages and the likes, by attempting to generalize that which I have experienced and imagined in Chicago, I have violated a social code, and as such I am an outcast. Thus, it is obvious that if I return to such an environment, I can obtain little in the way of material, I can enter into rapport with few people, and I can learn little."

Farrell concluded by arguing that "a writer can be cut off from . . . the milieu of his formative years, and still he need not be cut off from . . . his sense of people, his capacity for fresh receptivity and fresh assimiilation." . . . For "there is life to be assimilated, there are impressions to be received no matter where a writer happens to be, even if he happens to be alone with himself in a room, or alone with himself in a woods" or even "if he lives in New York, and was born in Chicago."[28]

Surely in this essay Jim Farrell is right about the gulf between his values and those of many persons in the Studs Lonigan neighborhood. He is right about their feelings toward him. He underplays the extent to which some of his characters—by no means all of them—are closely patterned after real persons. His belief that he is forevermore an outcast from Chicago is too pessimistic. And his implied confidence that he can creatively assimilate any environment, such as New York City or Paris, as thoroughly as he absorbed and utilized impressions of his boyhood neighborhood, is not confirmed by his later writings, excellent as they are in many respects.

Opinions about the merits of *Young Lonigan* and about its author which originated in the 58th Street and University of Chicago communities carry the special edge of familiarity with Farrell and the neighborhood he wrote about. They also simplistically foreshadow some opinions of "outside" reviewers writing from beyond the Chicago area. Some of those critics tell us that the book is no novel, that it is a case study, a photographic account masquerading as fiction, the product of a cloacal mind, and at best a writer's notebook from which Mark Twain might have created an epic of boyhood. But others tell us that *Young Lonigan* is not a social tract, not a case history, not research in the sexual psychopathology of American boys, but rather a classic of serious realistic fiction, a literary performance emphasizing the texture of the language. It is written, we are told, with an undercurrent of potential tragedy and is so true to the way boys' minds work that its title might well have been "Young Everybody." Likewise, the trilogy that *Young Lonigan* introduces has been condemned as being completely outside the Christian-Humanistic tradition, a work steeped in documentary philosophic determinism, without hope, without myth, without technique, and peopled by comic-strip characters. The trilogy's author, some say, is a *merde*-writer, a muckraker of his past, a man consumed by hatred who never had an adult experience, an uneducated, clumsy, repetitive naturalist deserving ritual slaughter.

But over the years *Studs Lonigan* has gone through innumerable editions, foreign and American. It continues to be read, discussed, taught, and republished. It has appeared on television. It has profoundly influenced a small galaxy of later writers. My personal evaluation of *Studs Lonigan* has little if anything in common with the negative opinions noted in the preceding paragraph. Rather, it approximates that of Paul Binding expressed soon after Farrell's death. Binding wrote that the trilogy "is not only among the great novels of the century, it is unsurpassed by any other."[29] It is an American classic.

[1] When Eddie Ryan was a senior in high school, "a couple of the priests had advised him and the other fellows in his class against going to the University." Even so, Eddie's enrollment there "didn't mean much to old friends, and if he saw any of his high school classmates, as he did occasionally, mostly by accident, they asked few questions about his courses and progress, and little was said of it in his family" (*The Silence of History*, pp. 51, 209). Before he lost his Catholic faith and decided to become a writer, Danny O'Neill in *My Days of Anger* (p. 185) recorded that "Everyone in the family was proud of him for working his way through school. No one at home ever called the U. an A[merican] P[rotective] A[ssociation] place." When Danny tells his family he is an atheist, they are hurt. His uncle Ned curses him and calls Danny's atheistic arguments "goddamn crap." His uncle Al sorrowfully tries to reason him out of his new belief. His grandmother laments: "Jesus, Mary, and Joseph! Me grandson runs with the tinkers and the heathens" (*My Days of Anger*, pp. 218-20).

[2] "Since I Began," completed 17 July 1975, pp. 4836-37, misnumbered for pp. 2236-37. Eddie Ryan is warned by some of the older neighborhood fellows "that he'd better be careful because if you read too many books, you might be locked up as a nut just the same as you might be given a bum's rush to the booby hatch if you pulled your pudding a lot." Hostility to Eddie grows when it becomes known that he has lost his religion and will not go to mass. It grows even more "when word got around that he was doing very well . . . This went to show what kind of a place it was over there on the Midway, and a couple of the fellows argued that they weren't honest, them professors over there, and they were giving young Ryan them fancy marks because he was an Irish Catholic boy from the Catholic schools, and you watch and see if they didn't get him away from the Church with them methods" (*The Silence of History*, pp. 51, 209).

[3] Ibid., pp. 2230 (misnumbered 2830), 2243. In Farrell's tale "All Things Are Nothing to Me" (*SS, pp. 263-76*), Joe [Joe Cody] who has lost his Catholic faith after five liberating quarters at the university, tells this tall tale to his humorless Aunt Maggie. Joe is torn between the fear of hurting his family if he reveals his atheism, which would mean "that he would be forever estranged from the world of Fifty-eighth Street," and "because he was choking with hypocrisy"—his need to cast off the lies of his old faith and live openly according to his new convictions. Joe's conflict accurately reflects Farrell's.

In *The Silence of History* (p.51) Farrell explained that "A few of the old women [of the neighborhood], and others as well, were convinced that the University was an A.P.A. institution, or, as the old women claimed, a place of the Devil."

[4] "On Being a Writer in America," Special Collections Department, University of Pennsylvania Libraries. In Farrell's novel *The Dunne Family* (1976), Eddie Ryan's Uncle Larry thought that Eddie "was never going to get anywhere" by choosing writing as a career. Eddie's Aunt Jenny "thinks Eddie will not amount to anything. A writer! Where did he get the nerve? Why, she could be a better writer than he could. She could write rings around him. He was a little snot" (p. 102). In *Lonely for the Future* (1966), Eddie's Uncle Larry "laughed at him, called the books he brought home to read 'dirty,' and laughed at the manuscripts of stories that Eddie had tried to write and left lying around the apartment" (p. 185). In *My Days of Anger*, Uncle Ned said "Cripes, I saw something he had written. Nothing but thighs, and breasts. Cripes" (p. 353).

[5] "James Weber Linn—A Memoir," *Chicago*, 5 (Oct. 1955), p. 57. In "The Call of Time" Eddie Ryan notes that to many neighborhood people a career in writing was "a sissy's work." To them "it was funny to want to become a writer," but "there was nothing funny about becoming a lawyer, a businessman, an engineer or an embezzler" (Vol. 1, p. 873; Vol. 2, p. 74).

[6] Letters, Stern to Farrell: 9 Aug. 1931; 10 Oct. 1931; undated; 13 Jan. 1932. Farrell repeatedly recorded that *Young Lonigan* sold a disappointing 533 copies. In a letter of 16 Jan. 1932 to James Henle, Farrell spelled the name Gillegan as Gilligin.

[7] Reviews in Chicago newspapers were generally favorable: Llewellyn Jones in the *Chicago Evening Post*; Fanny Butcher in the *Chicago Daily Tribune*; James Weber Linn in the *Chicago Herald and Examiner*; Vincent O'Brien in the *Chicago Times*; and Tom Mariano in the *Chicago Daily News*. Writing to Jim and Dorothy on May 20, 1932, Joe Cody reported that he had seen no "knocks" of the book in the Chicago press.

[8] Farrell's 1933 notebook titled "Notebook—Novel—Am. Ex. Company," entry dated April 26, pp. 26-28.

[9] "Since I Began," completed 12 Feb. 1973, pp. 34-35.

[10] Helen Farrell Dillon to Branch, 7 July 1994. Farrell's sister Mary seconded this judgment, according to Mrs. Dillon.

[11] Raymond Hilliard [Harry Rooney; Kemil] recalled that at this time "a kind of a favorite sport was to identify the incident or person from the novel." Hilliard was two years behind Farrell in St. Cyril High School and like Farrell played end on the football team. A 1928 graduate of Notre Dame, he began an M.A. degree in English at the University of Chicago that fall. In 1929 and 1930 when Farrell lived at 7046 Euclid Avenue, Hilliard lived across the court from him and the two often went to the campus together. He recalls Farrell at this time feverishly peddling his short stories in the face of mounting rejection slips. Hilliard became the Director of the Chicago Public Welfare Office. In 1946 he was named New York City's Commissioner of Relief. (Interview, Raymond Hilliard, 28 Dec. 1955.)

[12] Letter, Farrell to Branch, 27 July 1976. In *The Road Between* the character Pinky Cullen is loosely based on O'Keefe. Pinky tells Bernard's brother Art that "'Writing a book like that—why, it's like spitting on your mother's dead body!'" Later, in an invented scene occurring at the wake of Bernard's father, the drunken Pinky confronts Bernard, calls him a "yellow sonofabitch" who "did me an awful trick, writing about me," and unsuccessfully tries to stab Bernard with a knife (*The Road Between*, pp. 175-76, 358-59).

[13] From a conversation with Dorothy and Jim Farrell, 10 June 1957. Joe Cody also noticed that the initial resentment of some of Farrell's friends who were included in the book soon changed to a kind of pride (Interview, Joseph Cody, 3 April 1956).

[14] Referring to the lifelong emotional ties between Jim Farrell and his brothers and sisters, Helen Farrell Dillon wrote: "I think all my brothers and my sister were proud of Jimmy but they did not have the bond between them that Jimmy and I had, because of both of us being with the Dalys. We went to Church together, school together, Xmas shop-

ping, shows. He took me to parties as a young boy and always treated me with his loving kindness. I think I saw a side of Jimmy that not many people did. He was a beautiful person" (Letter to Branch, 24 Aug. 1994).

[15] Letter, Earl Farrell to Farrell, 29 April 1932.

[16] Letter, Helen Farrell Dillon to Branch, 9 Aug. 1994.

[17] Letter, Farrell to James Henle, 1 April 1936. Bernard Carr's older brother Jim Carr, in *The Road Between*, confides in his fiancée Gerry: "'I wouldn't say it to anyone else—I'm ashamed of that book. When I see the name of Carr on it . . . I feel like hanging my head. That's the honest-to-God truth, Gerry.'" Gerry "hated that brother of his, Bernard" (pp. 179-80).

[18] Interview, 19 June 1970. In *The Death of Nora Ryan*, Eddie's aunt Jenny thinking of the Danny O'Neill novels, asks her sister Nora Ryan: "Eddie was such a darling boy. Why did he write the way he did about us?" Jenny resentfully believes that Eddie was making money "by writing lies about her. . . . My God, after the way they had worshiped that boy, that he should bite them like a snake in the grass. Those lying books he wrote." Steve Ryan reflects that even though some characters and situations in Eddie's books "were based on members of the family and things that had happened, Eddie was not a newspaperman. He added lots of things. An artist had a right to do this. But it certainly made it hard for the rest of them when they tried to explain this." Resentment was mixed in with the pride Steve felt for his brother (pp. 93, 108, 241, 339). Helen Farrell Dillon remarked in a recent letter: "There are parts he has in some [of his books] that isn't how I knew it." She and her sister Mary agree that "a lot is fiction" (Letter, Helen Farrell Dillon to Branch, 9 Aug. 1994).

[19] "Linn's Line," *Chicago Daily Times*, 20 Apr. 1932 and 6 Feb. 1934.

[20] Special Collections Department, University of Pennsylvania Libraries; "Linn's Line," *Chicago Daily Times*, 6 Feb. 1934.

[21] "James T. Farrell," *English Journal*, 26 (May 1937), pp. 347, 348.

[22] Letter, Felix Kolodziej to Farrell, 25 April 1932; letter, Edward Bastian to Farrell, 14 May 1932. Lasswell was assigned to the course as the instructor, replacing a colleague at the last minute. In 1930 Farrell characterized Lasswell as "one of the most brilliant younger men on the faculty" (Farrell to Joseph Niver, 22 Mar. 1930).

[23] Writing from Paris, Bastian praised the novel's truth to boyhood in Chicago as he had known it. To his mother he repeated the observation, and urged her to have relatives read it. (Letter, Bastian to Farrell, 25 May 1932).

[24] Letter, Farrell to Branch, 28 July 1960. While Stern was writing his novel *Star's Road* (1932), Farrell advised him in a letter of February 21, 1932, not to take any advice about his book from Mary Hunter, James ("Jack") Sullivan, or any of their Chicago friends because, he said, they knew nothing about literature. "Also," he added, "don't forget that in Chicago, the minute you have success, you meet with envy and jealousy on every side."

[25] Letter, Bastian to Farrell, 26 Aug. 1932. Farrell responded: "It's all right by me. A person's task is not to convince somebody else that one is good, but to convince oneself, and that is a difficult enough job" (Letter, Farrell to Bastian, 31 Aug. 1932).

[26] Letter, Ruth Jameson to Farrell, 2 May 1932.

[27] Likewise, in a more personal vein, Farrell wrote in his 1933 diary: "I don't feel that Communism as a philosophy and as a way of life will ever have a great appeal to the educated Catholic, if the latter has been sincerely & deeply Catholic. In that case he has gone through the sometimes terrific struggle of living in the terms of a unity. Communism is likewise a unity and is truly a way of life. An emancipated catholic knows the contradictions that [come into play] once one sincerely embarks on a way of life within the terms of an enclosed and imposed unity" (pp. 94-95; the bracketed words are the author's reconstruction of a portion of a line omitted from the copy).

[28] "Notes by James T. Farrell, Volume One, 1935," pp. 513-15.

[29] "Chicago Masterpiece," *Books and Bookmen*, Sept. 1979.

Chapter Six: Afterword

JAMES FARRELL LIKED TO TELL THE STORY of the college English professor who, upon meeting him, was surprised that the author of *Studs Lonigan* said "these" and "those" and not "dese" and "dose." *Time* magazine called Farrell a "rough, tough" person.[1] Even Farrell was susceptible to the notion that he might have ended up like Studs Lonigan: his introduction to the Modern Library edition of his trilogy concludes "There but for the grace of God go I." He once wrote that Sister Magdalen had saved him from becoming a tough.

But even if Sister Magdalen had not benignly pushed him toward self-recognition, Jimmy Farrell would have become James T. Farrell. Even as a boy, his intellect was latently too vigorous, his will—masked by his shyness—too formidable, his need for approval too acute and enduring, his goals too lofty, his self-scrutiny too intense, and his perception of the worth and weaknesses of those he knew too penetrating for him to have become a second Studs. As a boy, he loved physical activity and sports—baseball, football, boxing, wrestling, running—and he always boasted of his strong upper body and shoulders. But in the mid-1920s he came to believe that the training and use of his mind, rather than athletic ability, was all-important for him, and soon afterwards he discovered his true calling.

For the remainder of his life Farrell read voraciously. He thought creatively about cultural and social issues. His anger flared against tyranny and injustice, and when his fighting instincts were aroused, he flayed "the local boys" (the Stalinists), or "the Philistines," or the censors—whomever he perceived as enemies of free human development. He was unrelenting in the pursuit of his personal literary goals. As a critic, he defined his standards and exposed what he saw as literary ineptitude (as in his review of Jack Conroy's *The Disinherited*) and the distortion of critical integrity through adherence to partisan ideology (as in his review of Granville Hicks's *The Great Tradition*).

He once remarked that his personality was "centrifugal." It was true. His ideas popped like a string of firecrackers; he was prominent in a surprising variety of literary activities and social movements; and he established personal and intellectual ties with an astonishing number of people, both famous and ordinary. But also, like the boy walking down 58th Street oblivious to everything but the baseball box scores in the evening papers, the man could be absorbed in the present moment—any moment—soaking up an immediate perception and storing it in his memory for later use, to the sometimes irritating exclusion of peripheral concerns.

Jim Farrell proved to be a complex and fascinating friend in the three decades that I knew him. He could be generous and cooperative in matters of import to both of us. He helped an extraordinary number of writers find publishers for their poems and tales and novels. He was capable of large and selfless kindnesses and sustained loyalties. Nonetheless, in his personal relationships Farrell was a man of pronounced likes and dislikes, often intuitive in kind. Having once been a sensitive boy who had suffered rejection, as a man he was proud of his success. He was determined to build on his fierce independence exactly as he alone saw fit. He spoke and wrote with thorny integrity. He took pugnacious stances —some saw him as pushy and boastful—and displayed no desire to "network" for personal gain. When his hard-won intellectual footholds were attacked, or when his writing was savaged by religious, political, and academic opponents, his old boyhood team of sensitivity and rejection reared up. Hard driven by his formidable ego, it could ride roughshod over even close relationships. Farrell would strike back when he perceived himself and his work as the victims of deliberately organized hostility which, in fact, they sometimes were. Yet he also recognized the symptoms of paranoia in his personality.

Farrell's diaries reveal that even when he was not defensive, he could make extremely harsh judgments of mere acquaintances and even of intimates. His scorn sometimes led to contempt. Occasionally, he recognized this failing and admitted his mistake. For example, on February 24, 1953, he penciled a marginal comment opposite his self-justifying analysis of a 1935 letter from Nadine ("Deene") Young, one of his many mistresses. He wrote: "My comments on this were wrong, cold and clouded by love of Hortense. I am a little ashamed." Deene's letter, in fact, had been exemplary in its feeling and phrasing.[2] In his latter years, whether he had been the victim or the victimizer, Farrell made up with many people with whom he had fallen out.

Perhaps other admirers of Jim Farrell and his art will agree with me that his seeming inability to set and observe limits was simultaneously a character strength and a character flaw that had profound implications for his writing. As we have seen, that inability was essential to what he *did* accomplish. But it also created whirlwinds he could not tame. The adverb "too" often comes to mind in thinking of his career. Was not his initial ambition when he began his university studies—to learn everything and to be everything—too great? Just as he drank too much when he drank, and smoked too much when he smoked, in his latter years did he not write too much too constantly and too hurriedly to attain the level of literary excellence that he sought in those novels which post-dated the O'Neill-O'Flaherty series? Haunted by the certainty of death's finality, acutely aware of time's swift passage, and driven to complete his envisioned "Universe of Time" series of novels, tales, and plays, the older Jim

Farrell strove mightily and, perhaps, too hastily—a criticism he always strenuously disputed.

Many memories and impressions of the man inevitably come to mind: his volcanic monologues; his persistent, aggressive controversies; his intuitive insights; the incredible range and accuracy of his memory; his probing self-analysis; and his compulsive composition, any time, anywhere. What's more, Farrell was a highly social individual. The following memories of two episodes illuminate that side of his personality and are typical of the man who made Studs Lonigan a household word.

In December 1955, some three months after Farrell's remarriage to Dorothy Butler Farrell, my wife and I were part of a New Year's Eve party bringing together Jim Farrell, Dorothy, and members of their families. We had gathered in the Chicago apartment of Mrs. Margaret Butler, Dorothy's mother, at 53rd Street and University Avenue. It was interesting to observe the novelist who had created an intricate mosaic of his family surrounded by its members who could join him.

That night Dorothy acted as hostess. With her red hair shining, she flickered among her guests. Farrell was simply Jimmy to all. He and his family were comfortable together. Like Dorothy, he moved easily about the room, but sometimes with a hesitant purposivness. His approach to others was sensitive and somewhat tentative, but clearly he was a man who knew what he thought. As he spoke, his gestures were often quick, abrupt, and decisive. When he listened, he listened intently.

Casually dressed and of medium height, Farrell at fifty-one was still obviously muscular and moderately heavy through the shoulders and chest and in his lower body. His hair, once very dark, was lined through with grey. His eyes were big behind the thick lenses of his horn-rimmed glasses, and later that night he had to use a magnifying glass to look up the telephone number of his friend Ray Schalk, the famous old-time White Sox catcher. His face was becoming lined. The night before, he had not gone to bed until 6 A.M., following long talks with relatives and rounds of whiskey in Mrs. Butler's kitchen. Up shortly after noon, he had spent most of the afternoon writing, filling the blank pages of school composition notebooks. That evening he showed off his work. One notebook held a novel in progress, another a short story or two, a third a literary essay, and a fourth the sly ruminations of his alter-ego Jonathan Titulescu Fogarty.

When asked about his current writing, he took center stage and dramatically brought three of his tales to life—one baseball story and two of his "foreign" tales, especially the story of a deteriorating marriage as told in "It's Cold in the Alps." He spoke with pride of the large number of his tales with European settings. He explained his work as chairman of the American Committee for Cultural Freedom. He had been elected to that office just one year before. And recently at the meeting of the international organization in Nice, he had delivered $10,000 collected in America for the relief of writers and artists who were refugees from despotic regimes. While Farrell held forth, Dorothy sat listening. She smoothed her green taffeta party dress over her knees with her hands, like a little girl at a party.

That evening Farrell's close bonds with his brother Earl, Earl's wife Loretta [Molly Ryan], and their son Bill [Andrew Ryan], and with his sister Helen Farrell Dillon, were evident, as was his easy-going companionship with Matt Dillon [Jack Boyle], Helen's husband—a blunt, articulate worker in a locomotive factory. Matt was an aggressive union man like Farrell's father, and an outspoken supporter of Walter Reuther of the C.I.O. Farrell obviously was on good terms too with Helen's son Jimmy Dillon [Eddie Boyle], an expert young bowler, and with Dorothy's younger sister, Virginia [Caroline Brown; Alice Healy], whom he had known for over twenty-five years; but to Virginia's lawyer husband, Robert Livingston [Leonard Tannenberger], he showed a marked coolness. Sometimes Farrell's attention turned to Mrs. Butler and her companion Timmins [Merkle],[3] both of whom often lingered in the kitchen laughing and talking. These two aged Irish ladies retained their effusive manner, and, Farrell noted with a childlike wonder, had lost their sense of time.

Farrell's constant, protective concern for fifteen year old Kevin [Tommy Ryan], his and Hortense Alden Farrell's [Phyllis Ryan's] son, was noticeable. In a room filled with the babble of voices stimulated by rounds of drinks, with Jimmy Dillon's occasional piano playing, and with women's laughter coming from the kitchen, Kevin and his two cousins amused themselves by pitching pennies and playing poker and chess. Farrell joined in those games when not moving restlessly from one person to another, chain smoking and talking. Once he insisted that Kevin abandon poker to watch a television program on the Bolshevik revolution. When Kevin left the apartment to run an errand on unfamiliar Chicago streets, his father anxiously scribbled Mrs. Butler's address on a scrap of paper for Kevin to carry with him.

As everyone watched the coming of 1956 in Times Square on T.V., there was a final round of drinks, boisterous kissing of the women at the stroke of midnight, and then the calling up of absent relatives. Farrell talked at length on the telephone with his sister Mary [Catherine O'Neill; Frances Ryan] and his brothers Joe [Dennis O'Neill; Leo and Luke Ryan] and Jack [Robert ("Bob") O'Neill; Steve Ryan].

The reality of Jim Farrell's closeness to his family

was not unique to a New Year's gathering. As a guest in my house a few years later, he drank himself into a melancholy mood and, around 2 A.M., poured out his loneliness to brother Earl over the telephone. Still later, at an American Studies convention in East Lansing where he was a featured speaker, he rushed off, fearful and distracted, upon learning that his brother Joe and Joe's wife, Rose [Florence Ryan], had been injured in a highway accident.

Whatever shortcomings Farrell's family may have found in him, or he in them, it was evident that his caring involvement with his brothers and sisters and their families was deeply grounded. It was apparent why he never wanted to forget where he came from.

On Farrell's fifty-fourth birthday my wife and I gave him a baseball that he came to treasure. It was signed by Walter ("Smokey") Alston, the manager of the Brooklyn Dodgers. The story behind that gift begins in the summer of 1957 when I spent an evening with Jim and Dorothy Farrell in their apartment, a block or two from the Hudson River and just off Broadway. It was the night Farrell proclaimed he was swearing off hard liquor. A call came from Phil Locke, the editor of the *Dayton Daily News*. He and Jim had met in my home in 1956. The two men liked each other, and Farrell had written a Fogarty piece for him on my kitchen table. Like Jim, Phil was a passionate baseball fan. He boasted that he "collected" ball parks. Visiting New York, Phil had called to invite Jim to see the Dodgers play the Cubs next evening in Jersey City. When Jim put me on the phone, Phil invited me too.

The next evening, after a delicious dinner prepared by Dorothy, we three took a cab to the Holland tube and then a long bus ride to Roosevelt Stadium. Jim had traveled with the Dodgers during their spring training season. He knew the Dodger players, the coaches, and "Smokey" Alston, the manager. As it happened, Alston lived just outside my home town, Oxford, Ohio, and his was a familiar face in town.

A couple of days later I wrote home to my wife, Mary Jo: "We got to the ball park forty-five minutes before game time. Jim first routed out his friend the Dodgers' Publicity Director, introduced Phil and me, and talked vigorously with him for ten minutes about Dodger prospects and home office management. Then with Phil and me in tow, he stormed down through the grandstand and boxes. He vaulted over the gate leading onto the playing field, where the Cubs were warming up. A startled usher standing nearby blurted out that the gate was unlocked. Eager but a bit dazed, Phil and I followed through the gate, trailing him into the Dodger dugout. There sat Smokey and a line of players. I shook hands with Smokey, met many players, and recognized others, like Sal Maglie, while Jim enthusiastically made the rounds.

"After about fifteen minutes of this, we three big shots returned to the stands. Jim insisted that we go up to the press box on the roof, so we went up by elevator. There Jim spoke with two or three reporter-friends, and we enjoyed a great view of the field below. On the way down, we stopped for a beer, then went to our box.

"It was Bayonne night at the Jersey City stadium. The Bayonne mayor, the high school principal, and the beauty queen were being presented on the field, while the crowd laughed, applauded, and jeered. Jim soon discovered that the two other persons in our box were Bayonne city fathers, Council members who worked with the mayor. All through the game, which ended about 10:20, Jim was a fountain of baseball lore and wisdom oddly intermixed with political advice directed toward those two guys, who loved it and came alive. Within minutes, we were all drinking beer, Phil paying the tab, and paying it again and again and again until he whispered apologetically to me near game's end that he was almost out of cash and had only traveler's checks left. After the last out we bid fond farewell to our Bayonne friends, Jim throwing his arms around each of them and exchanging addresses with them.

"And the game? Well, the Dodgers blanked the Cubs in a five-hitter thrown by their new 20-year old pitching star Don Drysdale, a big fellow who fanned nine Cubs. Ernie Banks was the only Cub who hit him solidly. Duke Snider with a triple and Gil Hodges with three hits took care of the Cubs. That afternoon Phil had watched the Milwaukee Braves beat the Giants 9 to 8 at the Polo Grounds in a very different kind of game. It had nine homers, including two by Red Schoendienst and one each by Willie Mays and Hank Aaron. Jim had lots to say about all those guys.

"A little unsteady on his feet, Jim informed Phil and me that we would now meet the entire Dodger team in its locker room. After ten crazy minutes of looking for it, we saw about twenty men lined up in a long hallway outside the locker room door. Jim, with Phil and me in tow, barged past them, but halted momentarily near the door as big Don Newcombe, splendidly dressed and combed, burst out. Jim shook his hand, introduced us, then went through the door as someone said "Hey, you can't go in there." Jim didn't even hear it. Phil and I looked helplessly at each other, then Phil said: "Let's go, we'll never have another chance," and we lunged through, right into the middle of the entire team, all of them naked or half dressed, and all feeling very good. Jim took us in hand and told each player we met who Phil Locke was and who I was. He talked about their spring training trip, the Dodgers' chances, and old-timers.

He renewed his energy by tapping the supply of beer set out for the players. During all this, I was impressed by how cordial the men were, not only to Jim but to Phil and me. It was a real pleasure to talk with Duke Snider and Gil Hodges, both of them intelligent, friendly guys.

"We were in the locker room about 45 minutes, and Jim exulted in every second of it. When Phil and I finally got him out, everybody but two janitors had left. Outside the ballpark there was no bus, no cab, no person. We walked until we came to a bar. Inside I ordered three beers and Jim proclaimed our predicament. A young fellow down the bar, 19 or 20, in a T-shirt and tough looking enough for Charley Bathcellar's poolroom, offered to run us downtown in his car where we could catch a ride back to Manhattan. We piled into his car, he roared off, and a car full of teen-agers immediately followed and tried to pass him. Our driver shook his fist at them and crowded their car over to the roadside to a standstill. Phil and I were ready to jump out and run, but Jim just lay back unconcerned in the rear seat.

"Our driver told off the teen-agers, started out again, and the other car meekly turned off the boulevard. This kid, we then learned, was a reformed delinquent and drag-racer who had often been picked up by the police. Once, he said, they had plastered his back with scotch tape so that the marks of the rubber hose they beat him with would not show. But now he was a Mounted Volunteer, part of an un-uniformed adjunct to the police department. His special task was to patrol that stretch of highway for speeders and drag-racers.

"Jim, wide awake and fired up once more, began talking about delinquency and gave this kid all sorts of advice. Jim asked permission to quote him on the scotch tape business for an article on delinquency he was writing. When we got to the subway station, we could hardly tear Jim away from his new young friend. Excited, he wanted more beer. We went into a bar and before we left I ordered two rounds.

"Jim became depressed. He began talking about bad experiences from his past and sobbed out that he was in danger of becoming disillusioned with the people, the country, with democracy itself. Phil told him he must not feel that way. Once we were back on the street, the light from a hot dog joint reminded us that we were hungry, so we had two rounds of dogs and coffee. Jim's knee had become painful—a few days ago he had tripped on a rug in his apartment. Phil and I decided we should take a cab, not the subway, all the way back. Luckily, one was outside. The driver would not accept Phil's traveler's check, but he was willing to take the sum of money in my wallet.

"On the ride back, Phil asked Jim for his impressions gathered from his recent Middle East trip. For the remainder of the trip Jim discoursed vehemently on the accomplishments of the state of Israel in the face of dangerous, uninformed hostility from Arab factions, all of whom he vigorously denounced. Most unsettling to him was what he considered to be the stupid leniency of U. S. policy makers—including his friend Hubert Humphrey—toward the Arabs, who he believed respected only force. Jim spoke with extreme feeling. As I listened, I watched with interest the cabbie's changing expression while he took it all in.

"We went up with Jim to his apartment, where Dorothy, obviously worried and in her dressing gown, met us at the door. Jim wanted us to come in and eat and drink. We said "Thank you, another time," and fled down the hall. Phil and I went back to our hotels by subway, stopping at the shuttle station for coffee and doughnuts. I fell into bed, broke but happy, at 3:45 a.m. It was a heluva good ball game.

"Consider this, Mary Jo. If Phil and I had gone by ourselves to the game, we would have had none of these experiences. We would have met none of these persons. Something in Jim makes things happen. Something in him opens up to people, draws them out toward himself with a magical force that can become engulfing, overwhelming. Do you see Danny O'Neill in this? Studs could not make happen what he really wanted, and he lacked the force and the magic to break out of his constricted world. But not so the character Danny-Bernard. He could shape events, and he kept expanding his human contacts."

[1] Vol. 67 (23 Jan 1956), p. 37.

[2] "Notes by James T. Farrell, Volume One, 1935," pp. 417-18.

[3] Beatrice Timmins (always called "Timmins" by the Butlers) came to the Butler household as a live-in servant in 1910 shortly after Dorothy's birth. An Ohio born Irish girl, she had settled in Chicago during the 1893 Columbian Exposition. She became like a second mother to Dorothy and her younger sister Virginia, and a close companion to Mrs. Butler. After Mr. Butler's death in January 1925, she refused to take more pay for her many services but continued to live, as a family member, with Mrs. Butler and her two daughters. In 1955 she was in her late eighties. She died not long before Mrs. Butler's death in 1959 (Interview, Dorothy Butler, 2 Nov. 1994).

Abbreviations

ADW	*A Dangerous Woman and Other Stories.* N. Y.: Vanguard, 1957.	*Lonely*	*Lonely for the Future.* N. Y.: Doubleday, 1966.
Anger	*My Days of Anger.* N. Y.: Vanguard, 1943.	*$1,000*	*$1,000 a Week and Other Stories.* N. Y.: Vanguard, 1942.
Baseball	*My Baseball Diary.* N. Y.: A. S. Barnes, 1957.	*OSS*	*An Omnibus of Short Stories.* N.Y.: Vanguard, 1957.
"Call"	"The Call of Time." Uncompleted and unrevised typescript of a novel.	*RAF*	*Reflections at Fifty and Other Essays.* N. Y.: Vanguard, 1954.
CGP	*Can All This Grandeur Perish? and Other Stories.* N. Y.: Vanguard, 1937.	*Side*	*Side Street and Other Stories.* N. Y.: Paperback Library, 1961.
CS	*Calico Shoes and Other Stories.* N. Y.: Vanguard, 1934.	*Silence*	*The Silence of History.* Garden City, N. Y.: Doubleday, 1963.
"Distance"	"The Distance of Sadness." Uncompleted and unrevised typescript of a novel.	*SL*	*Studs Lonigan.* N. Y.: Random House, Modern Library ed., 1938.
"Dut"	A fragment of Farrell's typescript of his abandoned book on Studs Lonigan intended for Dutton Publishers.	*SS*	*The Short Stories of James T. Farrell.* N. Y.: Vanguard, 1937.
		TWIMC	*To Whom It May Concern and Other Stories.* N. Y.: Vanguard, 1944.
F&S	*Father and Son.* N. Y.: Vanguard, 1940.	*Vicious*	*French Girls Are Vicious and Other Stories.* N. Y.: Vanguard, 1955.
GP	*Guillotine Party and Other Stories.* N. Y.: Vanguard, 1935.	"Young"	"When Time Was Young." Uncompleted and unrevised typescript of a novel.
No Star	*No Star Is Lost.* N. Y.: Vanguard, 1938.	*YL*	*Young Lonigan: A Boyhood in Chicago Streets.* N. Y.:Vanguard, 1932.
JD	*Judgment Day.* N. Y.: Vanguard, 1935.	*YMSL*	*The Young Manhood of Studs Lonigan.* N. Y.: Vanguard, 1934.
Judith	*Judith and Other Stories.* Garden City, N. Y.: Doubleday, 1973.		

Appendix A: The Farrell and Daly Families

THE FARRELL FAMILY

PATERNAL GRANDPARENTS OF JAMES T. FARRELL:

James Farrell (dates undetermined)
[James O'Neill; James Ryan]

Honora Kelly Farrell (1840-4/12/1872)

Married April 1870

PARENTS OF JAMES T. FARRELL:

James Francis Farrell (3/21/1871-11/24/1923)
[James O'Neill; John "Jack" Ryan]
(Only surviving child of James and Honora Kelly Farrell)

Mary Daly Farrell (9/22/1874-1/9/1946)
[Elizabeth "Lizz" O'Neill; Nora Dunne Ryan]

Married 19 April 1899

JAMES T. FARRELL AND SIBLINGS:

William Earl Farrell (3/27/1901-11/24/1980)
[William "Bill" O'Neill; John "Jack" Ryan]

James Thomas Farrell (2/27/1904-8/22/1979)
[Daniel "Danny" O'Neill; Edward Arthur "Eddie" Ryan]

(Married **Dorothy Patricia Butler** 4/13/31 and 9/10/55. Married **Hortense Alden** 1/12/41.)

Helen Honora Farrell (6/16/1906-1/19/1995)
[Little Margaret O'Neill; Clara Ryan]

Joseph Edward Farrell (6/25/1908-8/12/1986)
[Dennis O'Neill; Leo Ryan; Luke Ryan]

John Anthony Farrell (6/10/1910-10/7/1984)
[Robert "Bob" O'Neill; Steven "Steve" Ryan]

Mary Elizabeth Farrell (8/27/1911-)
[Catherine O'Neill; Frances Ryan]

Francis Edward Farrell (5/23/1914-6/21/1918)
[Arthur "Arty" O'Neill; Vincent Ryan]

(Mary Daly Farrell had fifteen pregnancies and eight stillborn children, including one set of twins and a son delivered in 1918 whose name would have been Edward.)

CHILDREN OF JAMES T. FARRELL:

Sean Thomas Butler Farrell (12/9/31-12/13/31)
(Son of James T. Farrell and Dorothy Butler Farrell)

Kevin James Farrell (10/3/40-)
(Son of James T. Farrell and Hortense Alden Farrell)

John Steven Farrell (9/21/47-)
(Son of James T. Farrell and Hortense Alden Farrell)

THE DALY FAMILY

MATERNAL GRANDPARENTS OF JAMES T. FARRELL:

John Daly (1840-12/1910)
[Tom O'Flaherty; Joseph Dunne]

Julia Brown Daly (7/1845-10/2/1931)
[Mary Fox O'Flaherty; Grace Hogan Dunne]

Married before 1869

MATERNAL GRANDPARENTS' CHILDREN:

James Daly (3/6/1868-9/12/1869)
[John O'Flaherty]

John Emanual Daly (12/7/1869-6/1870)

Thomas Richard Daly (8/26/1871-8/4/1961)
[Al O'Flaherty; Richard Dunne]

Mary Rose Daly (9/22/1874-1/9/1946)
[Elizabeth ("Lizz") O'Neill; Nora Dunne Ryan]

Julia Bridget Daly (12/22/1876-12/13/1879)

William John Daly (2/9/1879-12/8/1941]
[Ned O'Flaherty; Larry Dunne]

Margaret Ann Daly (12/1881-5/10/1882)

Ellen Julia ("Ella") Daly (6/10/1883-4/9/1959)
[Margaret "Peg" O'Flaherty; Jenny Dunne]

Elizabeth ("Bessie") Daly (3/13/1886-5/16/1911)
[Louise O'Flaherty]

Appendix B: Two Farrell Letters

In 1930 Farrell had sent many short story manuscripts and excerpts from what would become **Young Lonigan** *to Samuel Putnam, then the associate editor of Edward Titus's* **This Quarter***. Putnam published the tale "Studs" in* **This Quarter***. Soon after, he left Titus's employ to establish his own magazine, the* **New Review***, leaving Farrell's other manuscripts in Titus's hands. He suggested to Farrell the possibility of publishing a volume of his work. Farrell responded by briefly characterizing his "kid novel," soon to be sent to Clifton Fadiman at Simon and Schuster. Kroch's large Chicago bookstore was on Michigan Avenue.*

Jan. 31, 1931
Chicago, Ill.
2023 E. 72nd St.

Dear Mr. Putnam:

Thanks for the acknowledgment. I received by the same mail, twenty dollars from Mr. Titus for the story. There was evidently some confusion as to whether or not it had ever been printed. I am getting the mss back. The reason for this, instead of sending them to you from T. Q. is that I have thought of a number of revisions which I should like to try, and want to reread them all before resubmitting them for publication. I think this would be better. I'll send what is likely back to you as swiftly as I can, and in the meantime I'll probably have other material.

Rel to a volume; I'd be very pleased to have you bring one out for me, but it would probably be highly impractical, and I wouldn't want you to stand any losses for me. I have finished a novel. It's forty thousand words, and deals with kids after the manner of those fragments you saw. Originally, I planned to have it six hundred type-written pages. But then I decided that that style would not carry so long a volume without repetitiveness, so I made it a kid novel, and if I can get it printed, I'll do a sequel three or four years hence when I could come back to it fresh. Anyway, I'm sending it to Simon and Schuster who showed a mild interest in my work two years ago.

Have you communicated with Kroch's yet about your N. R. The kid running the magazines there is trying to push experimental magazines, and has a window display. He says there is an increasing interest in them. If you send me a few contents pages, I'll send them around where there might be a little publicity gotten. Unfortunately I lost the last one.

Thanks again, for your friendliness,
Very sincerely yours,
J. T. Farrell

When Farrell wrote the following letter, he suspected that Dorothy was pregnant, as she soon proved to be. Virtually without funds, he was getting no encouragement from American publishers for work he was submitting. The letter reveals the status of the "Young Lonigan" manuscript early in 1931 and Farrell's assessment of his novel. It also suggests the important role he assigned to the milieu—the Studs Lonigan neighborhood—while creating his novel. Harold Salemson was the editor of the Paris little magazine **Tambour** *in 1930 when it published Farrell's "In the Park" and "My Friend the Doctor." Putnam forwarded Farrell's letter to Ezra Pound, his associate on the* **New Review***, after pencilling at the top of page 1: "Dear Ezra, For your amusement & edification. Please return."*

2023 E. 72nd St.
Chicago, Ill.
Feb. 10, 1931

Dear Mr. Putnam:

In my last letter to you, I mentioned a novel which I had finished, and which was on the order of those fragments you'd seen a year ago. I'm thinking of sending it to Covici Friede. If a letter of yours would be of any assistance to me there, would you kindly send one. At present the novel is at Simon & Schuster, but I'm pretty sure of having it rejected because I just received a letter to the effect that it was over-emphasized, crudely written, that the irony was over-stressed (I didn't know it had any irony) and that while the material was genuine, I went at it with both hands. From this I naturally conclude that it won't be taken. I don't think the criticisms are at all true. S & S might suggest a re-writing but I doubt it, and I doubt if I could afford to go through this process, unless I was advanced something. Thus I expect to have the book back in about two weeks. I'll hold it a week and then mail it to Covici Friede, and by that time they'll have had your letter if you think it advisable to send it.

I've taken the liberty to ask you to do this for me, because I'm in a tough spot, and have my back pretty much up against the wall. If something doesn't break for me soon I'll probably have to let all my writing go hang. Also the book is more or less unconventional, and I know enough to know that the publisher's racket doesn't open its arms to such work. The book itself is around forty to forty-five thousand words, and I think it is pretty tightly put together, though it has no plot. It represents the life of kids in middle class Chicago, with implied criticism and representation of the institutions supposedly directing the kids' lives. It's style and manner is that of those fragments you saw, although I had to eliminate the playground scene which you liked best. The other two which you saw, the boy and girl in the park, and dribbling the soccer ball are kept, rewritten several times. The crudity of the writing is, if anything, the crudity of the material. It is a piece that will probably bump right square into most people's prejudices, and that's another reason I've requested your letter. I planned to try Coward McCann and Jonathan Cape Smith, if Covici's turns it down, though it stands a fair chance (I imagine) there inasmuch as it's new Chicago stuff, and they don't seem to be afraid of printing books that might have a few strong or supposedly obscene words in it.

If you do write them a letter, could you leave room open so that I might be free in case S & S do the totally unexpected and offer something on it. Say something to the effect that I am contemplating sending it there.

I know that my asking this is a taking of liberties, but I don't see much chance of getting the book accepted unless it is through influence. I've got no faith in the publishing business, and its conception of literature. It seems only accidentally connected with literature.

I am working on more stories to send you, and might have one long one in the mail this week. Also, I received several friendly letters from Harold Salemson who is in New Mexico doing translations, etc.

Thanking you, I am

Very gratefully yours,

James T. Farrell

(Letters published with permission of the Princeton University Library.)

Bibliographic Note

PAGE CITATIONS to the three novels of the *Studs Lonigan* trilogy refer to the 1938 Modern Library edition, perhaps still the most widely available printing of this work. Whenever possible, citations to other of Farrell's published books are to the first edition.

"Since I Began" is the title Farrell selected for his autobiography. He wrote it longhand in spiral notebooks, and made at least four different starts from the mid-1960s until the time of his death. The notebooks most useful for the present work cover Farrell's life from 1915 to April 1931 when he and Dorothy Farrell went to Paris. With stenographic help at home, he made typed copies—sometimes only partially completed—of the notebooks. The notebooks and their typescripts are deposited in the Farrell archives in the Special Collections Department of the University of Pennsylvania Libraries. The citations from "Since I Began" in this book are nearly always to the holograph notebooks. Their page numbering is frequently erratic.

In addition to the "Since I Began" notebooks there are literally hundreds of Farrell's relatively brief autobiographical papers that deal directly with his own experiences and his family. These may be found in the Pennsylvania archives and other locations. An unfinished work on *Studs Lonigan*, intended for Dutton Publishers, is often quoted in this book. Other projects ongoing at his death and useful to Farrell's biographers are a series of biographical sketches of his well known friends and a series of papers explaining the origin, background, and meaning (as he saw it) of his short stories and novels. Thousands of letters by Farrell and replies by his correspondents are deposited in his Pennsylvania archives. Copies of many of these as well as many of his holograph and ribbon copy letters may be found in other collections as well.

A number of unrevised typescripts of Farrell's unpublished and uncompleted novels were useful in writing this study; in particular: "The Call of Time," "When Time Was Young," "The Distance of Sadness," "Innocents in Paris," "Paris Was Another Time," and "After Eddie and Marion Went Away."

Index

Page numbers in boldface indicate photographs. Italicized names in brackets denote names of real life persons, institutions or places. Bracketed names in plain face denote fictional names. All entries are for the main text only.

Abelman, Henry [*Albert Halper*], 84
Administration building, Washington Park, **54**
Allen, Norman [*Albert Dunham*], 32
Alston, Walter ("Smokey"), Brooklyn Dodgers manager, 90
American Committee for Cultural Freedom, 89
American Express Company, and Farrell's father, 53, 69, 73
American Protective Association (A.P.A.), 39, 81
Anderson, Margaret, 32
Apartment building, the Lonigans', Wabash Avenue, **11**
    Michigan Avenue, **22**
    Red O'Connell's, **18**
Art Colony, Hyde Park, **32**, 33, 84
    Jackson Park, 32

Barnard, Harry [William ("Bill") Hallsberg], 83
Barnes, Elizabeth ("Lizzie") [Kate Moore Nolan; Kate Dolan; Margaret ("Maggie") Doyle], 81
Barnes, Jim [Gerry Nolan, Jim Dolan, Jim Doyle], 81
Barnes, Tommy [Tommy Doyle], 21
Baseball game, Washington Park, **23**
Bastian, Edward [Alvin Dubrow; Bob Estrelle], 84
Batcheler, Charley [Charley Bathcellar; Bert Calkins], 11, 26, 27, 50, 91
Bathcellar, Charley [Charley Batcheler], 11, 26, 27, 50, 91
Berger, Leo [*James Henle*], 33
Bergman, Dr. Adam [*Dr. Ben Lewis Reitman*], 55
Billiard Parlor and Barber Shop, Bathcellar's, **26**
Binding, Paul, and evaluation of *Studs Lonigan*, 85-86
Boathouse, Washington Park, **24**, **25**, 54, 76
Bobbitt, John, and appraisal of *Young Lonigan*, 84
Bodenheim, Maxwell [*Benjamin Mandlebaum*], 32, 33
Borax, Helen [Helen von Borries], 12
Borax, Ralph [Ralph von Borries], 12, 19
Boston Red Sox Baseball Team, 69
Boyle, Bishop [Bishop Burke], 55
Boyle, Clara Ryan [Helen Farrell Dillon], 89
Boyle, Eddie [James ("Jimmy") Dillon], 89
Boyle, Jack [Matthew ("Matt") Dillon], 89
Brockton, Wallie [John Loughman], 55
Broda, Walter [Felix Kolodziej], 31
Brodsky, George [Bertrand Glass; Bertrand Gold], 84
Brooklyn Dodgers Baseball Team, 90
Brovid, Walter [Felix Kolodziej], 31
Brown, Caroline [Virginia Butler], 30, 89
Brown, Marion [Dorothy Butler], 30, 33
Brown, Sad-Puss [Jim ("Shorty") Clark], 2
Bryan [Myron O'Higgins], 44
Buckford, Dick [Dick Buckley], 19, 23, 38
Buckford, Young Horn, 19
Buckley, Dick [Dick Buckford], 23, 70, 71
Bug Club, 55
Bughouse Square, 32
Buildings, neighborhood, 11-33
Burke, Bishop [Bishop Boyle; Bishop John O'Toole], 55
Burns, Elizabeth, 24
Butler, Dorothy Patricia (Farrell) [Marion Brown; Anna Brown; Marion Healy; Elizabeth Whelan; Elsie Cavanagh], 30, 32, 33, 63, 65, 83
Butler, Margaret ("Maggie") [Tessie Healey], 83, 89
Butler, Virginia (Livingston) [Caroline Brown; Alice Healy], 30, 89

Caldwell, Professor Herbert [*Professor Charles Hartshorne*], 63
Calkins, Bert [Charley Batcheler], 26
Calumet Avenue, 25, **28**, 29, 50, 52, 69, 73
Campus Catholic Club, 32
Carmon, Walt [*Carl Warton, New Masses editor*], 65
Carney, Doris [*Katherine Dunham*], 33
Caron, Joel [Ed Lanson; Roger Raymond], 82
Caron, Paul [George Raymond], 24, 32, 41, 82, 84
Carr, Doris [*Katherine Dunham*], 33
Carter Practice School, 52
Carter Public School, William W., 11, 12, **16**, 32, 71, 72, 76
Central Pool, Washington Park, **55**
Chamberlain, John [*Carl Jensen*], 2

Chekhov, Anton, 53
Chicago Herald-Examiner [*Chicago Questioner*; *Chicago Scope*; *Chicago Chronicle*], 31, 63
Chicago White Sox Baseball Team, 24, 26, 51, 69, 72
Church, Corpus Christi [Crucifixion], 12, 68
    Crerar Memorial Presbyterian, 51
    Greek Orthodox, 51, 70
    Methodist Episcopal, 51
    St. Anselm's [St. Patrick's], 11, 12, 13, **14**, **15**, **16**, 39, 50, 52, 54, 68, 70, 71, 73, 74, 75, 76
    SS. Constantine and Helen Greek Orthodox, 51
Clark, Jim ("Shorty") [Shorty Leach; Sad-Puss Brown], 2
Club, Bug, 55
    Dill Pickle [Sour Apple], 32
    Slow Down, 32
    Uasia, 32
Cobb Hall, 30, **31**
Cody, Joseph ("Joe")[Jim Gogarty; Peter Moore], 23, 38, 52, 81, 83
Cohen, Davey, 16, 27, 50
Collins, Tubby [Tubby Connell], 38
Comiskey Park, 4, 26, 69, 70, 72
Connolly, John [*John Loughman*], 55
Conroy, Jack, and review of *The Disinherited*, 88
Conservatory, Washington Park, 54
Cottage Grove Avenue, 25, 30, 54
Cottage Grove Avenue gang, 28
Cotton, Professor [*Professor Einar Joranson*], 30, 61
Couditch (Kuditch) Culture Center [Schmolsky Culture Center], 33, 63
Creative Writing Program, Iowa, 5
Cube theater [Square Circle; Diagonal], 33
Cunningham, Bridget Feeney [Mary Lonigan], 11
Cunningham, Frances [Frances Lonigan; Elizabeth Jennings], 11, 12, 13, 30
Cunningham, Loretta [Loretta Lonigan; Teresa Jennings], 71, 82
Cunningham, Patrick F. [Patrick ("Paddy") Lonigan], 11
Cunningham, William ("Studs") [William ("Studs") Lonigan; Jud Jennings], 11, 38, 39, 40, 45, 56, 63, 70, 71, 72, 81, 82
Curley, Vinc [Vincent Curry], 27, 40
Curry, Vincent [Vinc Curley], 27, 40

Daly, Bart [Richard Parker], 43
Daly, Ellen ("Ella") [Margaret ("Peg") O'Flaherty; Jenny Dunne], 11, 13, 40, 69, 70, 74, 76
Daly, Julia Brown [Mary Fox O'Flaherty; Grace Hogan Dunne], 4, 11, 28, 51, 63, 69, 70, 74, 75
Daly, Mary (Farrell) [Elizabeth ("Lizz") O'Neill; Nora Dunne Ryan], 12, 28, 40
Daly, Thomas Richard [Al O'Flaherty; Richard Dunne], 11, 40, 52, 63, 69, 70, 72, 73, 76
Daly, William J. [Ned O'Flaherty; Larry Dunne], 12, 23, 55, 76
Dawson, Gertrude [Dorothy McPartlin], see Dorothy McPartlin
Delaney, Bill [Bill Donoghue], 18, 38
Delaney, Dan [Dan Donoghue], 18
De Paul University [St. Vincent's University], 53
Devine, Catherine ("Cabby") [Cabby Devlin], 82
Devlin, Cabby [Catherine ("Cabby") Devine], 82
Dewey, John, 41, 44, 53
Dickson, Dick [Jack Jones], 32
Dill Pickle Club [Sour Apple Club], 32
Dillon, George, 83
Dillon, Helen Farrell [Little Margaret O'Neill; Clara Ryan Boyle], 12, 40, 52, 56, 70, 72, 73, 74, 82, 83, 89
Dillon, James ("Jimmy") [Eddie Boyle], 89
Dillon, Matthew ("Matt") [Jack Boyle], 40, 89
Divine Word Fathers, 5
Dr. Martin Luther King Drive (formerly South Park Avenue), 1, 2, 4, 12, 18, **23**, 44, 63, 66, 72
Dolan, Kate [Elizabeth ("Lizzie") Barnes], 81
Dollard, Stewart, 70
Donoghue, Bill [Bill Delaney], 18
Donoghue, Dan [Dan Delaney], 18
Dos Passos, John, 53
Doyle, Jim [Jim Barnes], 39, 81
Doyle, Margaret ("Maggie") [Elizabeth ("Lizzie") Barnes], 81
Doyle, Tommy [Tommy Barnes], 21, 28, 38, 39
Dreiser, Theodore, 53
Drexel Boulevard, 54

Drumm, Ed, 76
Dubrow, Alvin [*Edward Bastian*], 84
Dugar, Andrew [Andy Le Gare], 12, 13, 70
Dugar, Mr. [Mr. Le Gare], 13
Dugar, Sid, 12, 13
Dunham, Albert [Norman Allen; David or Daniel Carr or Carney], 32
Dunham, Katherine [Doris Carr; Doris Carney], 32, 33
Dunne, Grace Hogan [*Julia Brown Daly*], 11, 66, 82
Dunne, Jenny [*Ellen ("Ella") Daly*], 82
Dunne, Larry [*William John Daly*], 82
Dunne, Nora (Ryan) [*Mary Daly (Farrell)*], 82
Dunne, Richard ("Dick") [*Thomas Richard Daly*], 82

Egan, Frank [Weary Reilley], 12, 17, 63
Eisenberg, Dr. Dan [*Dr. Ben Lewis Reitman*], 55
Elevated train, 1, **25**, 26, 27, 29, 50, 51, 54, 70
Emerson, Ralph Waldo, 53
Estrelle, Bob [*Edward Bastian*], 84
Euclid Avenue, 5, 63, 66

Fadiman, Clifton [Tommy Stock], 63, 64
Falk, Bert [*Samuel Putnam*], 65
Farrell, Dorothy Patricia (Mrs. James T.) [Marion Brown; Anna Brown Marion Healy; Elizabeth Whelan; Elsie Cavanagh], 30, 32, 63, 65, 81, 89, 90, 91
Farrell, Earl (William), see Farrell, William Earl
Farrell, Francis Edward ("Frankie") [Arthur ("Arty") O'Neill; Vincent Ryan], 73
Farrell, Helen (Dillon) [Little Margaret O'Neill; Clara Ryan Boyle], 12, 40, 52, 56, 70, 72, 73, 74, 82, 83, 89
Farrell, Hortense Alden (Mrs. James T.) [Phyllis Ryan], 89
Farrell, James ("Jim" or "Big Jim") Francis [James Francis O'Neill; John ("Jack") Ryan], 12, 28, 40, 68, 69, 70, 73
Farrell, James Thomas [Danny O'Neill; Eddie Ryan], 1-10, 38-44, 63-77, 88-91
    academic record, parochial school, 68, 76
    acting at Cube theater, 33
    adulation, craving for, in childhood, 68
    Armistice Day, impact of, 39, 75
    anger, at man's existential predicament, 53
    anti-Stalinism, 84
    art colony participation, 32, 33, 84
    artist's goals, 40, 41, 63
    atheism, 53, 57-58
    athletics and fame, 68, 69
    aunt Ella, and relationship to, 11, 13, 40, 69, 70, 74, 76
        and her drinking problem, 70
    authors read in boyhood, 74
    autobiography, 33, 38, 40-41, 43, 56, 67, 70
    baseball interest, 2, 4, 24, 26, 51, 54, 56, 68, 69, 70, 72, 75, 88, 89, 90-91
    and Bible characters, 74
    bohemianism, 4, 32, 33
    boxing, interest in, 69, 70
    boyhood, 1-10, 38, 40, 53, 57, 63-77
    boyhood religious convictions and conflicts, 75-76
    Bug Club, 55
    Butler family's reaction to *Young Lonigan*, 83
    Catholicism, 3, 44, 50, 53-54, 57, 75, 81
    characters, fictional, 2, 41-42, 82, 88
        vs. nonfictional (Note to the Reader), 2
    and Chekov's writing, 53
    child of two families, 69-70
    Communism, 33, 55, 84
    confidence, lack of in boyhood, 68
    criticism of his novels, 3, 81, 84, 88, 89
    Cube theater, 33
    and Cunningham, William ("Studs"), 11, 38, 39, 40, 45, 46, 56, 63, 70, 71, 72, 81
    and Daly family, life with, 69, 70
        see also Daly family members
    and Danny O'Neill, creation of, 38
        see also O'Neill, Danny
    death, of brother, "Frankie," 73
        of mother, 40
    and De Paul University, 53, 81
    Depression Era, effect of on his writing, 33
    destiny, concepts of human, 43
        undefined sense of, 76
    and Dewey, John, 41, 44, 53
    diaries, 88
    disillusionment, with people and democracy, 91
    and doctrine, Catholic, 44, 53, 81
    and dogs, as pets, 44, 56, 72, 73
    drinking habits, 89, 90, 91
    early years, childhood, 1-10, 69
    and editors, 63, 64, 65
    education, Catholic, 53, 54
        De Paul University, 53, 81
        University of Chicago, 30-31, 53, 81
    existential predicament of man, 52
    eyesight, 12, 68, 72
    and Fadiman, Clifton, 63, 64
    family reaction to novels, 83
    family relationships, 69, 70, 76, 89-90
    and Father Gilmartin, 75
    and father, relationship with, 40, 67-70
    and father's drinking, 70
    and fighting, 70, 71
    football, interest, 69
    fraternity, high school Alpha Eta Beta, 71
    freedom, emotional and intellectual, views, 53
    friends, University of Chicago campus, 84
    girls, relationship with, 56, 68, 70, 71, 76
    goals, literary, 88
    and Gorky, Maxim, 53
    and grandmother Daly, 63, 69, 70
        see also Daly, Julia Brown
    and Gross, George, correspondence, 40
    and Halper, Albert—thesis of writing, 84
    happiness in childhood, 69
    and hoodlums, amateur, 42
    hostility following publication, 84-85
    and human development, 41-42
    idealism, 76
    identity, seeking of, 76
    and influenza (1918), effect on family, 74-75
    introspection, 68
    Irish-American groups, attitude toward, 50
    Irish, shanty, attitude toward, 42
    Israel, and the state of, 91
    "Jimmy the Genius", 36
    and Le Barr, Gladys, 56, 71
    manuscript, first, acceptance of, 31, 63, 65, 81-82
    marriage, 33, 89
    matriculation, as Danny O'Neill, University of Chicago, 28
    and Mead, George Herbert, 41, 53
    memoirs, 33, 70, 76
    and Mencken, H.L., correspondence, 53, 69
    metamorphosis, from "Jimmy Farrell to "James T. Farrell," 81
    and Middle East trip, 91
    and mother (Mary Daly Farrell), 12, 28, 40, 51, 69
    motivation behind Studs, 40
    and neighborhood,
        acceptance in, 70
        appraisal of his work, 81
        attitudes toward Farrell, 81
        bourgeois, 53
        concepts of, 51
        described, 51
        escapades in , childhood, 70
        ethnic groups, 50, 52
        ethos, 53,
        friends, 70
        horizons beyond the, 53
        importance of the, 43
        interstitial, defined, 52
        liberation from the, 53
        parties, 71
        preoccupation with the, 63
        reaction to his becoming a writer, 81
    and nephews, William ("Bill") Farrell; James ("Jimmy") Dillon, 89
    and *New Masses*, 65

and New Year's Eve (1955), 89-90
and New York City, 63, 64, 85
objective method, in writing, 42
and Palmer Method diploma, 74
and Paris trips, 53, 65, 81, 84, 85
and patriotism, 19, 51, 72
personality, basic, 68, 76, 88, 89
and Pound, Ezra—recommendation, 65
prejudices, 5, 52
prize fighting, interest in, 69
and Professor James Weber Linn, 31
and Proust, respect for, 84
publication of first novel, 65, 81-82
   of first story, 31, 63
and publishers, 63, 64, 65
purpose, as a novelist, 53
and Putnam, Samuel, editor of *New Review*, 65
racial groups, consideration of, 21, 22, 23, 50, 52
and radicals, political, 33
reading, boyhood, 74
realism, photographic, 3, 83, 85
and reality, 41
rejection of Studs Lonigan manuscript, 64
religious commitment, 75
reporter, campus, 63
reunion, with neighborhood boys, 82-83
Saratoga Springs and Yaddo, 15, **81**
school life, 76
siblings,
   Francis ("Frankie") Edward, 73
   Helen, 12, 40, 68, 69, 70, 72, 73
   John A., 28, 40, 73, 81, 82, 89
   Joseph E., 28, 49, 73, 81, 89, 90
   Mary, 28, 40, 73, 89
   William Earl, 28, 40, 68, 72, 73, 81
and Sister Bertha, 73
and Sister Magdalen, 14, 25, 44, 45, 68, 73-74, 75, 76
slum theory, rejected, 1, 42
and son, Kevin, 89
and spelling bee, 71-72
and Spinoza's aphorism, 53
and spiritual poverty, 42, 43, 44
sports, interest in, 2, 16, 24, 29, 30, 39, 52, 54, 55, 56, 68, 69, 70, 82, 88
teen years, 50
tolerance, 55
Trilogy and, see under **WRITINGS**
and Uncle Tom Daly, 69, 70, 76
and University of Chicago, C-Shop, 35
   Cobb Hall, 30-**31**
   Coffee Shop, **31**, 32
   enrollment in and course work, 30-31, 81
   neighborhood attitudes towards, 81
   professors and friends, reaction to *Young Lonigan*, 83
values, 42-45, 53
and Washington Park, influence of, 24, 57, 72
wife, Hortense Alden, 89
   Virginia Butler, 33, 89
and Wilson, Woodrow, idolization of, 72
and the working class, 42
and World War I, impact of, 5, 19, 51, 72, 73
wrestling, interest in, 69
writer, decision to become, 33, 63
WRITINGS:
   "Autumn Afternoon," 20, 68
   "Between Heaven and Hell," 83
   "The Bride of Christ," 73
   Calico Shoes and Other Stories, 23
   "The Call of Time," 66
   Can all This Grandeur Perish and Other Stories, 26, 28
   Collected Stories, 83
   "Comedy Cop," 33
   "Comrade Stanley," 33
   "Curbstone Philosophy," 26, 28
   The Death of Nora Ryan, 46, 47, 48, 83, 87
   "The Distance of Sadness," 66
   The Dunne Family, 82, 86

"Equal to the Centuries," 83
Father and Son, 14, 24, 28, 29, 39, 40, 60
French Girls Are Vicious, 44, 45, 57
Gas-House McGinty, 33, 47, 65
"Getting Out the Vote for the Working Class," 33
Guillotine Party and Other Stories, 15, 26, 80
"Helen, I Love You," 23, 38, 68
"It's Cold in the Alps," 89
"Jewboy," 65
"Jim O'Neill," 28
Jonathan Titulescu Fogarty satires, 89
Judgment Day, 15, 27, 30, 34, 38, 39, 45, 47, 63, 77
Judith and Other Stories, 80
"Kilroy Was Here," 43, 44, 57
Lonely for the Future, 24, 27, 86
"The Merry Clouters," 24
My Baseball Diary, 72
My Days of Anger, 31, 32, 39, 57, 58, 61, 86
New Year's Eve/1929, 33
No Star Is Lost, 27, 60, 80
A Note on Literary Criticism, 84
An Omnibus of Short Stories, 20
"The Open Road," 32
"Pie Juggling in the Loop," 31
Reflections at Fifty and Other Essays, 63, 64
"Reverend Father Gihooley," 13, 14, 15
The Road Between, 86, 87
Side Street and Other Stories, 47
The Silence of History, 30, 31, 34, 36, 58, 61, 79, 86
"Sister," 44, 45, 76, 77
"Slob," 63
"The Social and Aesthetic Values of Literature," 53
"Studs," 2, 18, 34, 38, 39, 42, 43, 63, 64, 65
Studs Lonigan: A Trilogy, mentioned 1, 2, 3, 4, 5, 33, 34, 40, 41, 43, 46,
   47, 48, 59, 60, 63, 64, 65, 66, 77, 81, 82, 83, 85, 88
   narrative method, 3-4
   origin and composition, 63-67
"The Stuff That Dreams Are Made Of," 41
"Three O'Clock Fancies," 83
"The Universe of Time," 88
"Wedding Bells Will Ring So Merrily," 26
"When Time Was Young," 66, 83
A World I Never Made, 46, 48, 83
"The Writer and His Source Material," 84
Young Lonigan, appraisal of, 84
   acceptance, 84
   censorship, 84
   critiques, 84, 85
   completion, 63
   manuscript, reading of, 84
   mentioned 3, 5, 14, 17, 18, 20, 21, 22, 26, 27, 29, 38-39, 50, 52, 63,
      64 ,65, 77, 79, 82, 83, 84, 85
   origin and composition, 63-67
   reaction of University of Chicago faculty and friends to, 83
   reaction of family to, 83
   reaction of Hyde Park Art Colony members to, 84
   reaction of neighborhood to, 81-82
   rejection of, 64
   and Mark Twain, 85
   publisher, seeking, 65
   reviewed, 84
   success, 84
The Young Manhood of Studs Lonigan, completion of manuscript, 65
   mentioned 5, 14, 17, 18, 19, 21, 22, 24, 27, 28, 30, 34, 35, 39, 40,
      44, 51, 53, 60, 63, 64, 65, 75, 79
   origin and composition, 63-67
   publication, 65
   revision, 65
and Yaddo, 15, **81**
Farrell, John ("Jack") Anthony [Robert ("Bob") O'Neill; Steven ("Steve")
   Ryan], 28, 40, 73, 81, 82, 89, 90
Farrell, Joseph ("Joe") Edward [Dennis O'Neill; Leo Ryan; Luke Ryan],
   28, 40, 73, 81, 89, 90
Farrell, Kevin [Tommy Ryan], 89
Farrell, Loretta [Molly Ryan], 89
Farrell, Mary Daly [Elizabeth ("Lizz") O'Neill; Nora Dunne Ryan], 12, 28,

40, 51, 69
Farrell, Mary Elizabeth [Catherine O'Neill; Frances Ryan] 28, 40, 73, 89
Farrell, Rose (Mrs. Joseph E.) [Florence Ryan], 90
Farrell, William ("Bill"), William Earl's son [Andrew Ryan], 89
Farrell, William Earl, usually known as Earl [William ("Bill") O'Neill; John ("Jack") Ryan], 28, 40, 68, 72, 73, 81
Feeney, Bridget [*Mrs. Patrick F. Cunningham*], 11
Feeney, Torch [*Harold ("Red") O'Keefe*], 16
Fifty-eighth (58th) Street, 1, 2, 4, 11, 16, 17, 19, 21, 24, **27**, 29, 50, 58, 63, 66, 67, 68, 81, 88
Fifty-eighth Street Cardinals, 24, 30
Fifty-eighth Street Station, **26**
Fifty-fifth (55th) Street, 1, 2, 50
Fifty-seventh (57th) Street, 1, 2, 4, 11-13, 20, 54, 84
Fifty-seventh Street Art Colony (Jackson Park Colony), 32
Flanagan, Mickey [*Mickey McCarthy*], 26
Fly Casters' Pool, Washington Park, **54**
Fogarty, Jonathan Titulescu, 89
Forty-fifth (45th) Place, 28
Forty-seventh Street Monitors, 14, 24, 30, 39
Freeman, Martin Joseph, and Farrell, 83
Freer, Catherine Anne [*Mary Louise Hunnell*], 30

Gang, Cottage Grove Avenue, 28
    Fifty-eighth Street, 24, 28, 38, 64, 81
    Indiana Avenue, 16, 18, 28
    Kenwoods, 25
    Merry Clouters, 24-25
Gardiner [*John Monroe*], 31-32
Garfield Boulevard (55th Street), 1, 50, 51
George the Greek, 26
Georgis, Takiss ("Pete") [*Christy, the waiter*], 27, 81
Gilhooley, Father Michael [*Father Michael S. Gilmartin*], 3, **13**, 15, 17, 22
Gillen, Wils [*Wilson Gilligin*], 39
Gilligin, Wilson [*Wils Gillen*], 81
Gilmartin, Father Michael S. [*Father Michael Gilhooley*], **13**, 15, 75
Ginn, Eva, and Farrell, 65
Gogarty, Jim [*Joseph ("Joe") Cody*], 23, 45, 57, 58
Goldman, Emma, and Dr. Ben Lewis Reitman, 55
Gorky, Maxim, 53
Gradek, Stanley [*Vladimir Janowicz*], 84
Grand Boulevard, 28, 54
Gunther, John, 83
Gus the Greek's restaurant, 27, 58

Haggerty, Paulie [*Paulie Harrington*], 16, 21, 26, 28, 29
Hallsberg, Bill [*Harry Barnard*], 83
Halper, Albert, 84
Hanrahan, Mickey [*Patsy McLaughlin*], 73
Harper Avenue, 33
Harrington, Paulie [*Paulie Haggerty*], 16
Hartshorne, Professor Charles [*Herbert Caldwell*], 63
Hayes, Roslyn [*Dorothy McPartlin*], 17, 30
Healy, Alice [*Virginia Butler*], 89
Healy, Marion [*Dorothy Butler*], 32, 33
Hebrew Temple and Community House, 51
Hemingway, Ernest, 33
Henle, James [*Leo Berger*], 33, 40, 65, 82, 84
Hennessey, Three-Star, 39
Hicks, Granville, and review of *The Great Tradition,* 88
Hirsch, Morris, 23
Hobo College, and Dr. Ben Lewis Reitman, 55
Hoffmann, John Wesley [*Mr. Thornton*], 30
Hunnell, Mary Louise [*Catherine Anne Freer*], 30
Hunter, Mary [Joan Jackson; Lenora Jackson], 33, 63, 84
Hutchinson Hall Coffee Shop, **31**
Hyde Park, 25

Ibsen, Henrik, and "The Master Builder," 33
Indiana Avenue, 4, 11-13, 14, 16, 18, 19, 23, 28, 39, 40, 50, 52, 54, 70, 71, 73, 76
Iowa Creative Writing Program, 5

Jackson, Joan [*Mary Hunter*], 33, 66, 84
Jackson, Lenora [*Mary Hunter*], 33
Jackson Park, 29, 76
Jackson Park Art Colony, 32

Jackson Park Highlands, 1
Jameson, Dr. Ralph [*Dr. James Roach*], 73
Jameson, Ruth (formerly Mrs. Vladimir Janowicz)[Barbara Morgan; Janet Ross], 84
Janeway, Mordecai [*Theodore ("Ted") Marvel*], 33
Janowicz, Vladimir [Comrade Stanley; Stanley Gradek; Jan Varsky], 84
Janowicz, Mrs. Vladimir (Ruth Jameson) [Barbara Morgan; Janet Ross], 84
Jennings, Jud [*William ("Studs") Cunningham*], 33, 66, 67, 82
Jennings, Julia [*Mrs. Patrick F. Cunningham*], 11
Jennings, Tom [*Patrick F. Cunningham*], 11
Jensen, Carl [John Chamberlain], 2
Johnson, Johnny [*Johnny O'Brien*], 12, 13, 16, 73
Johnson, Mr. [Mr. O'Brien], 12-13
Jones, Jack [Dick Dickson], 32
Joranson, Professor Einar [*Professor Kraft; Professor Cotton*], 30, 61
Joyce, James, 53

Keefe, Barney, 39
Kelly, Harold ("Red") [*Harold ("Red") O'Keefe*], 26
Kennedy, Kenney [*Kenny Kilarney*], 26
Kenny, Ed, and Farrell, 82
Kenny, Tim, 20
Kilarney, Kenny [*Kenney Kennedy*], 26, 28, 82
King of the Hoboes [*Dr. Ben Lewis Reitman*], 55
Kolodziej, Felix [Walter Broda; Walter Brovid], 31, 82, 84
Kraft, Professor [*Professor Einar Joranson*], 30, 61
Kuditch (Coudich) Culture Center [Schmolsky Culture Center], 33

"L" train, elevated, 1, **25**, 26, 27, 29, 50, 51, 54, 70
Lake Michigan, 5
Lagoon, Wooded Island, **20**
Lanson, Ed [*Paul Caron*] 41, 45
Lasswell, Professor Harold Dwight [Professor Pearson; Professor Donald W. Torman], and Farrell, 61, 83-84
Latham, Mary, 20
Leach, Jim ("Shorty") [*Jim ("Shorty") Clark*], 2
Le Barr, Gladys, 56, 71
Lederer, Loretta (Cunningham) [Loretta Lonigan; Teresa Jennings], 71, 82
Lederer, Louis [*Phil Rolfe*], 50, 82
Lederer, William L., 82, 83
Le Gare, Andy [*Andrew Dugar*], 12, 19, 25, 39
Le Gare, Mr. [*Mr. Dugar*], 13
Levin's Drug Store, **19**
Levinsky, Jawbones, 82
Lily Pool, Washington Park, **55**
Linn, Professor James Weber [Professor Paul Morris Saxon; Joseph Paxton Lyman], 31, 38, 63, 83, 84
Livingston, Robert [*Leonard Tannenberger*], 89
Livingston, Virgina (Butler) [Caroline Brown; Alice Healy], 89
Locke, Phil, and Farrell, 90-91
Lonigan, Frances [*Frances Cunningham*], 11, 13, 22, 30
Lonigan, Loretta [*Loretta Cunningham*], 30, 33
Lonigan, Martin [*Martin Cunningham*], 43
Lonigan, Mary [*Bridget Feeney Cunningham*], 11, 22, 33, 54
Lonigan, Patrick ("Paddy") [*Patrick F. Cunningham*], 11, 15, 22, 52, 54
Lonigan, William ("Studs") [*William ("Studs") Cunningham*], 1-5, 11-33, 38-45, 50-58, 65, 66, 67, 68, 71, 81-86
Loop, the, 1, 5, 17, 25, 39
Loretta Aacdemy, 30
Lott, Jr., George [Ray Taite], 2, 51, 63
Loughman, John [John Connolly; Wallie Brockton; Larry Norton], 55
Lovett, Professor Robert Morss [Lloyd Dunning Sheldon], 4, 38, 63, 83
Loyola Academy, **29**
Lyman, Professor Joseph Paxton [*Professor James Weber Linn*], 31, 66

McCarthy, Mickey [*Mickey Flanagan*], 26
McCarthy, T. B., 39
McDonough, John, 70
McGinty, Ambrose J. [*R. J. J. McManus*], 65
McGonigle, Alec [*James ("Jack") Sullivan*], 32
McLaughlin, Patsy [*Mickey Hanrahan*], 73
McPartlin, Dorothy [Roslyn Hayes; Gertrude Dawson], 17, 56, 70, 71, 74, 75, 76, 82
Mandlebaum, Benjamin [*Maxwell Bodenheim*], 33
Martin, Jim ("Fat"), 70
Marvel, Theodore ("Ted") [Mordecai Janeway; Bob Whipple], 33, 84

Mary Our Mother High School [*Mount Carmel High School*], 29
Matsoukas, Nicholas ("Nick") [Pete the Greek; Cyril Thearchos], 33
Maurer, Billy, 70
Mead, George Herbert [*Emerson Dwight*], 41, 53
Mencken, H. L., 53, 69, 74
Merkle [*Beatrice Timmins*], 89
Met Music Shop, 26
Metevier, Frances, 82
Michigan Avenue, 1, 2, 4, 11, 13, 15, 22, 23, 28, 39
Michigan Avenue Apartment Building, 5800 Block, **23**
Michigan Theater, **25**, 51
Midway Plaisance, 54
Monroe, John [*Gardner; Harry Oldering*], 31
Moore, Peter [*Joseph ("Joe") Cody*], 58
Morgan, Barbara [*Ruth Jameson*], 84
Moritz, Moe [*Sammy Schmalz*], 26
Mount Carmel High School [*Mary Our Mother High School*], 29
Murphy, Francis Xavier, 32

Neighborhood, amusement parks, 51
    apartment buildings, 4, 50
    barber shop, 26, 17
    black migration into, 52
    brothels, 3, 30, 31, 32, 51
    buildings, 11-33
    burlesque houses, 5
    churches, 3, 11, 12, **13**, **14**, **15**, **16**, 39, 50, 51, 52
    cliques, 70
    crime, 51
    drugstore, **19**, 27, 51
    environment, 3, 38, 42, 50, 52
    ethnic groups, 4, 21, 22, 23, 50, 52
    and Farrell, 63-77
    games, 51
    gangs, 14, 21, 24, 25, 28, 30, 38, 39, 64, 70, 80
    girls, 30, 71
    grocer, 23, 77
    hostility toward the University of Chicago, 81
    Irish, 50
    library, 33
    "L" train, 25, 26, 27, 29, 50, 51, 70
    movie theaters, 25, 51
    music shop, 26
    occupations, 52
    parks, 3, 50, 51
    playgrounds, 11, **16**, 51, 55, 56
    police, 51
    poolrooms, 3, **26**, 27, 39, 40, 42, 51, 91
    prejudices, 5
    prominent residents, Ring Lardner, 51
        George Lott, Jr., 51
        Mercedes McCambridge, 51
        Clarence Rowland, 51
    race riots, 52
    reaction to *Young Lonigan*, 81-82
    recreation, 51
    restaurants, **27**, 28, 51
    schools, 11, 12, **14**, 16, 22, 24, **29**, **30**, 32, 39, 52, 54, 71, 72, 76, 81, 82
    slums, 1, 3, 5, 42
    sports, 24, 29, 30, 39, 69, 82, 88
    stores, 2, 50, 51
    streetcars, 54
    theaters, 25, 51
    traffic, 51
New Masses, editor and *Young Lonigan*, 65
New Review [*This Age*], 65
Nolan, Jim [*Jim Barnes*], 39
Nolan, Kate Moore [*Aunt Lizzie Barnes*], 81
Norton, Larry [*John Loughman*], 55

O'Brien, Johnny [*Johnny Johnson*], 3, 12, 13, 16-17, 19, 52
O'Brien, Mr. [*Mr. Johnson*], 16
O'Brien, Paul ("Fat"), reaction to *Young Lonigan*, 82
O'Callaghan, Old Man, home, **18**
O'Connell, Red [*Red O'Connor*], 18, 38, 40
O'Connor, Red [*Red O'Connell*], 18, 38, 40

O'Dea, Paul, 70, 72
O'Flaherty family home, **12**, **13**, **23**
O'Flaherty, Al [*Thomas Richard Daly*], 12, 23, 24, 42, 52
O'Flaherty, Margaret ("Peg") [*Ellen ("Ella") J. Daly*], 12, 23, 28
O'Flaherty, Mary [*Julia Brown Daly*], 11, 12, 23, 28
O'Flaherty, Mildred [*Emma Wilkinson (Mrs. William J.) Daly*], 23
O'Flaherty, Ned [*William J. Daly*], 12, 23
O'Higgins, Myron [*Bryan*], 44
O'Keefe, Harold ("Red") [*Red Kelly; Torch Feeney*], 16, 81, 82
Oldering, Harry [*John Monroe*], 32
Olmstead, Frederick Law and Washington Park, 54
O'Neill, Arthur ("Arty") [*Francis ("Frankie") Edward Farrell*], 73
O'Neill, Catherine [*Mary E. Farrell*], 28, 29
O'Neill, Daniel ("Danny") [*James T. Farrell; Jimmy Farrell*], 2-32, *passim*; 38-45, 53, 54, 55, 56-57, 58, 68,82, 91
O'Neill, Dennis [*Joe Farrell*], 28, 89
O'Neill, Elizabeth ("Lizz") [*Mary Daly Farrell*], 12, 14, 28-29
O'Neill, James Francis ("Jim" or "Big Jim") [*James Francis Farrell*], 12, 14, 26, 28-29, 42
O'Neill, Little Margaret [*Helen Farrell*], 12, 23, 28
O'Neill, Robert ("Bob") [*John ("Jack") A. Farrell*], 28, 89
O'Neill, William ("Bill") [*William Earl Farrell*], 28
O'Toole, Bishop John [*Bishop Burke*], 55

Paris, 53, 65, 81, 84, 85
Parker, Richard [*Bart Daly*], 43, 82
Pete the Greek [*Nicholas ("Nick") Matsoukas*], 33
Philadelphia Athletics Baseball Team, 70
poolroom, Bathcellar's, **26**, 27
Prairie Avenue, 1, 16, 21, 25, 26, **27**, 52, 64, 68, 81
Publishers, 31
    Brewer and Warren, 64
    Covici Friede, 64
    Coward McCann, 44
    Modern Library, 88
    Simon and Schuster [*Wallingford and Wyndfall*], 63
    Vanguard Press [*Advance Press*], 33, 65, 84
    Smith and Haas, 64
Putnam, Samuel [*Bert Falk*], and Farrell, 65

Raymond, George [*Paul Caron*], 24, 32
Raymond, Roger [*Joel Caron*], 82
Reilley, Weary [*Frank Egan*], 12, 13, 14, 16, 17, 18, 19, 21, 28, 29, 39, 42, 63
Reitman, Dr. Ben Lewis [*Dr. Adam Bergman; Dr. Dan Eisenberg*], 55
Reuther, Walter, 89
Rogan, Walter, 70
Rolfe, Phil [*Louis Lederer*], 50, 82
Ross, Janet [*Ruth Jameson*], 84
Ryan, Andrew [*William ("Bill") Farrell*], 89
Ryan, Edward Arthur ("Eddie") [*James T. Farrell*], 24, 30, 31, 32, 58, 66, 67, 82, 83
Ryan, Florence [*Mrs. Joseph E. Farrell*], 90
Ryan, Frances [*Mary E. Farrell*], 89
Ryan, Leo [*Joseph ("Joe") E. Farrell*], 89
Ryan, Luke [*Joseph ("Joe") Farrell*], 89
Ryan, Molly [*Loretta (Mrs. William E.) Farrell*], 89
Ryan, Nora Dunne [*Mary Daly Farrell*], 82
Ryan, Phyllis [*Hortense Alden (Mrs. James T. Farrell)*], 89
Ryan, Steven ("Steve") [*John ("Jack") A. Farrell*], 89
Ryan, Thomas ("Tommy") [*Kevin Farrell*], 89
Ryan, Vincent [*Francis ("Frankie" Farrell*], 73

St. Anselm's Convent [*St. Patrick's Convent*], **14**
St. Anselm's High School and Community Center, 15
St. Basil High School [*St. Cyril High School*], **29**, 71, 82
St. Cyril High School [*St. Stanislaus High School; St. Basil High School*], **29**, 71, 82
St. Francis Xavier's Academy [*St. Paul's Academy; St. Matthew's Academy; St. Hilda's Academy*], **30**
St. Patrick's Convent [*St. Anselm's Convent*], **14**
St. Patrick's Grammar School [*St. Anselm's Grammar School*], 11, 12, **16**, 24, 39, 54
St. Paul's Academy [*St. Francis Xavier Academy*], **30**
St. Stanislaus High School [*St. Cyril High School*], **29**, 30
St. Vincent's University [*De Paul University*], 53
Saxon, Professor Paul Morris [*Professor James Weber Linn*], 31

Scanlan, Helen [*Helen Shannon*], 17, 23, 45
Scanlan, Lucy [*Lucy Shannon*], 3, 11, 13, 16, 17, 18, 19, 21, 24, 25, 28, 39, 71
Schmaltz, Sammy [*Moe Moritz*; *Toothless Nate*], 26
Schmolsky Culture Center [*Couditch Culture Center*], 33
Schuman, Frederick, 84
Shannon, Father [*Father Stanton*], 15, 39, 70
Shannon, Helen [*Helen Scanlan*], 17, 56, 71
Shannon, Lucy [*Lucy Scanlan*], 11, 13, 17, 71
Shearer, Earl [*Earl Shires*], 51
Shearer, Helen [*Helen Shires*], 17, 51
Shearer, Marion [*Marion Shires*], 13, 17, 71
Sheehan, Arnold [*Roland Powers*], 30
Sheldon, Professor Lloyd Dunning [*Robert Morss Lovett*], 63
Sheridan Road, 29
Sherman High School, 81
Shires, Helen [*Helen Shearer*], 13, 16, 17, 19, 29, 50
Silver Michigan Farm [*Silver Saddle Farm*], 52
Silver Saddle Farm [*Silver Michigan Farm*], 52
Simpson, Aunt Annie, 83
Simpson, Isabel, 83
Simpson, John, 83
Sister, Bernadette Marie, 14, 25, 72
    Bertha ("Battling") [*Martha ("Mauling")*], 14, 71, 73
    Carmel, 12, 14
    Cyrilla, 14, 71
    Magdalen [*Josephine*], 14, 25, 44, 45, 68, 73-74, 75, 76
    Martha ("Mauling") [*Bertha ("Battling")*], 14
    Teresa, 20
Sisters of Mercy, 30
Sisters of the Order of Providence, 14
Sixty-first (61st) Street, 13, **15**, 50
Sixty-seventh (67th) Street, 1, 34
Sixty-third Street, 1, 34
Slow Down Club, 32
Smith, Professor Thomas Vernor, 84
Soapbox orators, 55
South Dante Avenue, 29
South Park Avenue, 1, 2, 4, 12, 18, **23**, 44, 57, 63, 66, 72
South Shore, 50, 63, 66
South Side, 2, 52, 53, 67
Spinoza, Benedict, 53
Squibbs, Joe, 70
Stagg Field, 76
Stanley, Comrade [*Vladimir Janowicz*], 84
Stanton, Father [*Father Shannon*], 15, 70-71, 73
State Street, 72
Stern, Lloyd George Alfred ("Bus") [*Fred Morris*], 64, 81, 84
Stock, Tommy [*Clifton Fadiman*], 63
Stony Island Avenue, 1, 29, 33
Sullivan, James ("Jack") [*Alec McGonigle*], 32, 84
Swinburne, Algernon Charles, and Danny O'Neill, 57

Taite, Ray [*George Lott, Jr.*], 2, 51, 63
Tannenberger, Leonard [*Robert Livingston*], 89
Thearchos, Cyril [*Nicholas ("Nick") Matsoukas*], 33
Theater, Cube [Square Circle; Diagonal], 33
    Michigan, 25, 51
    movie, 25, 51
    Palm, 25, 51
    Prairie, 25, 51
    Vernon Avenue, 25, 51
Thirty-fifth (35th) Street, 72
<u>This Age</u> [*New Review*], 65
<u>This Era</u> [*This Quarter*], 65
This Quarter [<u>This Era</u>], 65
Thornton, Mr. [*John Wesley Hoffmann*], 30
Thrasher, Frederic, 52
Timmins, Beatrice [Merkle], 89
Titus, Edward W. [Robinson], and *This Quarter* [<u>This Era</u>], 65
Twain, Mark, and *Young Lonigan*, 85

Uasia, 32
Ulysses, and *Gas-House McGinty*, 65
University(ies), of Chicago, 1, 2, 17, 23, 25, 27, 32, 38, 53, 57, 76, 81, 83, 84
    De Paul [St. Vincent's], 53, 81
    of Iowa, 5

Varsky, Jan [*Vladimir Janowicz*], 84
Veblen, Thorstein, 53
von Borries, Helen [*Helen Borax*], 12, 82
von Borries, Ralph [*Ralph Borax*], 12, 70

Wabash Avenue, 11, 16, 22, 50, 52
Warton, Carl [*Walt Carmon*], 65
Washington Park, Bug Club, 55
    buildings, 54
    and Farrell's intellectual and spiritual development, 57-58
    mentions, 1, 2, 4, 12, 15, 17, 20, **23**, **24**, **25**, 26, 29, 30, 38, 41, 50, 54-62
    origin and location, 54
    sports and recreation, 54, 55, 56
Wells Street, 28
Wentworth Avenue, 69
Westcott, Glenway, 83
Whelan, Elizabeth [*Dorothy Butler*], 33
Whipple, Bob [*Theodore ("Ted") Marvel*], 33
Whitehead, Alfred North, 32, 53
Wilkinson, Emma [*Mildred O'Flaherty*], 23
Willingham, Marion [*Martha Dodd*], 32
Wooded Island, Washington Park, 2, 3, 17, **20**, **21**, **24**, 56, 71

Young, Nadine ("Deene"), 88

Publisher's Note

WHAT MAKES THIS BOOK IMPORTANT and special is not just the amazing visual record that the photographs provide, but the skill and care with which Edgar Branch addresses himself in the accompanying chapters to the Lonigan neighborhood as found in both fact and fiction, as well as to Farrell's formative years within it. This should not be surprising as Edgar Branch's relationship to Farrell was unique. He began a voluminous correspondence with Farrell in 1948 which lasted until the novelist's death, at age 75, in 1979. In the course of this thirty-one year exchange, Farrell candidly revealed much about himself, providing numerous insights into his development as a writer in addition to supplying ideas and crucial information about his early years in Chicago.

When Professor Branch informed Farrell in 1974 that he wanted to undertake the writing of his biography—which for reasons of health he eventually was prevented from pursuing—Farrell happily granted him full access to his vast archives at the University of Pennsylvania and appointed him his literary executor as well. In typical fashion, Farrell wanted it understood that he would impose no restrictions on the research or use of materials.

In originally discussing the publication of this book with me, Ed Branch used words like "booklet" to refer to the project—but not for long. It soon became apparent to both of us that in addition to the one-of-a-kind photographs, Ed had so much to share about the Washington Park neighborhood of Studs, Danny O'Neill, Lucy Scanlon and company that the book deserved—nay, begged—to be expanded. Ed heroically, at a time of life when most men are content to stay home and watch the grass grow, went on to write a wonderful introduction plus five enlightening fact and quote filled chapters in addition to the original chapter containing the documentary photographs. Needless to say, Edgar Branch's initially modest-sized project grew into a work of considerable scholarly importance and, I might add, charm.

Reading this book and studying its photographs have wonderfully deepened my own perceptions of the Lonigan neighborhood, the trilogy, and Farrell—the man and writer. Looking at the photograph of the vacant lot on Indiana Avenue, near 58th, for instance—where Danny O'Neill met Studs Lonigan for the first time, on 1 May 1915—produces an intensified sense of reality or living that rivals in quality some of my own deepest personal memories. The unanswerable mystery of just how a writer like Farrell was able to create such memorable meetings between imagined characters in vacant city lots and other nondescript locations of little obvious significance lies very much at the center of this book.

To Ed Branch we owe a special debt in that he has acted not just in an enlightened scholarly manner relative to the life and work of James T. Farrell and other literary figures, but also as someone who has followed the larger path that literature can set for us and went out exploring, investigating, on his own in an interested and conscientious fashion.

—Marshall Brooks